Schools Council
Research Studies

The Development of
Writing Abilities (11–18)

Schools Council
Research Studies

The Development of Writing Abilities (11–18)

James Britton
Tony Burgess
Nancy Martin
Alex McLeod
Harold Rosen

A report from the Schools Council Project
on Written Language of 11–18 Year Olds,
based at the University of London Institute
of Education, 1966–71

Macmillan Education

First published 1975
Reprinted 1977
Reprinted (boards and paperback) 1978, 1979

Distributed in paperback in the
United States of America and Canada by the
National Council of Teachers of English
1111 Kenyon Road, Urbana, Illinois 61801, USA

ISBN 0 333 17862 9 Boards
ISBN 0 333 24103 7 Paper

Published by
MACMILLAN EDUCATION LTD
Houndmills Basingstoke Hampshire RG21 2XS
and London
Associated companies in Delhi Dublin
Hong Kong Johannesburg Lagos Melbourne
New York Singapore and Tokyo

Printed in Hong Kong

Contents

Appendices

Tables and figures

Tables

Figures

Charts

Charts of the *audience categories* and the *function categories* will be found on the fold-out sheet which follows the index.

Preface

The proposal to inquire into the development of writing abilities in children aged eleven to eighteen was discussed in outline with representatives of the Nuffield Foundation in September 1964. By agreement among all concerned, the application was transferred to the Department of Education and Science, held over for the formation of the Schools Council, and approved by that body as a part of its initial English Programme in April 1966.

Three of us—Nancy Martin, Harold Rosen and myself—drew up the proposal. Bernard Newsome was appointed as the first full-time research officer on the project in September 1966, and at the same time our colleague in the London Institute English Department, Dennis Griffiths, joined the team. Alex McLeod was appointed as a second full-time research officer in September 1967. When Bernard Newsome left in September 1970 to direct the Schools Council project on English in the Middle Years of Schooling, Tony Burgess was appointed in his place, continued in a full-time capacity for two years and thereafter (on his appointment to a lectureship in the Institute English Department) on a voluntary basis.

In 1971, the Schools Council approved the establishment of a three-year development project—'Writing Across the Curriculum'—under Nancy Martin's directorship, to investigate in collaboration with teachers in schools the practical application of our research. The research team (now un-funded) have continued to work in collaboration with the development project and we have thus had the benefit of the assistance of the two project officers, Peter Medway and Harold Smith, in preparing this report.

Cynthia Barnes' name must be added to complete the roll: she was full-time secretary to the research project during its first five years and proved both an invaluable secretary and much more; she took, in fact, an active share in all the research procedures.

There are a great many others who have taken some share in the work—too many for me to mention them all. Mr John Dixon of Bretton Hall College of Education assisted us during a sabbatical term; Professor Merron Chorny of Calgary University during his year as a Senior Commonwealth Fellow at the Institute; Professor Wayne Booth of Chicago University, Dr Ruth

McConnell of the University of British Columbia and Professor Wallace Douglas of Northwestern University during sabbatical stays in London. Help was also received from Mr John Pride, now of Victoria University of Wellington (New Zealand), Dr Peter Wexler of the University of Essex, and Mrs Henrietta Dombey of Brighton College of Education. Mr Ted Wilkinson, HM Inspector, has been a constant source of assistance, advice and encouragement.

We have greatly profited from consultations with colleagues at the Institute of Education, notably Professor W. D. Wall and Professor B. B. Bernstein; with the Birkbeck College Applied Linguistics Research Unit (Dr Michel Blanc and his colleagues); with Mr Tom Brown of Moray House College of Education; with Mr Paul Lamb of Armidale Teachers' College; with the Nuffield–Schools Council Linguistics and English Teaching Project (Professor Michael Halliday and his colleagues); with the Schools Council Oracy Project (Dr Andrew Wilkinson and Mr Leslie Stratta); with the Nuffield Foreign Language Project (Mr Ramsey Rutherford); with the Schools Council Project on Language Development in the Primary School (Mrs Connie Rosen); with the Schools Council Humanities Curriculum Project (Dr Lawrence Stenhouse and his colleagues); and with Mr W. S. Harpin, Miss E. Louden and fellow team members of the University of Nottingham Project on the Development of Written Language in Primary School Children.

What we have tried to do here is to write a book for teachers, a book about writing in the secondary school which will at the same time stand as the record of our inquiry. As we explain in Chapter 3, the book covers only the first stage of the two-stage inquiry made possible by the Schools Council funding. We hope there will be stepping stones here that will assist further inquiries, as well as suggestions that will help teachers in drawing their own day-by-day conclusions as they deal with pupils' writing.

We have been at considerable pains to maintain our joint responsibility for the final text. Inevitably, however, the burden of first drafting the various chapters fell to various individuals, and here is the record: Chapter 1— Britton, Rosen, Martin; Chapter 2—McLeod; Chapter 3—Britton; Chapter 4 —Rosen (published in advance, in modified form, in *Educational Research*, Vol. 15, No. 3); Chapters 5, 6 and 7—Britton; Chapters 8, 9 and 10—Burgess; Chapter 11—Britton, Martin, Burgess.

We record in conclusion our gratitude to the teachers who have assisted as collectors or as assessors; to the Schools Council, both for their money and for their continued encouragement and unfailing patience (two other commodities often enough in short supply); and in particular to Mrs Sylvia Chirnside of the Schools Council Publications Section, whose editorial wisdom proved invaluable and whose tact and resourcefulness were inexhaustible.

JAMES BRITTON

The Schools Council and the publishers are grateful to the following for permission to reproduce copyright material:

John Wiley & Sons, Inc., for the diagram on p. 14, reproduced from pp. 353 and 357 of T. A. Sebeok, *Style in Language* (New York, 1960); Granada Publishing Ltd for the extract on p. 39, reproduced from D. W. Harding, 'Raids on the Inarticulate', *Use of English*, Vol. 19, 2 (1967); Holt, Rinehart & Winston, Inc., for the extract on p. 37, reproduced from pp. 125–6 of F. Smith (ed.), *Psycholinguistics and Reading* (New York, 1973); The Regents of the University of California for the extracts on pp. 56, 81 and 78, reproduced from pp. 19–20, 10 and 14–15 of E. Sapir, *Culture, Language and Personality* 1949); Basil Blackwell for the extract on pp. 75–6, reproduced from pp. 82–4 of J. Lyons, *Structural Semantics* (1963).

1 The background to the project

We classify at our peril. Experiments have shown[1] that even the lightest touch of the classifier's hand is likely to induce us to see members of a class as more alike than they actually are, and items from different classes as less alike than they actually are. And when our business is to do more than merely look, these errors may develop, in the course of our dealings, into something quite substantial. Yet, in the present state of our knowledge about the way we perceive differences and similarities, the process of classifying seems an essential stage on the way to understanding our environment, or indeed responding to it even in more practical ways: if we see somebody throw something at us we may well spend the split second wondering what category of missile it is—as well as ducking! In handling the objects of our world or relating to the people in it, we must classify as far as we can go, and one reason for an inadequate response is a failure to go far enough: if burning petrol and burning brushwood are simply 'fires' to us, we may use the wrong kind of extinguisher, and are only lucky if we don't.

It is easy to classify fires or missiles because we already possess a knowledge of the different categories which are available. There is, however, no satisfactory way of classifying pieces of writing. The serious consequences of this were brought home to the authors when, in a previous piece of work,[2] we undertook to experiment in ways of marking General Certificate of Education compositions. In the first place, we needed to build up over the course of a year a general assessment of a pupil's ability as a writer. We knew we wanted an 'all round' picture of his ability, but what kinds of task should we include? Writing a memo is different from writing a sonnet; writing a love letter is different from writing a letter to *The Times*. Again, writing about bombs is different from writing about combs is different from writing about tombs—and so we might go on. What was to constitute a relevant difference between one task and another? In other words, a naïve global sense of the ability to write needed to be broken down into distinct and comprehensive categories of task. We did the best we could—worked by hunch to produce something a little more adequate than the time-honoured text-book categories of narrative, descriptive, expository and argumentative. We arrived at eight assorted tasks which acted, so to speak, as landmarks but certainly did not attempt to map out the field.[3]

The seriousness of the consequences of taking an undifferentiated view were sharply demonstrated at a later stage in our experiment. For each of the candidates in our sample of five hundred we took a general assessment of ten pieces of written work (examples of the eight differentiated tasks and two pieces chosen from a range of tasks typical of a GCE paper) done at monthly intervals during the year in which the candidate prepared to take the GCE. We also had the marks candidates obtained for their composition in the GCE examination itself. Thus, we were in the unusual position of being able to make a direct comparison between the year's mark and the examination mark for five hundred candidates in seven schools, each assessment having been arrived at independently of the schools.

Examining boards in English themselves normally take a global view of writing ability: they present candidates with an assortment of tasks, some easier than others, and invite them to make their own choice of one, or occasionally two tasks. It is often claimed that the harder tasks (such as debating a controversial issue) are put in for the 'benefit' of the better candidate. Our records were able to show that it was, indeed, the better candidates on the whole who chose the harder tasks—we recognized them by their higher marks in the all-round assessment. But we were able to show also that they were penalized for doing so. In other words, though the examiners may have intended to make allowance in their grading for the ease or difficulty of the task chosen, they failed on this occasion to do so adequately: candidates who chose the more difficult tasks gained examination marks that compared less favourably with their all-round assessment marks than did those of the rest of the sample.

Many research workers, over a number of years, have looked for stages in the development of the ability to write, and have frequently proposed indices of maturity in writing. Their work in general has suffered from this same defect, a failure to make systematic differentiation among kinds of writing. To take a recent example, Kellogg Hunt[4] found a significant increase in the length of his 'minimal terminable unit' or 't-unit' (i.e. a main clause with its subordinate clauses, if any) in the writing of students from grades 4 to 12 (roughly ages ten to eighteen), basing his analysis on a thousand words of each student's writing regardless of topics or task; however, he found also that the measure gave very curious results when applied to the work of adult novelists (Hemingway and Faulkner). When one of the present writers[5] applied the measure to writings within function* categories, he found a mean difference between categories in the work of sixteen-year-olds greater than Hunt's difference between grades 8 and 12 (ages fourteen and eighteen).

* See Glossary on pp. 217–8 for definition of this word and others used in a specialized linguistic sense.

Moreover there was evidence to suggest that the more able writers were those who showed the greatest 't-unit' differences between one kind of writing and another.

Of course we hoped that any categories we devised for writing would be useful not only to researchers and examiners but also to teachers, particularly since it is probably in school that the global view of writing has its most insidious and powerful effects. Many teachers, we suggest, entertain the belief that an English teacher has only to teach pupils 'to write' and the skill they learn will be effective in any lesson and in any kind of writing task. As a result, it seems to us, a learning process properly the responsibility of teachers of all subjects is left to the English teacher alone, and the inevitable failures are blamed upon him. We would urge against this theory the belief that children learn to write largely *by writing* and that it is misguided to expect them to 'practise' in one lesson what they will actively employ in another: but that, of course, is a belief that rests on the assumption that writing cannot be regarded globally.

It is our intention in the present research to describe stages in the development of writing abilities. Clearly, therefore, a major part of the work will lie in finding satisfactory means of classifying writings according to the nature of the task and the nature of the demands made upon the writer; and, as far as possible, a way of classifying that is both systematic and illuminating in the light it sheds upon the writing process itself.

The rhetorical categories

That categories of writing exist is, of course, no novel idea. Indeed, if we are to judge by typical school textbooks of composition, we might say that varieties of the written language have been, until quite recent years, a preoccupation of the English teacher. A somewhat mysterious orthodoxy resulted in certain categories being presented to the learner as beyond question or debate; his problem was limited to acquiring the appropriate strategies for performing in them. Like so much else that found its way into the strange amalgam of the school English book, this orthodoxy has its history, though its disciples seem rarely to be aware of it. Its origin is to be found in the study of rhetoric which, despite vicissitudes, has continued as a basic discipline since classical antiquity, and turns up in various guises to this day.

In textbook after textbook four categories are discussed and their familiar names presented—*narration, description, exposition* and *argument*. They have shown a remarkable capacity for survival and have not been seriously challenged even in the recent revival of rhetorical studies in America.[6] They survive unscathed in the most influential of contemporary manuals, which states with confidence:

> We can see with only a moment of reflection that these four types of intention [to inform the reader, to change him, to convey to him the quality of experience, to tell him about an event] correspond to the four basic kinds of discourse: EXPOSITION, ARGUMENT, DESCRIPTION and NARRATION.[7]

In fact it requires only a little more than 'a moment of reflection' to appreciate that these time-honoured categories will not serve as a conceptual framework for the study of writing, though it requires much more time to provide a powerful and comprehensive alternative.

The four categories have evolved from the period when rhetoric broadened its realm of inquiry from persuasive oratory to all forms of written discourse; their point of origin in this form is to be found in Campbell, who wrote in 1776, 'All the ends of speaking are reducible to four', and went on to identify these ends as: to enlighten the understanding, to please the imagination, to move the passions, to influence the will.[8] By Bain's time (1866), the categories have a more familiar ring. Without supporting rationale he announced 'five leading kinds of composition, namely, Description, Narration, Exposition, Oratory and Poetry.'[9] In our own day Grierson, in the direct line of descent of this predominantly Scottish tradition of rhetoric, refers to the familiar four and asserts that they are based on 'a division which arises out of the fundamental division of experience'[10]—a bold but eccentric psychological criterion.

Small wonder then if the 'four modes of discourse' with their long history and *ex cathedra* tradition should seem unassailable. They have become so much a part of our thinking that they tend to occur whenever we discuss written composition, and what little research there is in the field accepts them without question.[11]

What then are the shortcomings of the rhetorical categories? First, it should be noted that they are derived from an examination of the finished products of professional writers, from whose work come both the categories and the rules for producing instances of them. The tradition is profoundly prescriptive and shows little inclination to observe the writing process: its concern is with how people *should* write, rather than with how they do. It can scarcely, therefore, be helpful in studying the emergence of mature writers from young writers. They had high ideals, the rhetoricians, and at their best they offer insights about language which remain valid, but, as I. A. Richards says of Whateley's *Elements* of 1828,[12] rhetoric aimed at mastery of the fundamental laws of language but what it actually provided was 'a very ably arranged and discussed collection of prudential rules about the best sorts of things to say in various argumentative situations'.[13]

It is the taxonomy itself that reveals the basic weaknesses. The categories, supposedly based on the purpose or intention of a given piece of writing, are seen only in terms of the intended effect upon an audience. Yet narrative can scarcely be seen as an intention in the same sense as persuasion or exposition might be. We can perceive widely varying intentions in different narratives such as a fictional story, a factual report of events, a scientific account of a sequence of events (the process of digestion, for example), and a narrative contained within an advertisement ('Their laughter turned to amazement').

More generally it can be said that the four categories are not equal in status. If it is the intention of a given discourse to persuade or to explain, then on this criterion the narrative and descriptive categories can be conflated with the other two. It is no difficult matter to find narrative or descriptive writing which has as its dominant function calculated persuasion or highly didactic explanation. Only by giving narrative and description sharply distinctive *functions* could the system be made consistent and workable. The concept of function, and how it relates to intention, is of course a difficult one—a matter we shall return to at some length in Chapter 5. Suffice it to say here that such central concerns as the effect on the writer of what he writes, the needs he is satisfying, his actual procedures—these are obscured rather than illuminated by the distinctions embodied in the rhetorical categories. Writing characterized as 'narration' and writing characterized as 'description' may well be performing the same function for the writer; on the other hand, two pieces put into the same category might well differ widely in the kind of demands they make on the writer: the broad category 'exposition' for example would embrace tasks as far apart as simple technical explanation and the elaboration of a complex theory. In the study of writing development vital distinctions of this kind would be completely lost.

There are other difficulties. If we attempt to use the categories, not for prescriptive purposes (for example, narrative is a category and this is how to narrate well), but as a sorting system which throws light on development, then it rapidly becomes apparent that many pieces of writing employ one mode to fulfil the functions of another. This is not, as we shall see, a difficulty that is easily overcome, since human beings soon discover means of disguising their purposes, and may have very strong motives for doing so. The system we are discussing, however, does not even acknowledge the difficulty and therefore rapidly breaks down as a practical instrument.

Finally, the system obliges us to assume that we are dealing with four major writing activities which correspond to fundamental mental activities, and that though we may encounter them only in an impure state, the pure forms exist as ideals—Platonic compositions, so to speak. Yet we must be concerned with what people actually write when they are performing, as far as we can judge, at least competently. We must base our model, in other words, on mature adult competence, if we are to trace stages in development towards that competence. No doubt the most uncomfortable of the categories, from this point of view, is that of description—despite the fact that its presence in the system has led to a strange form of school writing known as the descriptive essay. It seems to us that 'pure' description—something fit to be proffered as a model, a prescription—is very difficult to find in adult writing. Except at times in poetry, it almost always appears in conjunction with other kinds of discourse and takes a supporting role. Sustained description occurs mostly in narrative writing, and appears at points where the writer feels the need of it. Thus a descriptive passage of some length may introduce a narrative by 'setting the scene', though this may be a dying literary fashion: in contemporary fiction, the description tends to be inextricably interwoven into the narrative. More-over, standard definitions do not easily accommodate descriptions in which reality is treated as changing before the writer's eyes—a sunset for example—and they do not distinguish between generalized and specific description.[14] Finally, literary and technical description, so different in their functions and the demands they make of a writer, both fall into the one category.

Description, then, may be taken as representing in most extreme form the inherent weaknesses of the rhetorical categories and as illustrating most clearly why we were obliged at the outset to reject the system and look else-where.

The need for a multi-dimensional model

Our task was to create a model which would enable us to characterize all mature written utterances and then go on to trace the developmental steps that led to them. The traditional categories of rhetoric were, as we have argued, quite inadequate to such a purpose; another traditional scheme of categories, the notion of *genres*, was both too broadly diffuse and too exclusive to form a starting point. Since our central concern was with the development of writing in its relation to the development of thinking, we needed to focus upon the *processes* involved in writing. Obvious sources from which we might develop a model were therefore psychological and linguistic studies in child develop-ment. However, we could not expect to find anything here ready-made for us.

Since the fifties there has been a steadily growing awareness of the relation between language development and learning, so that studies of language have crept into a central position in diverse disciplines. In psychology we have drawn at many points from studies concerned with such general matters as concept-formation and cognitive growth. In linguistics, a great deal of work has arisen in a grammatical context and has therefore concerned itself with utterance at the sentence level; our evident need, however, was to characterize whole written utterances on as broad a basis as possible, taking into account as much as we could of the psychological processes and the social setting. We read with interest the more general developmental studies such as those by Loban,[15] Hunt[16] and Harris,[17] but were unable to derive from them the kind of theoretical model we were seeking.

There has been, of course, a great deal of research in America on the teaching of composition at all levels. In the main, however, these are empirical studies with a severely methodological or pedagogical intention and they yield little in the way of a theory of discourse. (There are exceptions, of course: we shall be referring in detail to the work of James Moffett,[18] and a recent study by Emig[19] shows some interesting parallels to our own work.) We found very little, either in America or elsewhere, in the way of general descriptive studies of the kinds of writing that school students actually do as part—and a large part—of their formal education.

It has been suggested recently[20] that the conclusions reached by a research worker owe a great deal to his own personality and personal past history. With this in mind we shall review the ideas and experiences that appear to us to have influenced us in arriving at a theoretical model, and attempt to relate them to particular sources where this is possible.

The school situation: its demands and limitations

The data of our descriptive and developmental study consisted of 2122 pieces of writing from sixty-five secondary schools by school students in the first, third, fifth and seventh years, drawn from their work in all subjects of the curriculum where extended writing was used (see Chapter 3 below). These pieces of writing were all set as tasks—in a non-pejorative sense—by the teachers. The tasks varied greatly, as did the writings, which we looked at very generally at this stage. At first sight some of the differences seemed to be accounted for by the demands of different school subjects and the conventions governing writing in those subjects. For instance, writings in history and in science were both informative but within this broad term different conventions obtained. Other differences seemed attributable to the differing expectations of teachers, and to varying relationships between students and teachers—but a more general problem lay behind these: the question of the degree of involvement in the writing task.

In terms of the school situation it is the problem of the set task and the extent to which the writer accepts it and makes it his own. When, and if, he makes it his own it would appear not to differ from a self-imposed task, that is writing that is voluntarily undertaken. As we met the problem in the scripts it was the difference between writings which we distinguished as being *involved* or being *perfunctory*. When involved, the writer made the task his own and began to write to satisfy himself as well as his teacher; in perfunctory writing he seemed to satisfy only the minimum demands of the task. When a writer wrote to satisfy himself as well as to fulfil the task, he seemed better able to bring the full force of his knowledge, attitudes and language experience to bear on the writing, which was carried to a conclusion on some sort of 'rising tide'. This quality of involvement was distinguishable in writing which permitted expressive uses of language or was in the poetic mode, but in other kinds of writing the

involved
perfunctory
impelled

conventions governing the impersonal language traditionally used for much school writing often made it impossible to distinguish between the perfunctory and the involved. It needs also to be said that children can often become involved at the extrinsic level of satisfaction at getting it right, or seeing a folder of work mount up, without being intrinscially involved in the writing and what it is achieving. These are differing levels of commitment though we cannot at this stage distinguish them; but that the notion of a rising tide of involvement is not merely whimsical was demonstrated by a number of pieces in which the writer seemed not to be in control of his writing but to be controlled by it. Here the topic had the writer by the throat, as it were, and its relevance to the task set was hard to determine. We called this writing *impelled*. We did not pursue these distinctions owing to lack of time, but we thought, and think, they are highly relevant to a study of the process of writing in general, and of particular relevance where closely defined tasks are increasingly set, as is likely to be the case in the later years of the secondary school.

Not unconnected with this involvement or alienation of students from their writing is the matter of the inadequate concepts and models of kinds of writing current in schools. The earlier of these models, in so far as the English lesson is concerned, was derived from the traditional categories of rhetoric described above and featured as a classificatory system for writing in most textbooks of English up to the 1950s. In the 60s a broad distinction between *personal* and *impersonal* (or *objective*) writing began to be made, and alongside this a focus developed on what was widely called (and still is) *creative* writing. Impersonal writing was dominant in the school situation, owing to the demands of the various school subjects for abstract and generalized writing, and to an implicit belief that progress in writing is associated with movement away from personal language towards more abstract and impersonal formulations. It is true, of course, that abstract writing is rooted in a knowledge of particulars and an ability to relate them, so one might expect age to be a factor in progress here. Furthermore, it is true that the ability to use the detached style of address appropriate to an unknown public audience is a relatively late development. On the other hand, it is clearly not true that expressive and poetic language belong to immaturity. The stress on creative writing (and the range of writings included under its great umbrella) developed in part as a reaction against the limitations and inadequacies of impersonal writing.

It was impossible to attempt to trace the development of writing abilities within a three-category system of classification as loose and accidental in origin as this personal/impersonal/creative model. Development in any of these modes could not be described or assessed except in terms of approximation to, on the one hand, textbook models for writing in science, history, geography; and, on the other, adult models derived from literary *genres*. Furthermore, these notions about kinds of writing and the models they related to left undescribed and unassessable, except in subjective terms, the great bulk of personal writings—such as accounts of individual experiences of all sorts—which were such a marked feature of the English teaching current in the 60s and onwards.

We needed therefore to find related sets of categories which would allow us to classify within a theoretical framework all the kinds of written utterance which occur in schools. In attempting this we were going beyond the views of Hirst[21] and others who ascribe the different kinds of writing to the concepts obtaining within the various 'disciplines', such as science, history, philosophy and so on. The weakness of this view of language differences is that since they are held to derive from the different disciplines they cannot account for writings which do not fall within certain subject boundaries, and they raise endless problems concerned with what is and is not a discipline. We were seeking a system of categories which would overarch the disciplines and which would be refined enough for us to be able to say, for instance, that a piece of writing in geography and a piece of writing in science, irrespective of subject, were alike (or different) with regard to function or audience or context. Given a refined and coherent system of classification it might then be possible to trace the stages at which school students acquire the ability to modify their writing to meet the demands of different situations and thereby move from one kind of writing to another.

Our focus on the process of writing

Our previous work on the multiple marking of compositions (referred to above, p. 1) had certainly directed our attention to the nature of the demands a writer has to meet. We were not disposed, therefore, to attempt a developmental study that merely marked out stages of progress in terms of a descriptive catalogue of the end-products. To quote from our 1966 document:[22]

When we write we are on our own. By premeditation we must arrive at the form of words which must thenceforward carry the whole of our meaning to an absent reader. What is the nature of the premeditative processes by which we arrive finally at a delayed action utterance? What strategies does a writer need?

The strategies a writer uses must be the outcome of a series of interlocking choices that arise from the context within which he writes and the resources of experience, linguistic and non-linguistic, that he brings to the occasion. He is an individual with both unique and socially determined experience, attitudes and expectations; he may be writing voluntarily or, as is almost universally the case in the school situation, he may be writing within the constraints of a prescribed task. This he either accepts and makes his own in the process of writing, or he perfunctorily fulfils his notion of what is demanded; and his choices are likely to vary from occasion to occasion and from task to task.

Would it be possible, we asked, to plot the variables—to distinguish the forces of which any given piece of writing is the result?

From our early discussions the following emerged as factors or features that it seemed possible for us to study within the limits of the design of our project:

(a) whether the writer became involved in the task set or performed it perfunctorily;

(b) his expectations with regard to the reader—usually the teacher (we came to call this set of expectations a writer's *sense of audience*);

(c) the teacher's expectations with regard to the class—as a group and if possible as individuals;

(d) *function*—that is, the demands that different tasks make upon the writer (a story, a poem, a history essay, a science report, etc.);

(e) the varying language resources which individual writers bring to their writing (how far, for example, these resources include reading experience);

(f) whether the writing is a means to some practical end or not.

If a written utterance is the resultant of variables such as these, we clearly needed to develop a model which would enable us to place any piece of writing at some point on a series of different scales or dimensions representing the variables. It was our intention to employ the model first as a means of characterizing a broad sample of school writings in all subjects, and secondly as a means of describing, in a four-year follow-up study, the development of writing ability on the part of selected pupils in five London secondary schools (see Chapter 3).

In Chapter 2 we shall consider in some detail the broader implications of our study of the process of writing.

The relation between speech and writing

It seemed to us that one very promising way into our investigation lay in considering the relationship between speech and writing—how the two processes differed and how they were alike.

Speech is constantly on the move, and the problem of all who have studied it has been to find ways of classifying the circumstances and directions of its moves. We drew on Sapir's[23] theory of the essentially expressive nature of all speech and the way in which it moves to a greater explicitness at the expense of its expressive features when the need to communicate increases. Expressive language signals the self, reflects not only the ebb and flow of a speaker's thought and feeling, but also his assumptions of shared contexts of meaning, and of a relationship of trust with his listener. He does not therefore need to be particularly explicit until he finds his listener does not understand or accept what has been said. Then the demands of the situation will cause the speaker to become more explicit, possibly more formal, and thereby edit out some of the expressive features of his utterance in order to communicate more fully.

We extended Sapir's notion of this movement of the expressive to include movement in an opposite direction from the referential or communicative— towards what we have called the *poetic*. Here the demands of shaping an utterance into a wrought verbal construct, such as a story or a poem, modify the expressive language no less than the demands of the communicative, but in very different ways. (For a fuller account of these processes, see Chapter 5.)

We thus arrived at a dynamic three-term scale (communicative–expressive– poetic) which might be used to distinguish very broadly one utterance from another across the whole range. It seemed to us to have important theoretical implications, but in practical terms it was still too broad to be adequate as a tool of analysis for our purposes.

In Sapir's notion of expressive speech being modified according to the demands of situations, we found a most important link between speech and writing. The writing of young children is often very like written down speech, and some writings by mature writers also have expressive features that make them seem nearer to speech than to writing. Clearly the degree of difference between speech and writing will vary a great deal, partly according to the demands of the situation (contrast a personal letter, for instance, with a history essay or a sociological article), and partly according to social conventions and the level of sophistication or personal taste of the writer. Expressive language interested us particularly, both because it represented some overlap between speech and writing, and because, looked at developmentally, it seemed to be the mode in which young children chiefly write. Its relationship to thinking, moreover, seems particularly direct and this suggests its importance as a mode of learning at any stage. It appears to be the means by which the new is tentatively explored, thoughts are half uttered, attitudes half expressed, the rest being left to be picked up by the listener, or reader, who is willing to take the unexpressed on trust. Its use is not, of course, always exploratory, but exploratory situations seem to call for it. Thus, a study of the expressive elements in writing has been a continuing thread in our work.

The work of Piaget and Vygotsky on inner speech has made a valuable contribution to our understanding of the way thought, speaking and writing interrelate (see page 39 below); George Mead's[24] concept of the process by which we internalize a 'generalized other' we have found helpful in relating a speaker's processes to a writer's. There are of course striking differences in the effect of context: writing is solitary, premeditated and a sustained act of imagination; there is no direct listener and no contemporaneous feed-back as in speech. Something has constantly to be envisaged and a flow of words kept going.

Vygotsky has observed that writing is remote from the purposes of the child, and children have somehow to acquire a sense of what it is for and what it is like, if they are to learn to do it. Little work[25] seems to have been done in tracing a young child's developing sense of the conventions governing the uses of writing. A child of three and a half in a nursery school kept asking her teacher for 'the handbag story'; what she wanted was for the teacher to turn out the contents of her handbag, identifying each object and saying what it was for. Older children would be likely to have learnt not to call this string of items 'a story'. Somewhere along the line, by experience rather than by definition, we acquire a notion of the differing forms of written language that serve differing purposes; and some of these modes will for a long time remain, in Vygotsky's words, 'far from the purposes of the child'.

Arriving at a multi-dimensional model

These, then, were our starting points and at the end of our first year's work we wrote the following:

Our central hypothesis is that development at the secondary stage should not be seen as progress in performing a single activity called 'writing', but rather that it expresses itself as the acquisition of new kinds of abilities—abilities which enable pupils to undertake successfully different kinds of writing. While certain accepted categories of different kinds of writing have been in use for centuries, they have proved in various ways unsatisfactory for our purposes. Our work up to this point has therefore been wholly concerned with devising a system of categories which will lend itself to the purposes of this research.

We see these categories not as a set of pigeon holes into one of which any piece of writing can be deposited, but rather as multi-dimensional, that is a piece of writing can be located at different places on a set of axes. We are not concerned to make judgements about the quality of the pieces of writing we are looking at but to consider above all *processes* and *functions*.

The work on these categories is not yet complete since our task was made more difficult and more protracted by the fact that no work of this kind has been undertaken in relation to sophisticated adult writing. In fact, most of the aid we have derived from the literature comes from work on speech and therefore requires modification and re-interpretation.

This was what we settled for—to look at process and function in order to develop a dynamic theoretical model; and, if this was to be both refined and coherent enough to do what we wanted, it had to be envisaged in multi-dimensional terms. A developmental model, however, presupposes some sort of end-point, presumably a model covering all kinds of adult writing (or to put it another way, covering the completion of the socialization process with regard to writing), and since no adequate description of the kinds of adult writing existed we needed both to produce such a model and to relate a developmental account of children's writing abilities to it. It became clear as we worked on this problem that we needed *first* to produce a theoretical description of the categories of adult writing, and *then* an account of children's writing which would show the dynamic of development towards these categories. We therefore used our initial sample of 2122 scripts (written roughly at the same time) as the basis for our general theoretical model of kinds of writing, and based our study of development on the four-year follow-up work in five particular schools (see p. 57), using the theoretical model as the chief instrument for assessing progress.

The term 'progress' is a difficult one to handle. One of the errors arising from a global view of writing is that judgements of good and bad quality are made without taking adequate account of differences in kinds of writing. Teachers are necessarily concerned with comparative judgement of quality—is this a good piece of work? Is it *better* than the last attempt? How does it *compare* with writing by other children?—and so forth. But we had to be concerned with quality in a different and more general sense. We had to envisage quality of writing as a stage in a process—the process of mastering different kinds of writing. We had, therefore, consciously to break the habit of using traditional evaluative norms of good and bad and focus on the criteria derived from our model. Thus writings by two children that in terms of stylistic criteria might be assessed as 'good', and 'merely adequate', might in our terms be held to have reached the same developmental point. For instance, two attempts by different children to write communicative rather than expressive accounts of, say, a field trip, might differ in quality in the normally accepted sense, but reveal a similar developmental stage of attempting to take account of the need of a reader for information.

We have said that much of the aid we derived from existing research came from work on speech, and in our search for a shifting-focus model for written language Jakobson's[26] notion of a hierarchy of speech functions was an important influence on our thinking. He identifies features common to any speech situation and suggests that function consists of a focus upon one of these features. Since any utterance may shift in focus from one feature to another he brings in the notion of a 'hierarchy of functions' present in any utterance: that is to say he envisages the possibility of determining a dominant function in any utterance. His model is set out in Table 1.

When a speaker's focus is on himself (the *addressor*) his speech will be, in Jakobson's terms *emotive*: Dell Hymes,[27] however, suggests the term *expressive* for this function and this certainly accords better with the notions we have taken from Sapir. When a speaker shifts his focus towards his listener (the *addressee*) or his topic (the *context*) his utterance is likely to move into the *conative* or *referential* respectively; again, when his focus is on the *message* (that is, on the exact words and their interrelationships), this represents a move into the *poetic*.

Table 1   Jakobson's hierarchy of functions[28]

Features:		CONTEXT	
	ADDRESSOR	MESSAGE	ADDRESSEE
		CONTACT	
		CODE	
Functions:		REFERENTIAL	
	EMOTIVE	POETIC	CONATIVE
		PHATIC	
		METALINGUAL	

The most obvious examples of *contact* utterances, or the *phatic* function, are the remarks, or noises, which someone in a listener role makes in a telephone conversation. Their purpose is to confirm that the channel is still working; if they do not come at regular intervals, the speaker is likely to say 'Hullo—are you still there?' When the focus shifts away from speakers, context and message to comment on details of the *code* (for example, 'That's an odd word to use—what do you mean?') the function has become, for the moment, *metalingual*.

Dell Hymes, in developing Jakobson's views, suggests that this model can at present be no more than a preliminary outline: 'as a guide for field work, its concern should be for scope and flexibility.'[29] He accepts Jakobson's notion of a hierarchy of functions derived from a focus on each of six features but finds it necessary to subdivide 'focus on context' into two functions, *referential* and *situational*. He points out that actual situations are far more complex than Jakobson's model might imply; this model, however, was important to us because it provided a dynamic classification for speech functions which might be adapted and applied to written utterances.

In adapting the model, we had to determine whether a particular piece of writing could be ascribed *as a whole* to a particular function, or whether there were functional shifts of focus within a sustained written utterance comparable to those we had observed in tape recordings and transcripts of conversations. Our experience of reading the scripts many times suggested that the first alternative was correct, and the subsequent history of the project bears out our contention. The degree of agreement in assigning a dominant function, both by team members and by teachers who assisted us, is described in Chapter 7 below. There is ample evidence to suggest that a writer sets out to do one thing in a way speakers seldom do: in other words, that one of the differences between speech and writing lies in the sustained attitude that a writer takes up with regard to features in the situation—a stance which, in favourable circumstances, he maintains to the end of his written utterance.

We were interested in exploring the relationships between the seven broad types of function suggested by Dell Hymes. Our conception of the expressive function as the 'matrix' from which a writer moves in one of two opposite

directions (towards the *transactional*[30] or the *poetic*), according to the demands
of different situations and his own response to them, provided the basic structure of our model, but it needed to be extended and refined to cover differences within the transactional and the poetic. In tackling this problem we
became interested in James Moffett's scale of abstraction: his 'I/It' scale of
varying relations between a speaker and his topic.[31] Moffett's notion of
'distance' is on the one hand temporal: for instance, we may experience an
event and comment upon it while it is happening, or, at one remove of distance, we may report it. This temporal move enables us to distance the event
in other ways: by relating it, for example, to other events, experiences or
ideas; by comparing it with similar events, classifying it, introducing relevant
reminiscences or items of historical context. At a further remove we may
theorize about the event or the classification of it and use this speculation to
produce other hypotheses. The significance of Moffett's scale for us was in
relation to the sub-categories of the transactional, and in applying it we
found we needed seven categories in place of his four (see Table 15 below).

It will be seen that our notion of expressive writing moving on occasion
towards, or into, the poetic enabled us to dispense with the terms 'personal'
and 'creative' writing: and our other spectrum, from expressive to transactional,
covers in a more precise way the difference between personal and impersonal
writing of an informative kind.

We have said (p. 10) that at the end of our first year we listed degree of
involvement, expectation, audience, function and individual resources of
language as the situational features which we intended to study. Of these,
function was clearly of outstanding importance, and we had been able to draw
on the considerable amount of work being done on speech functions. However, when we came to study the expectation of the writer as a response to the
expectations of his reader (which we later called a writer's *sense of audience*) the
literature was not so helpful. Joos,[32] for instance, categorizes five types of
speech situation which sharply affect both a speaker's language and the type
of response this provokes in a listener, but his scale (intimate–casual–conversational–formal–frozen) would not discriminate finely enough between
types of addressee, or reader. We were concerned with a particular class of
situation where the teacher, as setter of the written tasks, and as reader and
dominating influence on the writer's expectations, was apparently a constant—
that is, we needed to look at the effect of variations within the teacher–pupil
relationship, and therefore needed a set of categories which would discriminate between the teacher in different roles, and reflect the effect of differing
relationships both between the teacher and the class and between the teacher
and individuals within the class. Our audience scale had, of course, to go
beyond the teacher, and here we found parallels in the work of Moffett, whose
'I/You' scale (as distinct from the 'I/It' scale we have already referred to)
plots an increasing distance between an addressor and his addressee(s).

Eventually we formulated a set of audience categories which distinguished the manner in which the writer expressed a relationship with the reader in respect of the writer's undertaking.

While we were working on our two major dimensions of function and audience we also did a good deal of preliminary thinking about a third dimension— the language resources that a child draws on in order to write—but we were not able to develop this area of inquiry fully. In general terms, we wanted to know how a child gathers his resources from speech and uses them in the course of moving into the written language; how what he reads is brought to bear on what he writes; how the expectations of his teachers affect his capacity to move out of the written-down-speech situation; and the part that increasingly varied talk might have in the growth of his written language competence.

This third inquiry seemed to require a different kind of classification: perhaps the metaphor of a nest of Chinese boxes best illustrates our notion of how language resources in the early stages develop, each resource successively drawn on encompassing the others, and subsequently being differentiated to provide a repertoire of available uses.

At first it is important that a child should tap the resources gathered in *speaking*. For instance, many children's first writings are direct attempts at story-writing, drawing on their experience of listening to (and then reading) stories. This is, however, to assign a limited role to writing and a second start is probably required in order that writing may draw upon a variety of spoken resources and serve a range of purposes previously served by speaking. Again, some children's early attempts at writing take the form of written-down *dialogue*, which proves a poor way of, for example, reporting an experience or telling a story, since its constraints inhibit direct narrative, comment, reflection, parenthesis etc., which are all available in children's spoken language.

Moffett supports us in the belief that written down *monologue* forms the best basis for writing, that is to say an uninterrupted utterance able to be sustained in spite of the lack of stimulus from another speaker. After this foundation has been laid, internalized written forms derived from reading feed into the pool of (mainly spoken) linguistic resources on which a writer draws. Probably the first written forms internalized are those of narrative, since anecdotes and stories, spoken or written, are part of a child's social experience from the very beginning. Later, particular interests lead to particular reading, and it is these texts which are internalized, varying very much with the individual.

This highly selective internalization of the written forms of texts that interest a child is not of course sufficient to meet the demands of the subject curriculum in the secondary school. Much direct teaching goes on, supported by the study of subject textbooks, and it meets with varying success.

Any study along these lines of the resources upon which a writer draws at successive stages of his development would demand the analysis of a corpus of work from each writer, if not his total output, over a number of years. It proved, at all events, to be outside the scope of the present inquiry. We hope that one day such an inquiry will be pursued.

Finally, it should be said that, as we were able to develop only two dimensions (function and audience) systematically, our model is as yet two-dimensional; it is, however, theoretically multi-dimensional, and we have done enough preparatory work on other dimensions to be confident that further development is possible.

Notes and references

1   H. Tajfel and A. L. Welkes, 'Effects of a Classification on Judgments of Length'.
2   J. Britton, N. C. Martin and H. Rosen, *Multiple Marking of English Compositions*.
3   Ibid., pp. 35–8. (The tasks are defined on pp. 15–16.)
4   Kellogg W. Hunt, *Grammatical Structures Written at Three Grade Levels*.
5   H. Rosen, 'An investigation of the effects of differentiated writing assignments on the performance in English composition of a selected group of 15/16 year old pupils'.
6   See M. Steinmann (ed.), *New Rhetorics*, and W. R. Winterowd, *Rhetoric: A Synthesis*.
7   Cleanth Brooks and Robert Penn Warren, *Fundamentals of Good Writing*, p. 30.
8   G. Campbell, *The Philosophy of Rhetoric*.
9   A. Bain, *English Composition and Rhetoric: A Manual*, p. vi
10   H. J. C. Grierson, *Rhetoric and English Composition*, p. 136.
11   See F. W. Ballou, 'Scales for the Measurement of English Composition'; Z. E. Wiswall, 'A study of sentence structure in eighth grade composition'; J. C. Seegers, 'Forms of Discourse and Sentence Structure'; F. J. Schonell, *Backwardness in the Basic Subjects*; C. T. Ford, 'Development in Written Composition During the Primary School Period'; H. Bilbrough, 'The Effect of the Title upon Performance in English Composition; G. W. H. Gosling, *Marking English Composition*; J. C. Mellon, *Transformational Sentence Combining: A Method for Enhancing the Development of Syntactic Fluency in English Composition*.
12   R. Whateley, *Elements of Rhetoric*.
13   I. A. Richards, *The Philosophy of Rhetoric*, p. 7.
14   See Rosen, 'An investigation of the effects of differentiated writing assignments', pp. 331 ff.
15   W. Loban, *The Language of Elementary School Children*.
16   Hunt, *Grammatical Structures*.
17   R. J. Harris, 'An Experimental Inquiry into the Function and Value of Formal Grammar in the Teaching of English'.
18   James Moffett, *Teaching the Universe of Discourse*.
19   J. Emig, *The Composing Process of Twelfth Graders*.
20   T. S. Kuhn, *The Structure of Scientific Revolutions*.
21   P. H. Hirst and R. S. Peters, *The Logic of Education*.
22   J. Britton, N. C. Martin and H. Rosen, 'Abilities to Write', p. 30.
23   E. Sapir, *Culture, Language and Personality*.
24   G. H. Mead, *Mind, Self and Society*.
25   But see A. N. Applebee, 'The Spectator Role: Theoretical and Developmental Studies of Ideas about and Responses to Literature, with Special Reference to Four Age Levels'.
26   R. Jakobson, 'Linguistics and Poetics', in T. A. Sebeok, *Style in Language*.
27   Dell Hymes, 'The Ethnography of Speaking', in J. A. Fishman (ed.), *Readings in the Sociology of Language*.
28   R. Jakobson, 'Linguistics and Poetics', in T. A. Sebeok, *Style in Language*, pp. 353 and 357.

29   Dell Hymes, 'The Ethnography of Speaking', in J. A. Fishman (ed.), *Readings in the Sociology of Language*, p. 117.

30   We abandoned the commonly used term 'communicative' because, in a sense, any use of language may be said to imply some kind of communication. We use instead 'transactional', as a self-explanatory term in utterances where some transaction is involved, such as informing, recording, instructing, convincing, etc.

31   Moffett, *Teaching the Universe of Discourse*.

32   M. Joos, *The Five Clocks*.

2 The process of writing

The psychological processes involved in writing are not well understood. However, it was considered fundamental to this research project from the outset that it should be concerned with the processes by which writing is produced. It requires very little observation or introspection to reach the conclusion that these processes are very complex. Writing is often difficult, and not only for the learner: for some kinds of writing, in fact, the difficulties may actually increase as the writer becomes more proficient. We are all familiar with the struggle to express in writing what we have in mind, and we are also familiar with the very bad writing sometimes produced by very experienced and learned writers—bad, that is, when judged for its intelligibility or its consideration of the reader.

Writing is rarely just a matter of transferring spoken words to written words; nor is it often accompanied by saying the words out loud. Typically, in writing, what is in our minds becomes words on the page without any audible articulation; we have to hear the words in the head. There are, therefore, very considerable differences between the processes of speaking and the processes of writing. As Vygotsky puts it,

> Written speech is a separate linguistic function, differing from oral speech in both structure and mode of functioning. Even its minimal development requires a high level of abstraction.[1]

It appears that there has been very little systematic direct observation of fluent writers at work.[2] It is probable that there are very significant dissimilarities between fluent writing and learning to write, and that fluent writing involves a number of contrasted processes, notably those occurring during pauses compared with those going on when the pen is in contact with the paper. It may well be that some of the assumptions about writing implicit in various teaching methods will be challenged when we know more about these psychological processes.

A start can be made by shifting the focus, in the study of writing, away from the product and on to the process. It is, of course, much easier to study the product. The bulk of recent study of the spoken language has been concerned with speech—the product—rather than with the processes involved in speaking, in conversing, and in other forms of verbal interaction. This criticism can be applied even more forcibly to the study of writing, particularly the writing of children and adolescents. In literary studies there has been more interest in processes, some of it stimulated by the publication of writers' notebooks, letters and diaries, and by recorded interviews with writers such as those published by the *Paris Review*; a selection from these has recently been published.[3] D. W. Harding (see list of works in bibliography, p. 220) has made a major contribution over a long period to our understanding of the psychological processes of poets and novelists, and our research project has drawn heavily on his theories and suggestions.

We wanted to find out whether the things the professional writers say about themselves, and the things Harding has discovered and explained, are applicable to the writing of children and adolescents. Our general theory, partly presented in this chapter and developed more fully in other parts of this report, is that the similarities are much greater than the differences. But, in examining these studies of the processes by which some major works of literature have been produced, we found that there were some irreconcilable differences between the way writers work, and the way many teachers and composition textbooks are constantly advising their pupils to set about their tasks.

A recent American study suggests that the above observation might also be true of the teaching of writing in American schools. J. Emig[4] made a very detailed study of the writing processes of eight seventeen-to-eighteen-year-old high school students in Chicago. As well as studying a number of differently oriented pieces of writing from each of them, she invited them to compose aloud, 'that is, attempting to externalize their processes of composing', and also recorded interviews with them about their writing. Some of her findings would not apply to British children and adolescents, but many of her theoretical conclusions are similar in many ways to those of this research team. Her use of only two categories of writing, *reflexive* or inward-looking and *extensive* or outward-looking, we regard as too restricted for our purposes, but her study, published when our collection of data and formulation of theoretical principles was almost completed, has provided useful confirmation of many of our own findings, and insight into some aspects of the field that we had not been able to investigate.

In concerning ourselves with writing as a process, we are suggesting that such a perspective is of major importance in understanding how children's writing develops, and how the interaction of writers with readers, pupils with teachers, children with parents and other adults, and children with each other, influences and promotes the development of writing in all its functions. As writing becomes more complex and its varying functions become distinguished and developed, so too do the processes by which the writing is achieved.

The moment when one takes up a pen and begins to write stands at the point of intersection of a number of different mental and physical activities. Some of these are ended as soon as the writing begins, others are continued as the writing proceeds, while some, obviously, begin and end with the act of writing itself. If we can discover and describe these activities, and establish the dynamics of their relationships with one another, we shall arrive at a description of the process of writing—though we may have to qualify that statement when we realize that as soon as we set out to look upon writing as a process we find ourselves engaged in describing the many different processes involved in producing different kinds of writing.

Teachers have many reasons for being interested in writing processes. Their involvement with all the learning processes of their pupils requires that they understand how something came to be written, not just what is written. They can bring to their reading of a pupil's work all their knowledge of his life and his context, realizing, perhaps intuitively, that what they already know about a child and his thinking when they read his work enables them to understand and appreciate something that may be incomprehensible to another. In this respect, many teachers are far in advance of anything educational research has been able to offer them. However, in the classroom a teacher's attitude to writing processes is probably part and parcel of his total approach to children. There is rarely time to stop and think about writing processes and their particularities. It is for this reason that we hope, by concentrating our attention for the time being on those processes, to be able to provide some theoretical background for what is acknowledged to be good teaching. It is the purpose of this chapter to discuss some of the ways by which writing processes can be directly observed—though they are few—and further to consider means other than direct observation which can illuminate them—and they are many, too many for the job to be a simple one.

In the background of this discussion there lies our assumption that writing is intended to be read for itself—for what it says—and not, for instance, as a demonstration of the ability to master technical skills, such as calligraphy, spelling and punctuation. This is not to deny the importance of these skills, but they are not our concern at this point. It is fundamental to our conception of reading and writing that it includes the notion of a functioning human being putting himself 'in gear' with another in order to co-function over a limited period of time. All this may be said without making any claim to an exhaustive definition of what a functioning human being is. Our purpose is to declare that the 'indwelling of reader in writer', to borrow an expression from Polanyi,[5] is a necessary part of the process of writing to enlighten rather than to mystify.

We shall now consider two examples of typical secondary school writing assignments. A teacher of science may ask a class to carry out some experiments in a laboratory, then to record what they observe, to explain their findings in the light of their knowledge of the subject, and possibly to put forward questions or discuss the implications of whatever has been arrived at. Or a teacher of English may ask his class to read a short story and a poem, and then to write a story about anything that comes to mind after the reading.

It is likely that in both cases there would be a good deal of discussion or talk of some kind before anyone wrote anything down. The presentation of the task, and the discussion, are the means by which the teacher sets in motion the preparatory stages of the writing process.

If it works, and the writing actually gets written, a number of fairly complicated things have to happen. First, the new experience—the reading or the experimenting—has to be fitted into the whole hierarchical complex of what the pupil already knows, and what he thinks and feels about what he knows. The experience might appear to deny or call in question something he knows or believes or feels; this conflict, if it occurs, has to be resolved or at least held in suspense if the operation is to continue. Then, having made sense of the new experience for himself, he has to apply it to the writing assignment, which makes new demands on him. The act of writing itself, once begun, is now probably helping his thinking, but he must, while he thinks, continue to be aware of the demands of the eventual reader, in so far as he knows them, and these may or may not combine happily with the direction his own thoughts take him. These difficulties may arise even if he has no problems in comprehending and interpreting the task and manipulating his ideas. But what happens if he has? The science student may need to consult his friends, or his books or his teacher, as well as his memory, and whatever he receives from those sources has to be made to fit, again, into what he already knows and what he learnt from what he did. The English student may suffer a total or partial failure of invention. He too can consult his friends, his teacher, and his memory, but all three may fail him (in a way that they would be unlikely to fail the science student), because nothing they say will help unless he can turn it into a story he wants to write.

These examples may suggest that it is worth looking at the process of writing, in terms of two preliminary stages, as well as the writing itself; and, further, that the eventual destination of the writing (who will read it and why, and whether it is to be kept or discarded, and why) exercises a profound influence on the preparatory stages and the writing. We have therefore divided the discussion of our topic into three sections—conception, incubation and production—though we shall not expect to find that the distinction between them can always be sharply maintained.

The first stage: conception

Writing is a deliberate act; one has to make up one's mind to do it. The decision may be forced on one, but then one still has to agree to be forced, or to refuse. So the process begins with those events which lead up to this decision, however it has been arrived at. The conception process may be very brief (it is more likely to be so when one is under orders)—or it can be very long: autobiographical notes are full of writers who have spent years mulling over slowly crystallizing ideas. There is usually some specific incident—this may be a purely internal 'mental' incident—which provokes the decision to write. In school it is normally a request from a teacher, with a greater or less degree of incitement or coercion, stated or implied; it is characteristic of school writing that *a task is set*. However, the amount of choice the writer has in what he will write about, and how he will do it, varies enormously. There is perhaps less variation in choosing when he will do it, and even less in deciding whether writing is the best way of meeting the educational needs of the moment. Very often the teacher has fairly firm ideas about what he wants, and he can measure the achievement of the pupils against his ideal. If this is the case, it is likely that some aspects of the process will be closely controlled too. Pupils may be told, perhaps, to consult books A, B, and C, or to use as a framework the notes given on the blackboard, and thus their attention is, as it were, focused for them.

But, however controlled the situation, the writer is *selecting* from what he knows and thinks (unless pure copying is all that's wanted), and embodying that knowledge and thought in words which *he* produces, no matter how much he draws on the language of a book or of the teacher's notes. Many young writers realize their own need to be themselves in their writing, even within the framework provided for them. Source-book material may be used in various ways involving different levels of activity by the writer. (Degrees of copying are discussed later in this chapter.) But some school writing tasks leave more decisions to be made by the writer—such as requests to 'treat the topic in whatever way you think appropriate', or open invitations to 'choose any topic that interests you and write about it'—and in these the process is much less controlled. However, help or direction may be provided more subtly; if we showed a film of violence in the streets and then asked pupils to write whatever they liked, we should probably be surprised if the thought-into-word process didn't at least begin by treating violence. Of course school pupils, like adults, sometimes decide for themselves to write something they want to write, and their teachers may not even see what's written. Writing that is totally self-initiated is of great interest to us, not least because it provides an important link with mature adult writing. It is also likely to be accompanied by much greater involvement by the writer, and may have very much longer preparatory stages, and most of the processes mentioned here may be much more complex.

Whatever it is that provokes the decision to write, it may begin as an isolated event but it soon comes to be seen in relation to all the writer's relevant previous experience. His conception, the way he explains to himself what he must do, is influenced by his involvement or lack of it. There are degrees of perfunctoriness, even at this stage. Optimally, he summons up all his powers, his knowledge, his feelings and attitudes, and he may have to struggle to fit his idea of this current task into what he knows he must do. If the method to be followed is explicit and familiar, this stage may be momentary. If it is implicit or unfamiliar, he may need time to draw on the complex interrelations of his experience and its realization in language—and this includes, as well as his primary experience, all those other things he has heard about, read about, and imagined. Even if the task is something he doesn't care about, but must do, he must begin by trying to understand what to do.

The writer, we are claiming, must relate his task, somewhere, to his own *hierarchical construct system.* We have taken this term from the American psychologist George Kelly,[6] whose theories provided us with a very useful approach to the problems involved in understanding writing. In the case of a school task, it may be that the writer will feel some obligation to restrict his 'summoning up of powers' to his school experience, and he may discount everyday experience as not relevant. His school experience, particularly his up-to-that-moment experience of writing in school, will strongly influence his construing of his present task.

The ability to recall is now critical—we must, after all, rely on our memory, even though we know that only some items are recalled with reasonable accuracy, while others may have been altered or rearranged inadvertently. Some relevant items may have been lost without trace; that won't bother us, but we may if we are unlucky spend some time trying to recapture those things we know we know, if only we could remember them.

The way the teacher sets up the writing task varies enormously, but it is probably a potent factor in determing the writing process. We know that there is wide variation from writer to writer in all stages of preparing to write. Teachers usually make allowance for this, but sometimes feel constrained to offer the kind of guidance that implies that there is a best way of doing it. Variation in the degree of specificity of the task has already been mentioned; it is a curious feature of some school tasks that there is a high degree of speci-

ficity, but it is largely implicit, particularly in such things as the anticipated degree of formality of the language, or the kinds of items of personal experience that may permissibly be included (the gas evolved had a smell of bitter almonds) and those that may not be included (the gas evolved had the smell of garlic but this was caused by impurities in the zinc which we have been taught to ignore).

If the writing topic is rigidly defined, and even if there is some latitude or choice, the kind of demand or suggestion made may also vary. The teacher may or may not specify how the topic is to be treated; he may offer a detailed context for the operation or none; he may say what is the purpose of the writing task (test, significant data to be learned and remembered, recording of observations, presentation of opinion, or telling a story) or he may say nothing about it; he may suggest or imply the nature of the eventual audience (see Chapter 4), and the role relationship he appears to anticipate between himself and the writer (is it just for him to mark, or does he expect to enjoy it?—will he show it to the headmaster or put it in the form magazine, or in the dustbin?). He may make certain stylistic demands, suggestions or specifications about how the writing is to be presented: 'watch your handwriting and remember full stops'; 'avoid slang'; 'a geography essay is diamond shaped';[7] 'just write what comes to mind'; 'try to vary your sentence construction'. Alternatively, the suggestions and demands may be methodological: 'first make rough notes'; 'give reasons for all statements'; 'support your answer with relevant quotations'; 'don't bother with a rough draft—write it straight out'.

For the child who can barely manage the task, the conception stage can be harder than the writing itself. It is then that total bafflement can set in. He may ask very simple questions, or raise points that have already been answered, in the hope of finding some clue, or he may sit silently mystified for fear of displaying his ignorance. Recollections of past failures will tend to make him think that he is bound to misinterpret the task; he will imagine difficulties that aren't there. Teachers have dozens of ways of restoring confidence. A common one is to simplify the task and prop up the writer with detailed instructions. This may be the best way of making sure that the result is what the teacher wants, but it won't help if the next assignment is different. Alternative approaches, such as 'Do it in whatever way seems right to you', may not produce the kind of work the teacher had in mind, but it could encourage the baffled child to try to explain the task to himself, and help him towards the beginnings of a more confident approach.

So the conception stage is completed when the writer knows that he is going to write and he has formed some idea of what is expected of him—and, as well as having endeavoured to come to terms with all the demands and suggestions, and perhaps his recollections of how he did the last piece and how well or badly it was received, he is, one hopes, thinking a good deal about how he, himself, will present his knowledge and his ideas and perhaps something of himself too, to his reader, in such a way that he may be willing later to acknowledge it as his own.

The second stage: incubation

It may seem rather pointless to write at such length about the preparatory stages of writing when one knows that there are very many occasions in schools when pupils are set tasks and immediately take up their pens and write. Written examinations discourage extensive premeditation of the writing. Examinees often scribble a collection of feverish notes; it takes courage, or despair, to sit in an exam room just thinking. However, an understanding of the writing process demands that we pay attention to preparatory phases, and we can perhaps learn more from those occasions when the process is not so hurried. It is true, of course, that when a writer begins a task as soon as it is set, the conception and incubation processes are running concurrently with production. Writers then define and redefine the task, and plan ahead, and sort out their ideas, while they are writing, and it's very difficult, retrospectively, to separate the three activities. Sometimes a writer is able to make use of what has been incubated for some other purpose. In any case, even if there has been time for conception and incubation, these processes do not end when the writing begins—the redefining, the planning and sorting are still going on. Most of the verbalization of ideas probably occurs at the point of utterance. When we say we are thinking ahead, we may keep in mind that we are developing ideas and perhaps some general plan, but only the next few words can be continuously present in the consciousness of the writer as he writes. But no matter how much the actual writing, as it is produced, shapes thought and modifies our conception—and we certainly believe that it does so—we cannot ignore the pre-writing stages. There are two important reasons. The evidence of mature writers provides many examples of the way incubation works. Some particularly telling examples of this are provided by Harding in his article 'Raids on the Inarticulate'.[8] Another aspect of incubation is described by Graham Wallas in *The Art of Thought*, in which he quotes from Helmholtz, the German philosopher and scientist, an account of the way important new thoughts came to him in four stages; and yet another by Michael Polanyi in *Personal Knowledge*, in his discussion of tacit knowledge and formal articulation.

The other important reason for studying the preparatory stages is that it is in these stages that teachers seek to influence the writing of their pupils. Once they are writing, we do not interrupt them with advice, but we do a great many things before they begin, so the more we know about the way the writing process works in the early stages, the more influence we are likely to have. We may also learn more about when we should not interfere.

Two factors are likely to influence the kinds of planning and incubating that go on in a writer's mind. There is the need to get it right in terms of the facts of the case and what is generally known or accepted; these may of course be challenged or rejected but cannot normally be ignored. There is also the need to get it right with the self, the need to arrive at the point where one has the satisfaction of presenting what is to be presented in the way one thinks it should be done. Both these aspects of projecting thought into writing are always there but usually one predominates. Making a summary, or writing down memorized factual data, is likely to involve almost exclusively the first; a poem may be almost entirely concerned with the second. But the two aspects interact and it is rare for either to function at the optimum level unless that interaction is powerful. They stem, of course, from two aspects of language, everywhere acknowledged, perhaps best distinguished by the terms 'expressive' and 'communicative', though the underlying idea is related to the kind of distinction we are making rather loosely when we speak of personal and impersonal writing, to the much wider question of the interrelationship of affective and cognitive thought processes, to the foundations of language itself involved in Susanne Langer's discussion[9] of presentational and discursive symbolism, and, more recently, to Roger Poole's attempt[10] to reduce the question to one of subjectivity and objectivity.

As Gusdorf puts it,

It's not a question, then, of an inverse relationship between expression and communication. The two intentions of human speech are complementary. Pure expression, detached from all communication, remains a fiction, because all speech implies aiming toward others. To break silence, if only with a cry of anguish or a song without words, is still to address someone, to call to witness, to call for help . . .

Inversely, the idea of a communication without expression is senseless, because my language can never be absolutely expropriated. It would not exist unless a personal intention had initially brought it into being.[11]

A full discussion of the emergence of separate functions in writing will be found in Chapters 5 and 6. At this stage it is merely necessary to point out that the incubation of our writing must acknowledge both the expressive and the communicative functions, because each feeds the other. But what kind of help is commonly offered to children in school? Frequently it's called planning, and this in itself suggests that the communicative aspect is emphasized: concentration is directed towards the marshalling of significant data, logical ordering, precision, exclusion of the irrelevant, justification of assertion and possibly formal proof, and, very often, the exclusion of the writer's individuality from what he writes. At an earlier stage, when this kind of planning is thought to be too complex for the writer to attempt, the plan may be provided—the data supplied readily to hand, the attention sharply focused on the exact demands to be met. And something like this is of course sometimes necessary: we do need to learn how to arrive at a formally structured and coherent product.

Young writers' ways of planning their writing, and their attitudes to planning, naturally vary enormously. It seems clear that teachers are more strongly in favour of planning than many of their pupils. Here is a comment on planning by an eighteen-year-old girl:

. . . Before any big essay, for example in English literature, I think to myself 'yes plan an essay like Miss —— said' but I begin to plan it and then suddenly the urge to start the actual piece of written work is overpowering—and 'bang' goes the plan . . . I can rely on this happening every time without exception.

We collected many comments of this nature from older pupils. Many were strongly in favour of planning for some kinds of writing. That appears obvious and sensible, but the following, from another eighteen-year-old girl, adds a further element to the discussion:

I cannot bear writing to a plan. I can rarely be induced to write my own and the though of writing to someone else's plan fills me with horror . . . which probably explains why my work is generally disorganized and rambling.

There follow here two pages, very well organized and without rambling, on the differences she perceives between writing history and English literature essays. She then returns to the planning theme:

It has just occurred to me that when writing Literature essays I always scribble down all clever thoughts on paper first. Then sometimes I may even write a complete rough essay but usually I write the final essay, using the written facts as a guide to help me think out the argument. I do not know if 'clever thoughts' rate as a 'plan', but I thought you might like to know anyway.

This girl's method would suggest that planning, like the whole process, can best succeed when it becomes part of the writer's own feeling for the work. If a ready-made plan is offered as an aid, something crucial to the child's interpretation of the task—his assimilation of it to his own understanding—may not be given a chance.

This shows up clearly when the system doesn't work. Suppose a child has attempted to follow the plan offered, but the work he gives in does not make sense. He may offer us something which would be totally incomprehensible to a reader if he were unfamiliar with both the data and the writer. This could be because the child got the facts wrong, or because he didn't care whether it made sense or not—those are the hazards of the game. There is also the possibility that he didn't understand, or more likely, that his understanding was incomplete, and his verbalization did not adequately express what he did understand. Now 'understanding' and 'expressing' are not necessarily influenced by making and following detailed plans. *An essential part of the writing process is explaining the matter to oneself*—and that is a highly idiosyncratic affair. There are plenty of things we are sure we know but cannot articulate: 'tacit knowledge', Polanyi calls it. There are many more where we may still be working towards a satisfactory understanding, and others where we surprise ourselves by only realizing after we've said or written something that we've succeeded in bringing to light an idea we thought was only half-formed. And we vary enormously in the amount of confidence we have in our tentative formulations.

C. B. Cazden[12] puts it this way: 'Language is knowledge in our heads: speech is the realization of that knowledge in behaviour.' Without distorting her intention, we can extend this to cover writing as well as speech, and we have to ask whether this vital stage in the process, this explanation to ourselves—maybe possibly hearing the words in the head—is one that can be influenced at all in the incubation stage of writing. Without it, all the careful note-making and selection and arrangement of data can do very little. It depends on the expressive and the communicative aspects of language feeding each other.

It takes time to incubate one's ideas. But often in school the assumption seems to be that, unless writing is done at once, vital ideas or information will be lost. This is in marked contrast to the view expressed by many mature writers and thinkers. Nearly half a century ago, Graham Wallas wrote as follows:

But, in the case of the more difficult forms of creative thought, the making, for instance, of a scientific discovery, the writing of a poem or a play, or the formulation of an important political decision, it is desirable not only that there should be an interval free from conscious thought on the particular problem concerned, but also that that interval should be so spent that nothing should interfere with the free working of the unconscious or partially conscious processes of the mind. In those cases the stage of incubation should include a large amount of actual mental relaxation.[13]

We are clearly a long way from the sixteen-year-old examination candidate whose homework is often three or four pieces of written work every evening.

It may well be that there are some things we write best if we write them at once, in the heat of the moment, but it is unlikely that they would be writings we should regard as our best work. Yet children are constantly judged on the basis of such impromptu and instantaneous performances. Few teachers would be willing or able to allow their pupils complete freedom to choose when they are ready to write, waiting always until the ideas have 'come to the boil', but many are now doing so for a part of the writing, and also allowing a little more leg-room, in terms of time, for all written tasks.

The relationship of talk to writing is central to the writing process. It is no longer necessary to justify classroom talk as a means to anything else; it is properly valued in its own right, but this doesn't detract from our conviction that good talk helps to encourage good writing. It is probable that of all the things teachers are now doing to make their pupils' approach to writing more stimulating, and the writing itself seem a more integral part of the manifold activities of the classroom, it is the encouragement of different kinds of talk which is the commonest and most productive factor. Talk is more expressive— the speaker is not obliged to keep himself in the background as he may be in writing; talk relies on an immediate link with listeners, usually a group or a whole class; the rapid exchanges of conversation allow many things to go on at once—exploration, clarification, shared interpretation, insight into differences of opinion, illustration and anecdote, explanation by gesture, expression of doubt; and if something is not clear you can go on until it is. Whether or not the mind is partly engaged in thinking about what may be written later, there's

Challenger
Bereiter's
developmental
shift from
conversation
to
text

a good chance that the incubation of ideas is taking place, and from this the incubation of the writing is given a boost, by the widening of the conscious-ness if by nothing else.[14]

Not all classroom talk will directly feed into the writing process. Nor should it. Improvised drama may well provide starting points for writing, but that is not why we do it. If the drama is a success the actors are likely to feel that all that matters has been expressed. Discussion, too, valuable though it is in the incubation of writing, can sometimes have the effect of narrowing the field of vision. It's interesting sometimes to observe strong-minded pupils who opt out of a discussion and begin writing, at the point where they know what they want to write and further talk is a distraction.

One of the great values of talk in the writing process is that it permits the expression of tentative conclusions and opinions. To the extent that incu-bation consists of arriving at an understanding, working towards a synthesis, coming to terms with a general principle, it's a great advantage to be able to try it out. The process won't be complete until the writing is done, but the free flow of talk allows ideas to be bandied about, and opens up new relation-ships, so that explaining the whole thing to oneself may be much easier. The kind of question-and-answer session that is looking only for right answers is of limited value, because it assumes that the task is simpler than it really is. Right answers are usually to be achieved by repeating the words of others—the textbook, or the notes, or the dictionary—and they may not make any demands on the pupil's ability to understand, explain, interpret and generalize for himself.

We have not so far attempted to distinguish the incubation processes appro-priate to different kinds of writing. If Gusdorf (see p. 27) is right, one ought to consider the similarities before the differences, and our own work on ex-pressive writing (see Chapters 5 and 6) would tend towards the same view. In every kind of writing, defining the nature of the operation, devising ways of tackling it, and explaining its meaning and implications to oneself, are essential stages in which the mind engages. In the writing of young children, and in some kinds of more mature expressive writing, these stages may be rudi-mentary and their realization incomplete, but that only serves to reinforce our belief that the expressive and the communicative are intimately related. Sapir suggests that 'in all language behaviour there are intertwined, in enormously complex patterns, isolable patterns of two distinct orders. These may be roughly defined as patterns of reference and patterns of expression.'[15] The point is that the complex patterns and the intertwining come first, and the isolating of reference and expression emerge later. Applying Sapir's hypothesis to the preliminary stages of writing, we would want to say that in the emergence of any original thinking (including under 'original' ideas which are new to the writer but may be familiar to the teacher-reader) there is an expressive stage in that thinking whether the writing is ultimately informative, poetic, or persuasive. It is what the writer makes of these expressive beginnings that determines his thought processes as the written text is produced.

Teachers naturally steer their pupils in desired directions. They want their pupils to have a variety of 'communicative competences' in writing.[16] We have noted that a great deal of the planning carried out emphasizes the communicative aspect. But teachers of English and, increasingly, teachers of some other subjects, are concerned with those processes which lead to expressive and poetic writing.

During the middle sixties a strong movement towards creative writing developed in some English schools. It was assumed that, given some attractive stimulus, original, profound and beautiful writing would emerge, and teachers should do nothing to interfere with the 'free' expression of the creative imagination. It is true that a great deal of very good writing did emerge, and the influence of the movement has, on the whole, been favourable. It encouraged teachers to read what their pupils wrote for its own merits, and not with some hypothetical standard of perfection in mind. But all worthwhile writing is creative in one way or another, and imagination is not confined to poetry. Nor is the writing of poems and stories free expression: here the writer is subject to constraints of many kinds, though he may have more options open to him than, say, a research scientist or a court reporter.

Some extremist advocates of this approach to creative writing arrived at the point where evaluation become impossible. Everything was 'creative' and therefore everything was good. How then could progress be observed? Teachers of English often find it difficult enough to say precisely what they mean by progress, and the areas of disagreement are vast. But this particular dilemma need not have arisen. It arose from a confusion of process and product. The teacher is in no position to try to evaluate the psychological processes that go into the writing of a poem. But once the work is written, it is there to be shared, and we say what we want to say about it to the writer. That doesn't imply marking or grading; however, a proper response may include an appraisal of the work. The evaluation comes in the kind of interest we show in the child. All teachers' responses are evaluative. On the one hand, withholding of help that would be welcomed can be a disservice; on the other hand, comments offered may sometimes be unhelpful or even inept. This is a crucial issue, but a discussion of it would lead us well away from the matter of this chapter.

Moreover, we need to distinguish between getting the process going, and attempting directly to influence it so as to determine the kind of process. The first, largely in the conception stage, is the teacher's major concern; in the second we would want to tread very warily. We know that some young writers think a great deal, possibly over a long period, about ideas that are developing into poems and stories. Bernard Newsome[17] was able to trace the growth and transformation of a compelling idea in one girl's writing over a period of nearly two years, but the only intervention of the teacher in this process was discussion with her of each poem or story after it had been completed. It seems that the teacher's influence on processes of this kind is necessarily indirect and often unintentional, though it may be very powerful. It could well be strongest when the reading, talking and writing of a class and its teacher follow a progression, with a number of dominant strands weaving in and out. We might here be offering what Graham Wallas wanted writers to have—'an interval free from conscious thought on the particular problem concerned'.

So long as the teacher is the 'significant other', the audience to whom the writing is primarily directed, his influence on process will be strong. His preferences and dislikes will be considered, even if they are not always respected.

One thing that does not seem possible is the detailed planning of poetic writing. Once the conception has begun to emerge—what Langer[18] called the 'import' of the work—most children are ready to start writing. There will still be a place for insights, and illuminations that may alter and develop the work as it takes its shape, but these are much more likely to be produced as the writing proceeds. And they are so much the personal possession of the writer that the teacher has no place in their formation.

The third stage: production

The discussion of conception and incubation of writing has anticipated to some extent aspects of the study that more properly belong with production. This was unavoidable, as the preliminary stages look forward to the writing itself; also—as has already been pointed out—it is largely in these stages that teachers seek to influence the writing of their pupils.

The production stage, the crucial one as far as psychological processes are concerned, is the most difficult to study. The writer is, essentially, alone with his thoughts, his pen, and his paper. Any oral communication, even an appeal for assistance, is an interruption. He may be nearer, psychologically, to his eventual reader than he is to someone sitting beside him.

The insights, such as they are, that we can gain into processes at this stage come in three ways. We can learn a little from watching and listening to the writer at work; we can study what people say about what they do; and sometimes we can infer something about the process from the product itself, especially if we know a good deal about the circumstances under which the writing has been done.

It must be admitted, however, that it is not yet possible to present a coherent theory of psychological processes in writing. All we are able to do is to provide a number of hypotheses concerning various aspects of those processes, and even these hypotheses cannot be easily related to one another.

EVIDENCE OF PROCESS GAINED FROM DIRECT OBSERVATION

Children making a start on a piece of writing sometimes reveal useful clues to the ways their minds are working. Hoggart has suggested that

*[handwritten: Conversation w/ self *?, T]*

> Writing isn't simply a way we reach others. It is a dialogue with ourselves. Finding a tone to talk with begins with finding one that seems right to and for us. Talking to others begins with 'talking to yourself' and with 'being yourself in talking'.[19]

Knowing how to begin may be as much a matter of 'finding a tone to talk with . . . one that seems right to and for us' as of knowing what to write about.

During this project we had many opportunities for watching how some secondary school children set about their tasks, without ourselves having to take any part in getting the thing going, as that was done by the class teacher. It seemed that many children had developed certain strategies for making a beginning. Several of them always began by writing at the top of the page their name and the date and a title. Very neatly. It seemed to make them a little more comfortable. They often wanted to be told what title to put down. Some, we think, were put off if the answer given by the teacher was 'Put what title you like, or none at all.' It appears that the title may play a part in finding a way to begin, and if a title is chosen, it has some effect on the way the writing proceeds, even if no title has been stipulated by the teacher. On one occasion, when ten minutes' class discussion before beginning was suggested, the class, without any intervention by the teacher, decided that the appropriate title was 'Profile of 4A'. That class's writing on that occasion followed a fairly consistent pattern, in marked contrast to comparable classes given a similar task and left to find their own titles individually, where there was very much more diversity.

[handwritten: Ritual]

A common strategy was to ask a question: 'Can you write about . . .?' 'Does it have to be true?'—or even, 'Can I write what I like?' These may well have been requests for reassurance, mainly to have some kind of confirmation that, whatever it was they were thinking of writing, it would be acceptable. A few appeared to be thinking about anything but the writing they were going to do. They moved around the room, chatted a bit, complained about having to do it at all, 'mucked about', and then quite suddenly started to write.

It was often possible to see on their faces the moment when they knew how to start. One fourteen-year-old girl, one of the least successful in her year in a large inner London comprehensive school, having been given some pieces of writing about themselves by people her own age, and asked to do something similar, was quite baffled for several minutes and asked to have everything on the sheet read to her a second time. Then she suddenly said, 'Oh I see, you can just write down whatever comes into y'r 'ead.' An expression of calm delight—neither calmness nor delight played much part in her life—came over her face, and she wrote three and a half quarto pages in twenty minutes. The only interruption to the flow was asking for more paper. Here is how she began:

School

One Friday afternoon I whent out of school and I met my mum with her mate down the road. When I come along she said coming shopping. The woman said O ant she sweet and her boy was with her I said come on Mum lets go shopping then The she said Stop hurring your mother I said I can and I got smaked When I never with my mum I have a Puff or two Some people say how smart I am dressed and that I am kind.

It takes some time to analyse what it was that caused her commitment to this piece of writing. It is a series of apparently unconnected episodes, like this extract; the common feature of the episodes, however, is that they all contain other people's openly expressed opinions of her. She had in fact found her way into writing this piece in terms of herself as others see her.

It's not only girls like her who find making a start difficult. The opening paragraphs of this section (see p. 32) gave the writer of this chapter a great deal of difficulty. As he explains,

Originally the section began with what is now the third paragraph, in a slightly different form. Thinking about how to begin it was spread over about forty hours. After completing the section before, and making a rather guilt-inducing decision not to proceed at once, I spent a whole day doing other things, including reading parts of three books rather remotely connected with the subject, and talking for a few moments about it to colleagues. While walking in the street the following morning, the opening sentence in its original form—'Insight into the process of writing comes in three ways . . . '—emerged uninvited into my consciousness, together, of course, with the three part expansion of 'ways' which follows, but that remained at the tacit level until it was written down some three hours later. Even then, it didn't strike me as a very good beginning, and I recall a strong feeling that it should have been a great deal easier because it was the only thing I had to do at the time, and the conception and incubation processes, including jotted notes made over the past three months, had already been taken as far as they could go. I often throw away the first paragraph of things I write, and this one might have been discarded if it had not become part of this explanation.

After making a start, children sometimes decide that it won't do and begin again. The strength of their conviction that a new start must be made, even though the teacher may have made no complaints about what has been written, is sometimes remarkable. They are not easily persuaded to reconsider a decision to reject what they have done. Some seem to make a habit of rejecting their beginnings, and rarely complete anything. These may be timid children for whom committing themselves to paper at all—'finding a tone to talk with' and 'being oneself in talking'—imposes a severe strain.

This all seems to suggest that adolescent writers do have some sense of the

importance of the opening words, and perhaps they have begun to realize sub-
consciously the extent to which the tenor of the whole is influenced by the
beginning. Getting a start, then, involves both finding a way into the topic,
and making some kind of subjective decision about the appropriate way of
expressing it. It is possible that the greater the maturity of the writer, the
more difficulty he may have in making a start. The effect of the opening sentence on all that follows it is explored in an unpublished Ph.D thesis by H.
Rosen.[20]

Once there has been a good start, there is often a period of fairly intense concentration. Interruptions are resented, though young writers may sometimes
interrupt themselves by asking for assistance. But observation shows that the
writing is not continuous, nor is the rate of production regular. Pauses are
often longer than the time spent actually writing. We can see a writer scanning
back over what has been done, and possibly making alterations; this, even if it
takes up comparatively little of the pause-time, may be quite important. On
one occasion, four members of this research team tried writing with worn-out
ball-point pens. We couldn't, therefore, see what we had written, but we
used carbon paper so that what we wrote could be read later. We were acutely
uncomfortable. When we wrote letters to an absent member of the team about
what we were doing, and when we reported recent experiences in a straightforward narrative, we were able to complete the task with only a few blunders;
but when we tried to formulate theoretical principles, even on a topic very
familiar to us all, and when we tried to write poems, we were defeated. We
just could not hold the thread of an argument or the shape of a poem in our
minds, because scanning back was impossible. As we expected, the carbon
copies showed many inconsistencies and logical and syntactical discontinuities.
They were, in fact, useless.

So it seems that scanning back is needed to help the writer keep overall
control of what he is doing, as well as to make corrections and improvements.
However, a very much larger proportion of the pause-time is concerned with
what is going to be written next. We can observe writers, totally absorbed in
the task, gazing into space or at blank paper, pen in hand, sometimes for quite
long periods. These pauses tend to be shorter and less frequent in narrative
writing than in most other kinds. We have noticed also that many young
writers take up narrative form even when doing so means that they thereby
fail to do what they were asked, as when a child asked to write about 'Gangs'
devotes all his time to telling the story of what happened on one particular
occasion.

Direct observation can tell us very little about what is happening during
pauses, and why some kinds of writing produce more pauses. However,
Emig's[21] method of asking students to externalize their own processes provides useful evidence. Although the composing process is not likely to be the
same when one has to talk as well as write, there is much to be learned from

her method. Here is one of her subjects, Lynn, as recorded while writing. (Italics indicate the words she wrote down; the repetitions mean that she spoke them again, not that she wrote them more than once.)

> *He dances in front*
> *He dances*
> *He dances in front of the living room*
> *He dances* (sixteen-second pause)
> *He dances with an expression of utter bliss on his face,* I could say 'smack in the middle of the' (three-second pause)
> *He dances with an expression of utter bliss on his face directly in the path of any-one*—yes, this is going to be good—*entering the front door* . . .
> Now I think I can put something else in that sentence about 'He dances' (re-reads silently)
> I might make it, 'He dances with an expression of utter bliss on his face, his arms held open in greeting, directly in the path of, et cetera'

Data of this kind are even more valuable when supplemented by retro-spective comment from the writer. Emig's interviews with Lynn, presented in full in her book, are of exceptional interest. It would be well worthwhile to replicate Emig's work in England, possibly studying younger writers as well.

Some recent work by Frank Smith gives an indication of what we might learn by a more detailed study of what fluent writers do. Smith's theories derive from other sources besides direct observation, but they are noted in this section because they point towards some kinds of direct observation that might be helpful. In *Psycholinguistics and Reading*, Chapter 10, 'Alphabetic Writing—A Language Compromise', he discusses the ways in which the relationship between phonology and orthography is related to writing and reading, and in particular to the *different systems* employed in writing and reading. Basing his argument partly on the work of Chomsky and Halle[22] and Carol Chomsky,[23] he finds that fluent writers normally draw very little on the relationship between the sound of a word and its representation on paper. They relate orthography directly to meaning. Their 'immediate' process involves mainly their ability to draw on a repertoire of what he calls 'integrated move-ment sequences', that is, roughly, the ability to write large numbers of words, or substantial sections of words, as whole units. It is only in 'mediated' writing processes that the writer uses other systems to determine how to write a word, and these, in order of importance, are (*a*) spelling lists (that is, remembered correct spellings); (*b*) analogic strategies (for example, if telegraph ends with -graph, it is reasonable to suppose that photograph will end similarly); (*c*) sound-to-spelling rules. System (*c*), the only one given much prominence in most writing instruction even today, is placed last in importance by Smith: the implication is that we call in our knowledge of how sounds are represented by letters only if all else fails. Smith states:

Normal writing would be impossible if we had to stop and think about every letter individually, just as piano playing would be impossible if the pianist had to think about and play every arpeggio one note at a time.[24]

Smith's method, with writing as with reading, is to begin by giving us full an account as possible of what a fluent writer (or reader) does, and then discuss the means by which the reader may arrive at such fluency. He writes:

Incidentally, it is quite obvious with writing as with reading that written language is related directly to meaning, not to sound. We would be just as likely to write 'a none tolled hymn' as 'a nun told him' if we were writing down the sound of words.

As in the case of immediate word identification [in reading], I suspect that the development and use of integrated movement patterns for writing are both the natural objective and the ultimate achievement of the skill. A child beginning to learn to write his first word—his name, for example—begins with a number of unrelated shapes that he rapidly integrates into one continuous movement (even though there may be breaks where the pen is lifted from the page).

However, because of the additional information and effort that a writer must put into a word compared with the relatively effortless task of establishing a visual feature list, the majority of words are initially put together letter by letter, by copying from a visible model or through the intermediary of dictation or memory. In other words, some mediated form of word representation intervenes between first acquaintance with a word and an integrated movement sequence, even though readers can go directly to visual feature lists and immediate word identifications without mediated processes.[25]

Smith's work may suggest ways in which we might be able to make w less difficult. It is possible that much of the advice normally given to ch about how to write effectively would, if taken, increase the difficulties pose for instance that a teacher has been to some pains to get the p going by engaging the interest of his pupils in a topic to the point whe ideas are flowing freely. If he then makes precise stylistic demands, matical prohibitions and admonitions, and insists, for instance, on the l up in the dictionary of all words where the writer is in doubt, he may the conscious choosing and the mediated processes of the writer so muc the forefront of his mind that the production of ideas is interrupted point where it dries up. Fortunately children are very good at ignoring such stylistic advice and getting on with the job.

This is not to suggest that it is wrong to try to influence how children write, but merely to say that direct advice during writing is seldom helpful. Whatever influence can be exerted should come to the writer in other ways and at other times—at times when he is not actually engaged in writing. It is perhaps not too much to suggest that we learn to write by reading and talking —and by writing.

EVIDENCE OF WRITING PROCESSES DERIVED FROM WHAT THE WRITER SAYS

> *But words came halting out, wanting Invention's stay;*
> *Invention, Nature's child, fled stepdame Study's blows;*
> *And others' feet still seem'd but strangers in my way.*
> *Thus, great with child to speak, and helpless in my throes,*
> *Biting my truand pen, beating myself for spite,*
> *'Fool', said my Muse to me, 'look in thy heart and write.'*
>
> (from Sir Philip Sidney: *Astrophel and Stella*, sonnet I)

Here are some comments on their writing from some sixth formers:

. . . essays in English and History were the sort of thing I had to leave a long while for, sit down at home in silence, and really work at. Writing original pieces of any length has always been difficult, perhaps because I tend to start writing and see what happens, rather than formulate some synopsis beforehand.

One girl concluded her comments by saying, 'I write so that I can understand.' Another boy's comment was as follows:

I find about all my writing, whatever form it takes, it is never exactly what I meant to write. This is partly, perhaps, my inadequate handling of language, but also the inherent nature of language. What a particular word means to me might be totally different from its associations in another's mind. Abstracts obviously will have widely divergent associations, but even mundane concrete objects have different contexts, however minute, for each individual . . .

A boy who left school at sixteen and went to police college continued to send us writing for two years. His final piece included this:

Also it is easier to write the truth than to say it. And by re-reading one's work one can learn a lot about oneself . . . Earlier this year when I was revising for my Sociology O Level (which luckily I passed) I learnt that I write better without a plan. If I just pour my thought out on paper I build up a type of plan anyway. But if I try to jot down notes my mind goes blank.

These four young writers are just as aware as Sidney was of the complexities of the writing process. They suggest that the approaches they have worked out for themselves often take precedence over careful advice—offered to them. One wonders to what extent those who give this advice about working to a plan, structuring, concentration on clear thinking—actually follow it in their own writing. 'Always think out a sentence right to the end before you begin to write it' might seem a sensible thing to recommend to a pupil who is having trouble with sentence structure. But it is almost impossible to follow this recommendation. Try it now, by making your own comment on the assertion we have just made. If the sentence is more than twenty-five words, having thought it out, can you remember it exactly? If you can, did you finish writing it without wanting to alter what you remembered?

It is tempting to think of writing as a process of making linguistic choices from one's repertoire of syntactic structures and lexical items. This would suggest that there is a meaning, or something to be expressed, in the writer's mind, and that he proceeds to choose, from the words and structures he has at his disposal, the ones that best match his meaning. But is that really how it happens? Harding raises the doubt in this way: *D.W. Harding*

> The notion that in putting an experience into words we always start from a definite something and seek words adequate to convey it may be an over-simplification. It seems necessary to add that language and experience interpenetrate one another. The language available to us influences our experience at intimate levels and if we manage to convey experience precisely, that may be due partly to the fact that available modes of expression were influencing the experience from the start.[26]

It was suggested in the discussion of incubation that the understanding of ideas and experience, and the articulation of those ideas in words, proceed side by side but at different rates (see pp. 26–7). They are not one and the same thing, but neither are they separable. The best description of the dialectical interrelationship of thought and language is still probably that provided by Vygotsky.[27] Our concern here is to stress how intimately the thought-language dialectic is involved in the process of writing. In particular, the way Vygotsky defines inner speech is of crucial importance, not only to an explanation of the process, but also to understanding what will make writing easier.

He suggests that inner speech is not the interior aspect of external speech but constitutes an independent linguistic function. His idea as to how this function develops is perhaps our best approach to what he means by it. He believes that in infancy a child takes over external speech from those about him, discovers the value of talking to himself about what he is doing ('speech for oneself' in Vygotsky's term), and so develops a form of speech suited to this non-communicative function—a form which is at first spoken aloud but soon used silently, and which more and more frees itself from the restrictions of syntax (using, for example, predicates with no stated subject), and the restrictions of commonly-accepted word meanings. As it becomes inner speech, that is to say, as it becomes syntactically loosened and abbreviated and semantically individuated, the more meaningful it becomes to the user because he need not make himself intelligible to any listener.

It is as though, in developing inner speech, the child were building a bridge between external, communicative language on the one hand and thought on the other. Thus, in Vygotsky's words, 'Inner speech is to a large extent thinking in pure meanings. It is a dynamic, shifting, unstable thing fluttering between word and thought, the two more or less stable, more or less firmly delineated components of verbal thought.'[28] ✓

This intermediate plane between word and thought is clearly an actively *operational* area. Vygotsky speaks of the movement from inner to outer planes —'from the motive which engenders a thought to the shaping of the thought, first in inner speech, then in meanings of words, and finally in words.'[29] And when written language is the end product, he sees the journey as particularly strenuous: 'The change from maximally compact inner speech to maximally detailed written speech requires what might be called deliberate semantics— deliberate structuring of the web of meaning.'[30]

The four quotations from adolescents reflecting about their own writing are from pieces they wrote because we asked them to reflect—but how much is a writer, in general, aware of his own processes? In talking and in reading, one is probably very rarely troubled by any such thing. In writing, the possibilities for wondering about what we do are very much greater. We can think about our writing because it stays there while we think about it; sometimes its difficulty may make us reflect, and that reflection can include some concern or interest about how it came to be written at all. Moreover, we can go back on it, alter, reject, rearrange, and consider alternatives, and these editing procedures may prompt us to be curious about how we came to write it as we did, so that if we are asked we may be able to give some kind of account of how we went about it. But generally we don't pay much attention to these things. It seems certain that in the very early stages of learning to write there is a great deal of concentration on how the words in the head can be got on to the paper at all, at the very simple level of knowing what letters to use, and even, sometimes, how to make the letters. This is grappling with the difficulty, rather than awareness of process, and with luck it may soon diminish to the point where a child and his teacher take it for granted that, barring accidents and the occasional spelling problem, he can get down on the paper anything he knows.

This account of awareness of process is undoubtedly a great over-simplification, but it is the kind of rough and ready assumption we may have to work with if we are to get anything written at all. That is because such awareness is quite likely to have an inhibiting effect on getting on with the job. Conscious and deliberate choosing would appear to play a very limited part in what a fluent writer does. It is only when there is a difficulty to be resolved that the need to choose becomes conscious. Also, some younger writers are so limited in the kinds of choice open to them that they are unaware of any need to choose. They are unlikely to be dissatisfied with the way they have tackled something unless someone tells them that it should have been done differently.

If writing is uninterrupted and the going easy, one is barely aware of making selections and rejecting alternatives. In fact these words—choice, selection, alternatives—are inappropriate to the process when it is proceeding fluently, because they tend to imply that we hunt in our minds for words to express our thoughts, whereas, as we have seen, thought derives from language just as much as language derives from thought. But writing is not always fluent.

When the task is difficult or complex, or when the external constraints are strong, the fluent process is often interrupted by the need to make conscious choices—to select the appropriate word, to make sure of the punctuation, to keep the tone and level of formality consistent, to decide about intricacies of grammar and syntax. These choices become even more difficult if we are slightly uneasy about our mastery of what is acceptable in the particular context. Giving guidance through this territory has, as we know, been a major concern of teachers of writing for as long as writing has existed. For our present purposes, it is more interesting, in noting the enormously complex and varied discriminations that can be made apparent, to realize that very often we make them all continuously and very rapidly without knowing, and we may even feel that we produce our most original work when we can concentrate on the general import of what we are writing, and do not have to interrupt the flow to decide between the relative merits of one word and another, or to divert attention to grammar, punctuation, style or tone when we are working at full stretch on the ideas. Emig's claim that 'writing is one of the most complex processes man engages in' can now perhaps be justified.

It is not surprising that a writer rarely goes very long without pausing. Pauses and hesitations in speaking have been studied in great detail, notably by Goldman-Eisler.[31] Reading research has been greatly advanced by study of the cause and nature of pauses. The observation of pauses in writing has already been referred to (p. 35) but we must go on to say that, while the revising and recollecting function of pauses is of great importance, their planning function must surely be crucial. It is tempting to put it simply as, 'We pause while we decide what to write down next', but that doesn't help us to know how the decision is controlled. One obvious constraint on the writing process, the number of words or ideas that may be held in the consciousness at one time, will be discussed below in the section on memory. Clearly, though, part of what is going on during a pause is a struggle to 'get it right', and nearly everything in this chapter may be relevant to that struggle—getting it right for the topic, for the writer, and for the reader.

The effect of external constraints is relevant here too. The ways in which the audience and the function of the writing may or may not restrict the writer will be considered at length later, but in general terms we can assume that something that can be written down as it comes to mind will require fewer pauses than something in which there are specific demands to be met. The four young writers quoted at the beginning of this section give some support to our belief that, while learning how to meet demands and expectations is one of the essentials in the development of writing, there are plenty of occasions when making fewer demands and allowing something to be written as it comes to mind might result in something better—more interesting to read and more enjoyable and profitable to write.

EVIDENCE OF PROCESSES INFERRED FROM THE PRODUCT

Every reader probably at some time makes some inferences about the processes of writing from the product. It's very difficult not to. Understanding and enjoying what we read frequently involve bringing our knowledge of the writer and his experience—that is, his context—to bear on what he wrote. But for the writer the process may be one of 'de-contextualizing' his experience. A skilled writer often works to detach what it is he wants to communicate from his own specific context, so that a reader who does not share that context may still share the understanding and the satisfaction of the writer. Others, particularly some poets and novelists, are able to present individualized experience in such a way that it achieves a high degree of universality in the reader's response.

 However, this detachment of experience from the writer's context is one of the difficult things about writing. Many young writers cannot do it. They can only write for readers they know, and that is why the response to their writing is so dependent on the shared context of the undertaking. Further, understanding and enjoying their work is often also dependent on seeing how it came to be written. In other words, without insight into the processes we are not able to make a proper response to the product.

Here is an example from a seven year old boy:

When I was Little

I was scared for I wasnt used to it and as well as that things wornte as nice as they are because my Mur Mun came But even from that day to this I have never stayed to dinner

The 'it' he was scared of was school. The phrase 'because my Mun came' sums up a whole complex series of events, something like this: 'At first I was very unhappy and scared but things got a lot better ["as nice as they are"] after my mother made several visits to the classroom and discussed the whole problem with my teacher.' To take the intended sense we have to realize that the 'because' is linked to the words immediately preceding it, and not to the whole of the sentence up to that point, as it probably would be in more mature writing. The 'But' which introduces the last sentence makes an important contribution to the unexpressed thoughts in the background. It is there to tell us that even now the playground is rather frightening, especially during the lunch hour.

The feelings that went into the making of this short recollection—the remembered fear, the satisfaction that it is now safely in the past, and the final implied warning—are not revealed, merely referred to, but they are central to our understanding of the psychological processes involved. The piece of writing earlier in this chapter by the fourteen-year-old girl (page 34) is similar in that we cannot begin to arrive at an understanding of her meaning, let alone her processes, unless we know a great deal of the context.

In much school writing, the context that we as teachers know so well includes books and classroom experience as well as the individuality of the child's feeling and thinking. Another piece, written by the older sister of the boy quoted above when she was six, shows, in a very simple way, recent reading feeding the writing process.[32] After the teacher had read *The Iron Man* by Ted Hughes the children were asked to write their own story about the Iron Man, and this girl began:

One day the Iron Man was in his scrap-metal yard when the little boy Hogarth came by.

Hello Iron Man he said. I have come to ask your help. I will help if I can sais the Iron Man and his voice rumbaled like a thunder storm only much louder. Well said Hogarth the sky is falling and it was so low when we sent a space rocket up to the moon it only went 100 miles till it got there.

Well said the Iron Man if I help I will have to have a rocket made me but I dont think we will be abel to make one.

Of cors we will said Hogarth.

The Iron Man, the scrap-metal yard and the boy Hogarth all come from Ted Hughes. The rest is her own. We can make quite confident inferences here about the way the story and its characters have stimulated her imagination and at the same time allowed her to bring in her own ideas. There is a great deal still to be discovered about the psychological processes in children's make-believe play, fantasy, and imaginative story telling. This particular girl could write such stories much more fluently than she could tell them aloud, though the opposite was true of her brother. Schools generally encourage written stories but provide few opportunities for oral story-telling; this appears to be one area where the feed-in of talk to writing is cut off very early.

A good deal used to be taken for granted about direct relationships between what children were made to read and what they ought therefore to be able to write. We are beginning to discover, however, that, no matter how much we help, children need to find their own ways of processing ideas and information and feelings, and that they differ enormously in how they do it. Focusing on processes rather than products will help us to appreciate the different methods and strategies children adopt as they learn to use the writing of others to develop their own. If we have this appreciation we are unlikely to condemn writing as 'highly derivative' or even 'plagiarized' just because we can see very clearly the influence of the sources; the process of taking on someone else's thinking, and expressing it in one's own writing, may in fact have been a valuable experience.

Teachers derive great satisfaction from reading their pupils' work. It is, however, a time-consuming activity, and many are tempted to read hastily, or to read only part, or to tick and hand back. Inspectors and advisers have often recommended skip-reading as a way of turning aside the pressing demands of English teachers for more free time. We believe, however, that very close reading of children's writing is essential, because that is the best means we have of understanding their writing processes. Children value perceptive comments, responses and questions on their writing, but they quickly see through perfunctory approval and generalized faint praise. And it's worth remembering that for very many children, for many years, their teachers are the only readers of the bulk of their work.

As readers we respond first to what children actually write, not what they may have intended to write. But if the gap between probable intention and actual product is wide, that may help us to gain insights into procedural difficulties. Even slips of the pen, errors and omissions can give clues to children's thinking. A boy who wrote 'I don't really know what my parents were like at my act' probably meant 'at my age', but the error may give us a good hint about himself.

It is true that the inferences we can make as we read the work of children will be largely intuitive. This need not worry us. The better we know the children, the more apt our intuitions are likely to be. Often, in the course of this research project, our reading of the pupil's writing led us to make intuitive judgements. Some of these we were able to develop and discuss, and many of them contributed eventually to the hypotheses and theoretical formulations that are presented in the following chapters.

Other aspects of writing as process

MEMORY

It is clear that the part played by memory in writing processes requires much detailed study. There is very little that we can say with any degree of certainty. It does seem probable that under some circumstances the act of writing actually assists the operation of the memory, and also that some things are remembered more clearly and fully from the written record than from the spoken word, but we were not able to investigate these phenomena in our study. There is, however, one aspect of memory that does bear on a theory that has influenced much of our thinking.

We have made it clear that we believe the most significant processes in writing go on at the point of 'utterance', that is to say, the formulation, and the setting down of the words on paper, go on together and are interdependent. If this is true, one crucial aspect of memory would be how much can be held in the sharp focus of the writer's attention at one time. The theory that there are important distinctions to be made between the short-term memory and the long-term memory would, if accepted, at least give us something to start from. Frank Smith,[33] while admitting that the theory is contentious, has used it to explain some processes in reading. A proper application of the theory to writing has yet to be made, but it is possible to see one important way in which it might apply.

The short-term memory, it is claimed, can hold only about four or five separate items. Smith writes:

Because its capacity is very limited, short term memory is disrupted if new information comes in before the information it contains has been disposed of . . . there is no absolute limit to how long information can be kept in short-term memory, but because we constantly want to pass new information through the bottleneck of its limited capacity, its effective duration is only a few seconds at most.

The long-term memory, however, has no limitations of this kind. It has the very convenient property that information, ideas, feelings, and even vividly recorded experience, can remain there undisturbed for years. But it is not a reservoir, nor a warehouse, and as a data-bank it has certain peculiarities. We have all experienced the frustration of not being able to recall something that we know that we know. It is as if we cannot find what we want. We have to know our way about. We arrange what we keep, but we frequently alter the arrangement, and we have a more elaborate cross-referencing system than any computer yet devised—so we need special procedures, and we're not always sure what those procedures are.

When we are writing, the short term memory is drawing on the long-term memory, as successive bunches of words appears on the page. One of the limitations on composition, then, is the number of words that may be held at one time in the short-term memory. These are the words we 'hear in the head' as we write. What has just been written, and what is still to be written, can only be held there to a very limited extent. For someone just learning to write, the number of words in the short-term memory may be even fewer, for he often needs to have letters there as separate items. The fluent writer, however, can hold not only whole words and phrases, but meanings as well, and possibly even general intentions (which can scarcely be thought of as items), so that it is much easier for what is written to have coherence. If, on the other hand, the teasing out of the thought becomes particularly difficult, all the resources of the short-term memory may have to be concentrated on a few words. That is when a writer may lose the track of his thoughts, omit or repeat words, misconnect or blunder in some way.[34]

Clearly, memory as we have spoken of it here is part of the whole imaginative and constructive process. We arrange our experiences, and they then make more sense to us, and the 'sense' they make is our own contribution, not part of the direct experience. We compare what happens with what we think might happen. We even think about what we know can't happen. We tell stories. We guess, and compare, and make moral judgements. We create theories and works of art. We may, with Sartre 'conclude that imagination is not a contingent and superadded power of consciousness, it is the whole of consciousness as it realizes its freedom.'[35] It is what we choose to do with our consciousness of our experience. It is also, in a sense, what we choose to do with our memory.

USE OF WRITTEN AND PRINTED SOURCES FOR WRITING

The complex variety of ways in which we draw on the writing of others has been referred to elsewhere in this chapter. It may be helpful, in addition, to propose a kind of scale, which we might call 'degrees of copying'.

First there is purely mechanical copying in which the writer may not understand, nor even try to understand, what he writes. Another kind of pure copying is found when children repeat exactly what the book says because it is the easiest thing to do. A further stage is reached by those who copy out things because they like them, or because they concur, or think they are memorable or that they may need them later. And sometimes children are required to reproduce, as exactly as possible, something they have learned by heart. None of the above include any significant composing by the writer; this comes in only when he tries to reproduce the ideas of the original in his own way. A different kind of complication appears when he has to summarize or expand what he has read.

The writer's self comes in more when he draws on others in the sense of 'taking the reader round the exhibits', presenting parts of his assimilated reading that he thinks interesting or important, and very possibly presenting himself to some extent through the 'exhibits' he has chosen. This technique reaches its most sophisticated level, perhaps, in the early chapters of many learned works.

As the element of copying recedes the writer may still be drawing very heavily on other writers for the best possible reasons. He may want to write like some particular author because he admires him—the apprentice-to-master relationship—or he may need to present a writer's ideas and theories so that he can discuss them. Finally, some writers are able to draw on the work of several others in order to find a synthesis of their own. This last is rare in school work, but it can be found—and it can be fostered. It may well be that a writer has to pass through most of the stages mentioned before he can reach the last. The pawn becomes queen.

REVISION

Great writers and teachers of composition agree about very little, but a large proportion of both are fiercely insistent on the need for very careful revision. But when we look into it we find that revision covers nearly as many activities as writing itself. These activities have in common only the fact that in them the writer becomes the reader of his own work. He may even try to be a detached and critical reader, but it is perhaps more likely that, in any substantial revision, the writer–reader relationship is shuttling to and fro. The correction of obvious slips and errors, the minor mishaps of writing, need not concern us much, and the checking of data and references, once one has learnt how to do it, is a relatively straightforward matter.

Often, however, pupils are exhorted to check their 'language'. The checking of grammar, syntax, the tone and appropriateness of the language, is fraught with hazards for the learner, especially if he has any reason for being uneasy about what is appropriate in the particular context, or if the piece of writing is one on which he is being judged or tested. Tests of linguistic acceptability are apt to be so closely associated with subjective judgements about social acceptability that the young writer may learn to mistrust his own language and, by trying to be correct, stifle half of what he wanted to say. *Again*

It is a common and natural thing in revision to realize that one has got it wrong—that what one has written does not accord with one's present thinking, and that some degree of redrafting, as opposed to simple correcting, is needed. There is a distinction to be made, too, between those things that a writer alters because he has changed his mind and those where he feels he has not succeeded in representing his thought. In the latter case, especially, we are back once more with the dialectical interpenetration of language and thought (see p. 39). It is true that a writer may not completely know what he thinks until it is fully formulated in words, but it is also true that he can tell when the words he has used have not achieved the embodiment of his thoughts suffic- iently to provide the satisfaction he must feel before he is prepared to let the completed writing go to the reader. Revision, then, is not just a question of correcting and improving. It is also the final stage of the process by which a writer presents himself: every piece of writing can be, to some extent, a declaration, a tacit agreement with the reader that the writer accepts responsi- bility for his own creation.

In putting the finishing touches to any piece of writing, one becomes aware, once again, of the twofold nature of the whole process—the need to meet demands and satisfy the reader, and the need of the writer to satisfy himself, to do what he wanted to do. In holding the balance between these two forces, he learns a great variety of roles and strategies, and these must very largely be worked out anew for each new kind of task. School tasks often require that certain strategies should be acquired—summary-writing is a common if rather unlovable example—and sometimes some of the strategy can be taught. But the part that can be taught may be very small and is possibly trivial in relation to the task as a whole. A writer draws on the whole store of his experience, and his whole social being, so that in the act of writing he imposes his own individuality. One of the reasons why this study is so absorbing is that no two people can ever write exactly alike.

Notes and references

1   L. Vygotsky, *Thought and Language*, p. 98.

2   Now that TV cameras and videotape are fairly easily available, it is possible to study writers at work. The tapes, the completed pieces of writing, and the writers' retrospective comments might provide very useful information about what happens during writing.

3   Kay Dick (ed.), *Writers at Work: The Paris Review Interviews*.

4   J. Emig, *The Composing Process of Twelfth Graders*.

5   M. Polanyi, *Personal Knowledge*.

6   G. Kelly, *The Psychology of Personal Constructs*.

7   This was explained to one of us by a sixth form girl, whose geography teacher had used the expression to help his pupils follow his instructions—to begin the essay with a clear statement of the topic, to follow this with an elaboration and detailed examples, and finally to draw together the threads of the argument in order to return to the topic as originally stated. She had found the advice very helpful.

8   'The surprising length of time that some writers have wrestled with a piece of creative work without reaching what seems to be a central feature of the finished product comes out vividly in two experiences of Carson McCullers. [Only one of these is quoted here.] Of her first novel *The Heart is a Lonely Hunter*, she wrote:

> For a whole year I worked on this book and didn't understand it at all. All the characters were there and they were all talking to this man—but I didn't know why they were talking to him. Then one day, after working very hard on this novel I did not understand, I was walking up and down the floor when suddenly it came to me that Harry Minowitz (his name) is a deaf-mute and immediately the name was changed to John Singer. The whole focus of this novel was fixed and I was, for the first time, committed morally, ethically, and with my whole soul to *The Heart is a Lonely Hunter*.'

(Oliver Evans, *Carson McCullers: Her life and work*, London 1967, quoted by D. W. Harding in 'Raids on the Inarticulate', pp. 104–5.)

9   S. K. Langer, *Philosophy in a New Key*.

10   R. Poole, *Towards Deep Subjectivity*.

11   G. Gusdorf, *Speaking* (trans. P. Brockelman), pp. 56–7.

12   C. B. Cazden, *Child Language and Education*.

13   G. Wallas, *The Art of Thought*, p. 87.

14   These observations on the role of talk are brief. They are not an attempt to summarize the extensive and valuable recent work on the subject. See, for example, D. Barnes *et al.*, *Language, The Learner and The School*, especially the section on talk in 'A Language Policy Across the Curriculum', pp. 162–4.

15   E. Sapir, *Culture, Language and Personality*, p. 11.

16   See Dell Hymes, 'Competence and Performance in Linguistic Theory'.

17   J. Britton and B. Newsome, 'What is learned in English Lessons?'

18   S. K. Langer, *Mind: An Essay on Human Feeling* (Vol. 1), p. 77.

19   R. Hoggart, *The Reith Lectures*.

20   H. Rosen, 'An investigation of the effects of differentiated writing assignments on the performance in English composition of a selected group of 15/16 year old pupils'.

21   Emig, *Composing Process*, p. 58.

22   N. Chomsky and M. Halle, *The Sound Pattern of English*.

23   Carol Chomsky, 'Reading, Writing and Phonology'.

24   Frank Smith (ed.), *Psycholinguistics and Reading*, pp. 125–6.

25   Ibid.

26   D. W. Harding, 'Raids on the Inarticulate', p. 110.

27   Vygotsky, *Thought and Language*, pp. 119–53.

28   Ibid., p. 149.

29   Ibid., p. 152.

30   Ibid., p. 100.

31   F. Goldman-Eisler, 'Speech Analysis and Mental Processes',

32   The choice of writing by quite young children who were very well known to us (they were in fact the children of the writer of the chapter) was made to enable us to be brief, as well as to be quite sure that we did know the context pretty fully. The known context of the writing of secondary school pupils is often so wide that it would be a lengthy task to bring the readers of this report far enough into it to make discussion possible.

33   Frank Smith, *Understanding Reading*, p. 78.

34   If we are right in surmising that the writer of the following wrote 'outlook' when he intended to write 'outlet', then it might well be that the error arose because his attention was already focused upon the point he was to make in the following sentence —a point he drives home by italicizing the word 'saw':

Philip hadn't had many dreams of late years. Sleeping pills inhibited them; that was one of their side-effects, and a bad one, for dreams were an outlet for the sub-conscious mind, and if denied this outlook, it took revenge in other ways. In madness, perhaps. One *saw* things in dreams of course, and one was aware of conversations; but were these conversations conveyed by sound, or by the illusion of the dream? (L. P. Hartley, 'Fall in at the double', *Mrs Carteret Receives and Other Stories*, p. 48.)

35   Jean-Paul Sartre, *The Psychology of Imagination*, p. 216.

3 The research problem and procedures

<u>Aim</u>

Our proposal was originally formulated (1965) in the following terms: <u>our aim</u> was to undertake a developmental study of the processes by which the written language of young children becomes differentiated, during the years eleven to eighteen, into kinds of written discourse appropriate to different purposes—in particular, a study of the dynamic relationship, within these kinds of discourse, of personal to impersonal uses of the written language; and, finally, some assessment of the contribution of the spoken language to this development, and of the relation between writing ability and reading ability.

<u>Methodology</u> Our *method* comprised four different procedures, formulated in the following proposal:

1 *Preliminary.* To set up hypothetical categories of written discourse appropriate to the general needs of the individual in our society by (*a*) considering traditional categories, and suggestions arising from recent work, and (*b*) carrying out pilot analyses (statistical and linguistic) of samples of written work by children and adults.

2 *Synchronic sample of writing.* <u>Taking as wide a range as possible</u> of <u>written work by a representative sample of 500 boys and girls</u> aged <u>eleven to eighteen, and</u> having tested the validity of the hypothetical categories referred to above, to (*a*) <u>investigate the stages by which children acquire competence in these categories, and</u> (*b*) investigate the <u>developmental relationships between categories.</u>

3 *Diachronic sample of writing.* To reinforce and amplify the above investigation by analysing four years' written work produced by a representative sample of 100 children eleven years old at the outset, and 100 children fourteen years old at the outset. In particular, attention would be paid to individual patterns of development which the synchronic sample could not reveal.

4 *Sub-sample for detailed study.* Taking a sub-sample of not less than thirty boys and girls selected from the diachronic sample, to study the relationship between their development in written language, their use of the spoken language, and their ability in reading comprehension.

Work on this sample would be in collaboration with researchers in the other fields.

It is the purpose of the present report to cover the first two items in the proposal (though it will be clear that they did not remain as two distinct phases). The third item will be the subject of a further report; the fourth was not carried out, since the two researches in parallel (on spoken language and reading comprehension) did not in fact take place as originally planned.

Collecting our material

We needed a pool of material to represent as widely as possible the kind of writing work that goes on in schools—over the whole secondary age range, over the whole ability range and across the subjects of the curriculum. We decided that our target should be six pieces of writing from each child, and—since English work seemed likely to produce a greater variety among written tasks than any other subject—that two of the pieces from each child should be in English, and that each of the remaining four pieces should be taken from a different subject. In order to sharpen the age contrasts we asked only for work from the first, third, fifth and seventh years. And we set out to collect the work of as many classes as possible, so that any sample of 500 we might draw would be representative of a larger pool.

An article explaining our proposals was published in *New Education* on 19 October 1966:[1] it was addressed to teachers and included an invitation to readers to volunteer as collectors. The direct response was small, but judicious use of some 250 offprints brought us, by March of the following year, from three to six pieces of writing from each of 1664 boys and girls, from eighty-five classes in sixty-five schools of many types scattered throughout England.

From this we drew our sample of the work of 500 boys and girls: 2122 pieces in all. Again, for the purpose of sharpening contrasts (of ability this time) we allowed secondary modern school classes and high ability grammar school classes twice the average probability of being selected. To compensate for very small entries we made the same provision for boarding school and technical college classes (there was in fact only one of the latter). Seventh year girls were in short supply and we had to take into the sample the whole set of fifty-nine received, and this made it impossible to balance the years and sexes exactly. The composition of our final sample is shown in Table 2.

Each child was given a number from 1 to 500, as drawn; each script bore this number followed by the serial number of the class followed by a serial number for the subject (allowing numbers 1 and 2 for English): thus, script 500685 is the work of pupil number 500 in class number 68 in subject number 5 (religious education).

With each set of classwork had come from the collectors a brief indication

Table 2   Breakdown of sample in terms of
sex and year of schooling

	Boys	Girls	Totals
1st year	62	63	125
3rd year	62	63	125
5th year	62	63	125
7th year	66	59	125
TOTALS	252	248	500

of the context of the writing—details of the task set and a comment by the
teacher on the ability of the class in the particular subject. These details were
reproduced with each script, and the whole sample was scrambled (regardless
of child, class and subject) and made up into sets of 100. In this form the
scripts were delivered to the teachers and members of the unit who were to
process them.

Collecting our thoughts

It is interesting to look back now at the broad conception we had of our task
before we began working on the material. Notes made at the time of drawing
up the initial proposal included the following:

Assumptions. That written utterances vary from each other
  (*a*) in accordance with linguistic resources of the writer (lexical and syntac-
       tical, spoken and written);
  (*b*) in accordance with other abilities and characteristics of the writer—per-
       ceptiveness (selectivity, conscious and unconscious), power of logical
       thought, habitual modes of imagery, more general personality traits;
  (*c*) in accordance with the strategy (or principle of selection and organization)
       chosen by the writer which itself will vary with the writer's intention (real
       or ostensible), his relation to his subject, his relation to his reader(s)—de-
       tachment or involvement (respect, love, hate, fear etc.).

By the time the proposal was finally approved in April 1966, and a consultative meeting called of colleagues from all departments in the University
of London Institute of Education, our briefing paper described our intentions
as follows:

We propose to look for a development pattern in terms of kinds of writing and
our first task is therefore to identify such kinds.
   We believe that writing should not for our educational purposes be divided
simply into traditional rhetorical types, but that we need to find categories which
are based on valid criteria. Our experience suggests that there is likely to be a
hierarchy of kinds of writing which is shaped by the thinking problems with

which the writer is confronted. The kind of writing first used effectively by the young writer appears to be essentially personal; the last kinds to be acquired (if they ever are) are those scientific and social uses of language which appear to be essentially impersonal. What lies between is as yet uncharted territory.

The paper concluded with the hope that the 'inquiry would provide a "map" of uses of the written language', and that 'this might form a basis for further research and development work envisaged as part of the Schools Council English Programme'; further, that 'its findings should suggest many applications for all subjects in the secondary school curriculum, and in some cases, we would hope, form the basis for a language policy for a school as a whole.'

In October 1966 we held an invitational ad hoc consultative meeting and put our ideas before an august and on the whole encouraging assembly of linguists, psychologists, sociologists and other researchers.

Meanwhile, we instituted what was to be our continued mode of working. For a day or a half-day or an evening the team of five of us[2] would meet for discussion—working on pilot scripts collected the previous summer or on brief working papers prepared by team members. We met as often as possible, which worked out (even in the busiest times) at not less than once a week in termtime. We had frequent joint sessions with other research teams and consultations with interested visitors and experts.

It was at this time that we embarked upon the study of existing work that we have referred to in earlier sections of this report, testing out on scripts any ideas that seemed promising. Our focus was, as we have said, upon the *process* of writing, since we felt that a fuller understanding of process would lead to ways of construing differences between products that were psychologically meaningful.

We have already referred to our interest in the *timing* of the writing process (p. 35). When we discovered that the only experimental attempt to carry out such a timing dated back to 1946 and yielded nothing very enlightening,[3] we did in fact work out a procedure intended to produce a time-record matched word-for-word with the process of writing and revising a script throughout a single writing occasion. A colleague in the Department of Electrical Engineering at University College, London, studied our requirements and was prepared to produce a prototype electronic transmitting pen to meet them. This would have cost about £300 and would have required the purchase of a recorder unit costing roughly the same. Neither time nor money was available at the time to pursue this line of inquiry.

A working paper produced in January 1967 may serve to illustrate the stage of our thinking at this time:

A writing task

1   In an imposed task, scanning ahead (i.e. covering the field on the alert for an echo) is in terms of

(a) the reader's (teacher's) expectations;

(b) the formulated objective;

(c) relevant available experience;

(d) knowledge of linguistic modes felt to be appropriate (this knowledge will always be grounded in experience of the spoken language; experience of the written language is likely to have specific bearing with all but the least experienced writer and readers).

2   At some stage the writer may either

(a) make the task his own, i.e. identify his own purposes with the purpose imposed; or

(b) become involved in some other way, i.e. pursue his own (different) purpose; or, of course

(c) remain uninvolved.

3   When the writer has not made the task his own, he will probably turn to some linguistic 'package deal': i.e. his preoccupation is with *language*. Involvement of either kind—2 (a) or (b)—probably results in the writer projecting, at least in some measure, an image of himself (i.e. part of the process is a declaration of identity).

4   For:

(a) language, even written, is likely to imply a *person*;

(b) young children unconsciously act on the principle that people *are* as they *sound* (in talk);

(c) we criticize our own writing (even of fairly formal kinds) by saying 'it doesn't sound like me';

(d) this way of regarding writing may be useful in distinguishing personal letter-writing from other kinds: in letters we may envisage the addressee, 'tune in', and so create the impression of ourselves appropriate; in other kinds of writing we may set out to create a more public image of ourselves.

5   Involvement of either kind is likely to give an *exploratory* aspect to the writing process. Scanning ahead is probably mainly concerned with non-linguistic phenomena: the concern with language probably consists rather in looking back at what we have written so far (either to amend it or to go on from there). This suggests:

(a) experiment with writing when we can't see what we have written;

(b) this view of the process might explain why we find it difficult to write to a pre-made plan;

(c) query: in Luria's[4] dynamics of semantic systems experiment, could an *object* have provided the same kind of stimulus as a *word*?

(d) query: how do we account for the difficulty of beginning, 'finding a way in'?

(e) experiment with effect of interruptions on various kinds of writing task (e.g. write an article and letter by doing a bit of one and then a bit of the other etc. and noting the differences in getting back into each task).

By stages which, looking back, may seem laborious, we moved through a consideration of the task-oriented, self-oriented and reader-oriented aspects of writing to concentrate on the complementary nature of the processes of writing and reading: and so to our first formulation of a mode of classifying writings in terms of the writer's 'sense of audience'.

When the sample was ready, in March 1967, we tried out a technique which had been suggested to us from the work of George Kelly:[5] taking scripts, at random, three at a time we worked out as many ways as possible in which we could find two of them alike and opposed to the third. When scripts were taken from widely differing sets of work, the dimensions of judgement suggested by this method were likely to be very broad, general ones, when the three scripts came from the same task set to the same class, the dimensions were likely of course to be very fine ones. By inviting a number of teachers to take on these 'triads', or minimal value judgements, we collected a pool of bi-polar 'scales' at all levels of generality. For example:

> generalizing upon experience / particularizing an experience
> presenting a view / exploring to arrive at a view
> writer's *persona* close to self / *persona* remote from self
> interpreting experience shared by writer and reader / relating experience not shared by reader.

It seemed feasible to take at least the more general of these scales and ask judges to apply them all to a single set of scripts; from the ratings of the scales we might have hoped to arrive, by factor analysis, at a reduced number of scales that were actually operative as a common factor in the judgements made. However, initial trials suggested that the range of possibilities was so vast that we were discouraged from seeking a tenuous objectivity in this way. It seemed more promising to use the pool simply as a source of hypotheses to feed into our own thinking.

Arriving at operational category definitions

Two sets of categories had to be developed, those for function and those for sense of audience. We took first the *sense of audience* categories. These were developed by constant formulation and reference back to scripts to modify and refine our system of categories, to fill in gaps or remove overlaps, to clarify borderline distinctions—and so to arrive at category descriptions that could be effectively used, not by team members only, but also by teachers. We compiled a 'briefing document' for assessors, describing the sense of audience categories, which attempted to convey a full understanding of what was meant by any particular kind of writing and how it could be distinguished from other categories in the set. When the assessor understood the description he was asked to take account of the brief statement about the context of each script (that is, the teacher's note on how the task was set and his opinion of the class) and then to read the script, entering as fully as he could into the viewpoint of the writer, and, as a result, to allocate the piece of writing to a category. The process was therefore an intuitive one, an exercise in empathy.

We believe it is in the nature of language and the way we use it that we can find justification for such a procedure. As Sapir has put it:

'Actions speak louder than words' may be an excellent maxim from the pragmatic point of view but betrays little insight into the nature of speech. The language habits of people are by no means irrelevant as unconscious indicators of the more important traits of their personalities, and the folk is psychologically wiser than the adage in paying a great deal of attention, willingly or not, to the psychological significance of a man's language. The normal person is never convinced by the mere content of speech but is very sensitive to many of the implications of language behaviour, however feebly (if at all) these may have been consciously analysed. All in all, it is not too much to say that one of the really important functions of language is to be constantly declaring to society the psychological place held by all of its members.[6]

That spoken language is likely to be richer in what it offers to our intuitions than a written text must surely be true; nevertheless, we believed that there was enough in the written text to work on.

Thus it was our intention to employ in the categorizing process the reader's more or less implicit awareness of the established conventions as we ordinarily operate them between writer and reader in our society. Only then, as an independent process, were the classified scripts to be submitted to further analysis. And at this later stage we hoped in particular to identify the linguistic features in the writing that were the vehicles for these conventions. (Had we allocated the scripts on the basis of any such features, we should of course have short-circuited the whole undertaking.)

Our briefing document, then, grew and took shape, as we tried it out on fresh scripts and as we enlisted the help of teachers who had not shared in our discussions and whose trial allocations served to point out where the document was misleading or inadequate. As we have already indicated, we attached considerable importance to the *general usability* of the mode of analysis we were trying to devise. What we hoped for was something nearer to a clarification of experienced teachers' insights than to a specialist instrument designed for particular research purposes.

There came the day, finally, when the brief was ready for use. On 17 February 1968 we held a one-day meeting to which eleven teachers came in response to our invitation. The morning was spent in going over the document and discussing illustrative scripts. Each teacher then worked on scripts taken from the first three sets of a hundred: some completed twenty-five scripts, some three times that number. We were able later to compare their categories with the team's findings, and on this basis we recruited seven teacher-assessors. During the course of the following twelve months these seven teachers and members of the research team completed the classification by sense of audience of the total of 2122 scripts. Three judges were used for each script, at least one of them being a team member. (The decision to use three judges was based in part upon evidence from our previous multiple-making experiment,[7] and partly on that of an American experiment which, on a somewhat similar task, employed two judges only, but rejected cases where the two did not agree.[8])

We should add that the largest item in our research budget, salaries apart, was money with which to pay assessors who were not members of the research team.

Before classification by sense of audience had been completed we had begun devising our second set of categories, those of *function*. We followed a similar procedure, the briefing meeting (of eighteen teachers) being held on 6 June 1970, and the allocations being completed in time to put both sets of data through the computer in the autumn of 1971.

Meanwhile, of course, the work on stage two—a four-year longitudinal study of two classes in each of five schools—was occupying a great deal of our time. Collection of data, and co-operation with schools, began in 1967 and ended in 1971. Analysis of the data is still in progress and will, as we have indicated, be the subject of a later report—a study of the development in writing of three hundred children in five schools.[9]

Notes and references

1   J. Britton, N. C. Martin and H. Rosen, 'Abilities to Write'.
2   Of our two full-time research appointments, one was made in September 1966 and the second in September 1967.
3   J. A. V. Van Bruggen, 'Factors affecting regularity of the flow of words during written composition'.
4   A. R. Luria and O. S. Vinogradova, 'The dynamics of semantic systems', *British Journal of Psychology*, 50, pp. 89–105.
5   G. Kelly, *The Psychology of Personal Constructs*.
6   E. Sapir, *Culture, Language and Personality*, pp. 19–20.
7   J. Britton, N. C. Martin and H. Rosen, *Multiple Marking of English Compositions*.
8   A. C. Purves and V. Rippere, *Elements of Writing about a Literary Work: A Study of Response to Literature*.
9   [Note added for 1979 printing] Two individual studies that formed part of the stage two research have now been published: A. McLeod, 'This is what came out', *English in Education* 3, autumn 1969 (reprinted in M. Torbe and R. Protherough, eds, *Classroom Encounters*, Ward Lock, 1976); A. [Tony] Burgess, 'Story and teller', *Bulletin* (University of London Institute of Education), summer 1971 (reprinted in M. Meek et al., *The Cool Web*, Bodley Head, 1977). Burgess has developed the ideas in his article, focusing on expressive and informative writing, in 'Two functions of written language', Dissertation submitted for MA in Education, University of London Institute of Education, 1976.

4 Sense of audience

A young child will adapt his speech to his sense of the person he is addressing, either bowing to imposed constraints or recognizing and meeting some need in the other person. Thus he might refrain from addressing an uncle by his first name because it is explicitly forbidden to do so, or he might simplify his speech grammatically and lexically because his younger brother would otherwise not understand it. But when children begin to write, this process of adjusting to their audience presents them with new problems even though they may fail to recognize them. We want to suggest that one important dimension of development in writing ability is the growth of a sense of audience, the growth of the ability to make adjustments and choices in writing which take account of the audience for whom the writing is intended. This accommodation may be coarse or fine, highly calculated or totally intuitive, diffused through the text or explicit at particular points in it; but, whatever the form of its realization, a highly developed sense of audience must be one of the marks of the competent mature writer, for it is concerned with nothing less than the implementation of his concern to maintain or establish an appropriate relationship with his reader in order to achieve his full intent.

Before we proceed to an outline of the model which we propose for charting this development, we must undertake some exploration of the concept 'sense of audience'. After having done so we shall look at its operation in the specific context of school writing.

Writing may be looked upon as soliloquizing monologue. This way of looking at it seems reasonable enough. The 'others' are not there, they cannot interrupt, and who they are and what they are do not make themselves insistently felt at every turn. The writer need not retract, concede, bluff, cajole, placate, counter-attack, deny, nor acknowledge directions and fancies which are not his own. Writing, then, appears to emancipate the writer not only from the fragmentation or disruption of his discourse by the intrusion of others but also from the acknowledgement of the fact that he must accommodate to the needs of others.

Yet while we may perceive some truth in all this, we also know it to be an absurdly inadequate description of what writers do—indeed must do. In spite of the fact that a writer is physically isolated from his audience, the act of writing inserts itself into a network of social relationships which will make him say this rather than that—in this way rather than that—or perhaps suppress this and add that. An invisible audience will exert some degree of control on his writing, impelling him towards choices along every dimension of language. There are some circumstances in which this is so obvious that we need not linger on them. What we shall be referring to as *conative* writing would be a case in point: for when a writer is setting out to convince his readers to change their beliefs, attitudes or behaviour, he must represent to himself their present posture. A letter-writer will make choices which take into account not only his status/relationship with the addressee but also, so far as he is able, whatever conventionalized formulaic repertoire is available for expressing this relationship ('Dear Sir', or 'Mr Smith', or 'Smith,' or 'Joe', or 'Joe Smith'). A scholar at home in the intricacies of his field will in a popularizing article be under considerable compulsion to simplify, to explain and to make certain assumptions explicit. And so on: these are all examples in which the writer will have a lively representation of his audience in mind—or, if he does not, he will fail in his intent, of which he is likely to be highly aware. In such cases it is a relatively easy matter to detect the influences that the audience has had on a particular piece of writing, or at least some of them. In the same way, in the conversation game one of the players can act with fully planned intent—having decided 'to butter someone up', or 'to keep someone in his place', or 'to create a good impression' or 'to show I'm not a snob'.

How does a writer enter into contact with an audience whom he may not know or not know very much about? Here we must face up to a difficulty which is relevant to the problem which we shall face later: the specifically educational aspect of the sense of audience. The bulk of writing in our society is of a professional or quasi-professional nature. The practitioners are, in part, aided by the conventions, practices and 'house-style' of the agency for which they write, and by their experience of public communication in general. This would also hold true for internal documents which circulate in large organizations like industrial enterprises, the civil service, etc. Writers in this situation need never have pondered the problem of audience: they have merely, so to speak, to serve their apprenticeship. They adjust themselves to the ground rules. On the other hand, it is true that in a single issue of a journal the contributors may display varying capacities or degrees of willingness to adjust to their common audience. All speakers go beyond the conventional devices provided by the language (levels of formality, politeness rituals, status-acknowledgement formulae, etc.) because of their sensitivity to the feelings, attitudes and knowledge of others and their ability to divine what has been thought rather than expressed. In the same way, writers may follow their own personal sense of audience and even ignore established conventions. We may say, then, that sense of audience is well-provided for in the written language but that each writer must learn the system and must also learn how to make individual use of it.

Professional writing in general is addressed to a wide unknown audience, but there are kinds of writing which are addressed to very different kinds of audience which may be very limited in number, be personally known to the writer, and with whom he shares a special relationship. We therefore need to establish a set of writer–reader relationships which cover the whole possible range, even though only one of these relationships dominates published material.

Since the time of Aristotle, the studied adjustment of discourse to its audience has been a major concern in rhetoric. In 1776 Campbell[1] elaborated this attention to audience in two chapters, the first entitled 'Of the Consideration which the Speaker ought to have of the Hearers, as men in general' and the second dealing with consideration for the hearers 'as such men in particular'; he proposed that the speaker should consider how to shape his language to allow for the level of understanding, the imagination, the memory and the passions of the audience. Rhetoric was an educational programme preoccupied with prescriptions of how speakers (and, later, writers) *should* take their audience into account, suggesting in the manuals what devices might be resorted to and what tactics should be adopted. However, much—perhaps most—discourse is not the product of manifest intent nor do its authors operate with a vast array of rules inculcated by an explicit specialist training. Although the rhetoricians taught us that the audience contributes to the discourse, we now have to go much further than them and observe that adjustment to the audience is inherent in the social contract of all language use. Thus we do not learn our mother tongue and then follow this basic training with a course on audience rhetoric: the two run concurrently and are central to socialization in general. In speech we can rely on society to make a fairly good job of teaching a sense of audience: there are immediate penalties for ignoring the audience. In particular, the speaker runs into serious trouble when he has to adjust to an audience with whose needs he is unfamiliar or whose demands he has not been taught by life to meet. Within his own linguistic community the speaker can develop a delicate sense of audience; outside it he can run into difficulty. As Gumperz points out, the linguistic community is 'held together by the frequency of social interaction patterns and set off from the surrounding areas by weaknesses in the lines of communication.'[2]

A writer has options open to him. Seen as someone engaged in more than producing discourse which is intelligible and satisfying to himself, he becomes the performer of a social act in the arena of *context of situation*.[3] The effect of context of situation on speakers is readily apparent. We can detect without difficulty some of the ways in which they are influenced by the circumstances of time, place and possibly accompanying activities. At the centre of the situation will be the other participant or participants also being affected by the other features of the context of situation. (We might think of the headmaster addressing a morning assembly, and construct for ourselves a model of how this general notion operates in a specific situation.)

To this we can add that the speaker and his listener(s) are not hermetically sealed in their context but operating within the whole culture of their society. In fact we have taken as the major premise of our work on function that for language to function effectively there must be 'tacit acceptance by both speaker and hearer of all the relevant conventions, beliefs and presuppositions'.[4]

But this picture is an idealized one and leaves out of account several features which loom large in the light of our preoccupations with writing rather than speech, and with one particular context, namely school. To the latter point we shall return. For the moment let us say that writers will differ greatly in the extent to which they are justified in making tacit assumptions and in their capacity to write in a way that accommodates these assumptions. In the speech context of situation the hearer is sharply in focus and indeed in most cases is likely to appear to the speaker as the major element, while for the writer this will not be true. The concept of context of situation has been shaped very much with speakers in mind and needs to be modified for writers. For the writer, it does not consist of the immediate environment, but rather of the universe of discourse he is entering (business letter, official document, short story)—the situation of writing this kind of thing in this sort of society for this sort of person. The writer, then, must construe his audience on the basis of clues which are harder to come by since they are on a more generalized plane. To put it another way, the writer does not, like the speaker, have the context of situation displayed before him, but must *represent to himself* a context of situation, and this includes his readers.

Dell Hymes[5] has insisted that in considering the linguistic development of children we need a broader view of what he calls 'communicative competence', which includes a knowledge not only of grammatical rules but also of 'speaking rules'. Some of these rules relate to addressor–addressee relationships which, he points out, begin to develop very early. He starts with the basic facts of social relationships rather than the basic facts of language. The communicative act grows out of these relationships and entails 'the selection and creation of communicative means considered specific and appropriate to it by the participants'. He suggests several areas for closer attention which do shed some light on our present concern. Firstly, *self-identity* is crucial to the kind of differentiated linguistic competence required of the individual in contemporary industrial society. Thus he shows the paradox of audience adjustment revealed by a black mother who said: 'You know, I've noticed that when the children play "school" outside, they talk like they're supposed to in school; and when they stop playing school, they stop.'

Secondly, he developed the notion of *sociolinguistic interference*. 'When a child from one background enters a situation in which the communicative expectations are defined in terms of another', misunderstandings and mis-analysis follow. In terms of audience we might see this most clearly displayed when the child moves from speaking to writing and perhaps again in the shift from the school exercise to the genuine communicative act. The ghost of the former audience is likely to haunt the new situation. Finally, Hymes sees that schools ask for special forms of communicative conduct (including writing) which bring with them their own hazards.

Indeed, since the beginnings of stratified society and the use of writing, it has been characteristic of the greater part of mankind that a desired or required communicative competence has confronted man as an alien thing, imposed by a power not within his control. In the complex circumstances of our own society it is hard to see how children can be expected to master a second system, complementing or replacing their own, if the process is not perceived as intrinsically relevant or enjoyable, preferably both.[6]

What is it that the writer must do if he is to exercise 'communicative competence' in respect of his audience in the context of situation peculiar to the writer–reader relationship? He must carry out a procedure of self-editing, of arresting, reorganizing and adjusting his message for his absent audience. He will be unable to do this unless he can *internalize* his audience. Mead[7] suggested that this was an essential part of all thinking. The individual must be able to call out in himself the responses which his gestures evoke from others. He begins by being able to internalize individuals and finally internalizes a 'generalized other' who speaks for society at large. This must be close to what the mature writer has to do when he addresses a public audience. We may say, then, that a writer's capacity to adjust to his audience is dependent on the degree to which he can internalize that audience. Piaget[8] showed how little the young child could do this because he 'has not like the adult the art of seeking and finding in the other's mind a basis on which to build anew'. And building anew is exactly what the full exercise of writing ability demands.

This is no place to examine the whole of role theory, but inevitably, having considered the process of taking the role of the other, we must look at the role taken up by the writer. In so far as a writer considers his audience to be in one role, his own role must be a complementary one. If he sees them as interested but uninformed laymen, he becomes the obliging expert. If they are seen as equals sharing a community of interest or concern he speaks as a peer. Furthermore we cannot rule out an element of role-playing (as distinct from role-taking); for a writer (particularly a school-pupil) might assume a role to which he has no acknowledged social claim, either for the purpose of practice, humour, or deceit or simply because it is demanded of him. He then sets up a fictitious top-stratum relationship with his audience beneath which there lies another. A schoolboy, for example, may set out to act the politician and treat his audience as citizen-voters when in fact they are his fellows.

Thus we conceive of the audience categories as a relationship between writer and reader.

The sense of audience in the school situation

Now let us look at the school situation and consider the application of our discussion to it. What is unique to this situation or more prevalent in it than is generally true?

The pupil operates within a context of culture which will exert an influence not only on the values he expresses but also on the ways in which he expresses them. It will also lead him to construe his audience (let us say, teachers) partly or wholly in the way in which his culture construes them. In some degree the pupil and teacher will share a common culture, but frequently there will be dramatic divergences—such as inner urban working-class pupil with parents from overseas, and university trained, suburban middle-class teacher.[9] The messages which flow from pupil-writer to teacher-audience will be affected by the extent to which they share common cultural assumptions and also by the extent to which the pupil is aware of how matters stand. Thus the pupil-writer may construe his teacher-audience naïvely, crudely or with considerably astute sophistication. We need hardly add that the pupil's sense of audience in this situation will be strongly coloured by the teacher's attitude to cultural divergence.[10] The most vivid demonstration of the effect of 'context of culture' is the change which comes over adolescent pupils' writing when it is genuinely directed to a peer-audience. Our research has revealed how dramatic this change is.[11]

If we look more closely at the context of situation we see that almost all the writing with which we are concerned is in the school domain. The act of written communication in this domain is in many ways unlike other similar acts even when they are apparently identical. For example, a pupil may be asked to 'account for the collapse of the Roman Empire' or to 'describe the transport system of France', both undertakings which we might expect mature adult writers to engage in. In school, however, the context is one in which this undertaking will be taken to be an 'exercise', one of hundreds the pupil will complete during his school career, the features of which he will learn as intimately as he learns the code of sanctions which his school operates. In this context he is likely to discriminate between a variety of tasks (note-taking, summarizing, 'essays', etc.), but, whatever the task, his audience will overwhelmingly be predetermined and sharply defined: the teacher, a known audience of one.

Ideally one of the goals of schools is that they should, wherever this is possible, produce writers who have developed the capacity to generate their own reasons for writing and to define their own audiences, which should include those which are large in number and unknown. In school, however, it is almost always the teacher who initiates the writing and who does so by defining a writing task with more or less explicitness. Not only does he define the task but also nominates himself as audience. He is not, however, simply a one-man audience but also the sole arbiter, appraiser, grader and judge of the performance. He becomes an audience on whom pupils must focus a special kind of scrutiny in order to detect what they must do to satisfy him. The peculiar feature of this relationship is that the pupil will see his teacher's response as a means by which his progress is being charted. It is part of a larger and more elaborate system of making judgements and not simply a question of the reader's pleasure or understanding or insight. Indeed the writer is frequently placed in the position of telling the reader what the latter already knows more fully and more deeply.

The fact that the pupil is subject to frequent demands for writing, some of which he finds distasteful or merely dull, may lead to his sense of audience taking on a particular complexion. His writing may be dominated by the sole consideration of meeting *minimum* requirements. In other words it may be shaped solely by the demands of his audience and not by the complementary pressure to formulate ideas in a way which satisfies the writer. The analogy here is hack-writing, and school becomes the writer's Grub Street. Readers will be aware that this sort of sense of audience can be finely tuned with arithmetic precision—the exact number of lines or pages.

We are well aware that other kinds of relationship exist between pupil and teacher, and also that pupils frequently *are* concerned to satisfy themselves as well as their teacher-audience. We try to accommodate these possibilities in our scheme. We are also aware that teachers often attempt to direct the sense of audience away from themselves by a variety of means. They may simply urge the pupil to *represent to himself* a general reader's difficulties of understanding or flow of sympathies or capacities for response. They may offer *stylistic advice* or *rhetorical precepts* which have a more general reader in mind, but this advice is not made explicit.

But whatever strategy the teacher adopts it is difficult for him to elude the stubborn reality of himself as audience, and he is likely, in our experience, to continue dominant in that role. Thus many pupil-writers have to operate a double-audience system which may give rise to particular tensions. Behind one audience stands the spectre of another. This will not always be so, especially when the writer actually enjoys the language game being proposed to him. Moreover, a distinction should be made between the feigning required for some specific fictionalized audience, and the gradual development both of the desire to reach out beyond the teacher and an awareness of how to do so. In other words the development of the pupil may be seen in terms of the move from 'the internalized other' (the teacher) to 'the generalized other' (the writer's unknown public).

Another way of looking at the teacher-as-audience is in terms of status. Normally in school the hierarchically ordered system will lead the writer not only to regard the teacher's demands as paramount but also as requiring a writing decorum which expresses the inferior status of the writer. The writer may reject his status by defying the rules of decorum. Similarly, a teacher may create a relationship which renounces his status and makes possible a different audience role. Whatever happens, the relative status of writer and reader will be set in terms of school relationships. The teacher's superior status is not marked out boldly like the ranks in the army, and we can detect variations as between teachers, and in one and the same teacher on different occasions. Similarly, the role the teacher takes up will vary; he may be instructor, collaborator, tester, wise adult or punitive arm. The pupil-writer may subtly accommodate to these different roles. Once again his maturity may well be marked by the development of the ability to abandon his inferior status and speak to adult peers.

Throughout his school career the pupil is provided with another source of awareness, his reading. From this he can learn strategies by means of which writers accommodate to their audiences (usually either the public at large or the school learner). This learning can be applied to any school writing but would be more readily drawn upon when the teacher encourages the pupil to direct himself to a more general audience.

Assumption

It has been our assumption so far that all writing will be influenced by the writer's sense of audience. There is, perhaps, one exception. When writing is seen as a mere task and the writer is indifferent to the demands of the teacher, or when in desperation he is merely stringing sentences together, he may produce a piece in which it is not possible to discern a hint of sense of audience.

CLASSIFYING THE SENSE OF AUDIENCE IN SCHOOL WRITING

We have by now given sufficient indication of the considerations which led us to attribute importance to the writer's sense of audience, and of general application of audience to the school situation. We can now pass on to the model which we evolved by means of which we could allocate scripts to particular categories, and thus use this dimension in the classification of school writing. The model is displayed schematically below and followed by an explanatory text; a diagrammatic representation is given in Figure 1.

SENSE OF AUDIENCE: CATEGORY SYSTEM

Definition: the sense of audience is revealed by the manner in which the *writer* expresses a *relationship* with the *reader* in respect to his (the writer's) *under-*

taking. The main divisions are self, teacher, wider audience (known), unknown audience: a full list of categories is given below.*

1 *Self*
   Child (or adolescent) to self

2 *Teacher*
   2.1 Child (or adolescent) to trusted adult
   2.2 Pupil to teacher, general (teacher–learner dialogue)
   2.3 Pupil to teacher, particular relationship
   2.4 Pupil to examiner

3 *Wider audience (known)*
   3.1 Expert to known laymen
   3.2 Child (or adolescent) to peer group
   3.3 Group member to working group (known audience which may include teacher)

4 *Unknown audience*
   Writer to his readers (or his public)

5 *Additional categories*
   5.1 Virtual named audience
   5.2 No discernible audience

Note (a). We have attempted to cover the full range of possible writing in school, while at the same time introducing special distinctions relevant to school writing. Most of the work we examine is inevitably assigned by the teacher and we would therefore expect most writing to fall in one of the subdivisions of category 2.

Note (b). For reasons we have, we hope, made clear we wish to focus attention on the reader, but since it is a relationship which we are classifying we have expressed categories in terms of both *writer* and reader; see, for example, category 3.1, 'expert to known laymen'. However, it is the second term, which refers to the reader, which is systematically varied; the first term names the general or usual complementary role of the writer.

The classifications

SELF

This is writing from one's own point of view without considering the intelligibility to others of that point of view; a written form of 'speech for oneself'. The writer himself must be the first-stage audience for any worthwhile writing; and some other reader must also be in mind except where

---

* For ease of reference, this list is also reproduced in the fold-out sheet which follows the index.

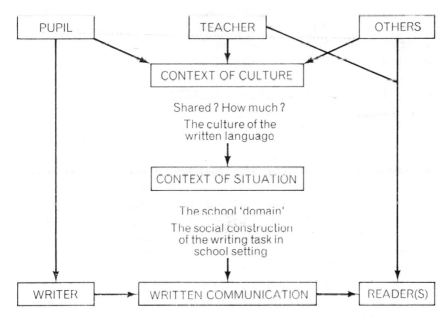

Fig. 1 Diagrammatic representation of the sense of audience in a teacher–pupil situation

(a) what is set down or explored is considered by the writer to be of no concern to anyone else (it might be mnemonic like a shopping list, record a stage in his thinking, or be preparatory to further activity including writing—graphically it may be very different from conventional written language); or

(b) what is set down or explored is regarded as a private concern, e.g. an entry in an intimate diary; or

(c) the exploration is so difficult or tentative that the writer could not afford to have anybody else in mind (i.e. is unable to operate the internalized other): he is using writing to discover what he thinks.

Assigned tasks may sometimes move into this category, particularly in the circumstances of (c) above. Some notes are likely to move into this category, where they may appear in two forms: (i) a diary-form entry where the writer comments on something which has interested him, or (ii) preparatory notes for an assigned task. (Here the teacher conditions the task but is not in mind as an audience to this preparatory version.)

2.1 CHILD (OR ADOLESCENT) TO TRUSTED ADULT

Only a mother understands the egocentric speech of the infant, and clearly the talking relationship with the mother is the general incentive that makes the infant talk. We transfer this to writing that can only go on because there is this teacher, this particular human being, who will understand what it is you are trying to say. It is writing that accepts an invitation because it comes from this particular person in whom there is confidence.

Because writing is a way of committing oneself, and because it is at first a difficult process, young children may rely upon the trusted adult reader in even the simplest piece of work. Later, the fact that this particular adult wants to hear *anything* you have to say may operate as a strong incentive, and a liberator, so that children who haven't written begin to do so simply because they now feel free to say what really matters. (See, for example, the black children's first pieces at thirteen or so in Kohl's *Thirty-Six Children*, 1972.) And in more ordinary circumstances adolescents may rely on this relationship in order to write dispassionately or objectively or critically about their families, etc.

The shaping responses of the 'internalized other' can be less heeded (and hence less of a brake) when a writer relies on the understanding of a particular trusted reader: writing for a trusted adult has therefore some affinity with the previous category, writing for oneself. Mead's distinction, that between the internalized other and the generalized other, is relevant here.

Teachers are likely to vary very much in their understanding of this role and their willingness to assume it. (It has been suggested that where they have established such a relationship but betray it by reading work out to the whole class without prior permission, the writers lose some of their directness and begin to show off to the class. In our terms this would be a move from category 2 to one form of 3.2, 'child or adolescent to peer group'.) We might speculate that, among assigned tasks, examples of writing for oneself will crop up more frequently in classes where the teacher has established the 'trusted adult' relationship and tries to work within it a good deal.

A role for the English teacher only? Not at all. Speculation in even a specialized intellectual field may need to rely upon this relationship—though it may not be possible for a reader to discern the fact. Of course, writing about personal relations is more likely to rely on the trusted adult than is writing on impersonal matters, and this would favour work in English lessons.

Preparing to distinguish category 2.2, 'pupil to teacher' from this one, let us sum up the pupil's attitude to category 2.1 writing as follows: 'My relationship with this particular adult provides me with an area in which I am free to operate, and I operate as myself.'

2.2   PUPIL TO TEACHER, GENERAL (TEACHER–LEARNER DIALOGUE)

Here the adult represents an audience which is an object rather than an area of free operation and the object has its teacherly characteristics which affect the pupil as writer.

Children may like or dislike, trust or mistrust teachers in general: the stereotype 'teacher' may often be what is felt as audience in category 2.2.

On the other hand, particular teachers may be liked or disliked, trusted or mistrusted—and also known or unknown (for example, if the teacher is new to the class). The particular teacher is likely to be there as an 'internalized other' in writing in this category. He may be a teacher who never takes the role described under category 2.1, or he may be a teacher who normally takes this role but on this occasion sets a task which is taken perhaps as rather more of a routine assignment, or more narrowly restricting as to area of concern. Thus the pupils may have a sense of audience which says 'We know what teachers in general expect of us, and to some extent how this particular representative embodies those expectations. This is our attempt to meet them.'

Distinguishing 'pupil to teacher, general' (2.2), from 'pupil to teacher, particular relationship' (2.3)
As a child in the secondary school comes to know his teachers he is likely to develop a personal relationship with one or more of them: a relationship that is fed by his growing interest in the subject taught. When this happens the pupil gains confidence both in the teacher as a person and in his own ability to operate within the subject field—and this will be reflected in his writing for this *particular* teacher. This category, 'teacher, particular relationship', is therefore, like 2.1, 'child to trusted adult', a personal relationship but also, unlike 2.1, a professional relationship based upon a shared interest and expertise, and an accumulating shared context.

In the course of teaching a class, a teacher is likely to build up a small group of pupils who hold such a relationship with him, and they may function as an elite group who form part of the audience felt by one of them in his writing (see also category 3.2, 'child or adolescent to peer group', but in 2.3 the role of the teacher is more central).

Distinguishing 'pupil to teacher, general' (2.2) from 'pupil to examiner' (2.4)
It is fairly widely assumed that, among the many things teachers do, their teaching function can be distinguished from their testing function. It is this distinction that we want to apply in defining 'pupil to teacher' as a different audience category from 'pupil to examiner'.

The basic difference seems to be that between, on the one hand, an ongoing process, an interaction between pupil and teacher, a continuing dialogue—and on the other, a 'show-up', a demonstration, an endpoint. In the teaching situation, a pupil looks, in his writing, to the response of the teacher and beyond that to his own activity to follow. He writes for a response; a genuine question, therefore, may be as appropriate as a statement, and a suggestion that invites development may be as highly valued as a conclusion. The test piece, on the other hand, is a culminating point rather than a stage in a process of interaction. (If candidates in the test situation ask questions, it will be because they are demonstrating their ability to frame the *right* or *approved* questions, rather than because they are seeking answers.)

A test may set out to measure what a pupil *can do* as well as what he *knows*, and here the teacher/examiner distinction may be more difficult to make. Thus:

(*a*) Suppose a teacher asks a first-year class to write a ballad, not as a test but as a piece of teaching. The poor performer may nevertheless find this an impossible task and his writing will show this. He cannot regard it as an 'invitation to be accepted' but only as a 'demand to be met'. It seems to us logical to regard this not as teacher-directed (the teaching miscarried in this case) but as coming within the category 'pupil to examiner'.

(*b*) When a piece of writing seems to offer back what the pupil has received—a mirror to instruction—this would also suggest 'pupil to examiner'. Where the writer seems to be *actively operating* within a task area this would suggest either normally, (i) pupil to teacher—especially where the writer tries to interest the reader or to write from his own interest; or occasionally, (ii) pupil to examiner, in the sense 'See how well I can operate!' Where the pupil seems to be copying straight from a textbook, or reproducing notes which the teacher has given him, the writing would again suggest category 2.4 because the pupil has taken the 'teacher as examiner' as the audience for the task as a whole (though this may not further affect what he writes). Exercises in précis, too, are likely to be of the form 'See how well I can operate'.

(*c*) The best exams in English may set out to test a candidate's ability to use language in optimum conditions, i.e. perhaps in circumstances modelled on the teacher–learner dialogue. In such cases an actual exam may call forth writing which we should rightly classify as 'pupil to teacher'.

(*d*) In an exam (unknown audience) the writer may take up the task as his own (a writer to his public) or may, availing himself of anonymity, use the situation as a confessional.

(*e*) The 'mock exam' presents a special case: in this 'show-up' teaching is likely to concentrate upon improving performance. We suggest that only where the writing seems to be strongly influenced by the teaching relationship (the teacher–learner dialogue) should it be regarded as moving out of the 'pupil to examiner' category.

Every interaction with someone else tells us something about that person; but when the interaction is between teacher and pupil, what a teacher learns from it leads not to a *verdict* but to further interaction. We need to distinguish writing aimed at a verdict from writing that is a link in a chain of interaction. The distinction being made is clearly not an organizational one but an educational one. There are many teachers whose everyday teaching consists in leaping from test to test. Work produced in these circumstances, while not examination work in the formal sense, is nonetheless likely to go into category 2.4.

3.1   EXPERT TO KNOWN LAYMEN

There is probably no need here to distinguish the teacher as layman from any other layman or group of laymen.

Essentially the writer will have chosen his topic, or it will have been suggested to him as an individual, as an expert. The writing will be explicit down to the non-expert level: that is to say more of the context will be supplied and less implied than would have been the case where an expert wrote for fellow experts. (This will distinguish work in this category from work in the 'pupil to teacher' category, where, however expert the writer may feel himself to be, he will assume that the teacher is even more of an expert.)

We have probably met writing of this kind in form magazines—in a 'hobbies section', to use the language of the *Boy's Own Paper* era. When the teacher sets an individually chosen or appropriately assigned 'hobbies' task, the result is not substantially different.

Where a task of this kind has been misassigned, is inappropriate for an individual, or the child has nothing in which he feels he can operate as an expert, the writing is likely to fall either into the 'pupil to teacher' category (where the child does his best to interest the teacher) or (in more desperate cases) into the 'pupil to examiner' category. Where expertise is based on written sources, the writing tends to move into the writer-to-public category (for example, a piece on cosmetics takes up the manner of women's magazines, or technical know-how may derive from manuals).

3.2   CHILD (OR ADOLESCENT) TO PEER GROUP

One of the things that good teachers do is to make children responsive to each other's efforts. (Probably in the best teaching this aim is subordinate to that of establishing a child-to-adult channel—but that is a matter of opinion, and certainly teachers will vary in what they set out to do.)

Writing to the peer group is familiar to most of us from form magazines: here sometimes it suffers from a kind of precocity, a pseudo-journalistic style, sometimes from extreme banality. But the influence of the teacher can move it from this level without substituting himself for the peer group as audience. Or he may function rather as spectator and adviser, or he may identify himself with the form's point of view and remain a member of the audience. A lot depends on genuine sense of freedom from censoring surveillance.

Another situation will also produce writing in a related category: here the peer group is the 'hidden audience', aimed at via the teacher and despite him. The in-group joke will be a sign of it. But the effect of the hidden audience has to *dominate* the writing (at the expense of the ostensible audience, the teacher) for a piece of work to go into this category.

3.3   GROUP MEMBER TO WORKING GROUP

For this category the teacher is likely to be regarded as a member of the group; the writing is likely to be a link in a chain of group activity the past phases of which will be taken for granted as a part of the initial context. The audience is seen in this respect to be a known audience. There may be other indications of this fact in the way the writer appears to take into account the views and attitudes of individuals in the group—perhaps anticipating their particular difficulties or objections. Sometimes, though not always, what is offered will be seen to be *material for the group to work upon*—a contribution to an ongoing activity.

This contribution to a joint undertaking is usually distinguishable from the 'expert to laymen' writing, but occasionally there can be a merging of the two—the joint undertaking may demand an expert's particular contribution.

4   WRITER TO HIS READERS (UNKNOWN AUDIENCE)

A writer who operates well in any of the categories will be, in the first instance, his own audience. Writing in which he functions as his own audience only at a minimum level is more likely to be in category 2.4 ('pupil to examiner') than in any other; and writing in this category is least likely to lead on to writing in category 4. On the other hand, pupils who operate well in categories 1 (child to self) and 2.1 (child to trusted adult) are likely to produce examples of category 4.

The move from any other category to this one is distinguished by the following characteristics:

(*a*) the writer's sense of the *general* value or validity of what he has to say;

(*b*) his sense of the need to supply a context wide enough to bring in readers whose sophistication, interests and experiences he can only estimate;

(*c*) a readiness to conform with and contribute to some cultural norm or trend;

(*d*) a desire to achieve an effect, or make an impression on readers in general;

(*e*) a sense that the writer's audience is not one with which he identifies himself in a personal way;

(*f*) a familiarity with adult writing of the kind he is attempting which seems a satisfactory model to the writer.

These characteristics are intended to be signposts, not the makings of a category definition. Other circumstances are likely to throw up poor work in category 4. Where there is a considerable gap between what a writer aims at and what he achieves, and where he is not aware of this gap, he may well produce naïve or pretentious or tedious writing with a public audience in mind.

5.1   VIRTUAL NAMED AUDIENCE

Sometimes children are asked to write a letter or address a piece of writing to a named person, or type of audience. In such cases, the writer may direct the piece towards the teacher, where it is likely to be a variety of category 2. But sometimes the writer may feel that the named person or audience is real to him, whereupon the writing may have an audience direction more akin to a personal letter than writing which has, as destination, the teacher. It would seem proper to distinguish these two cases.

5.2   NO DISCERNIBLE AUDIENCE

Occasionally there were scripts which could not be allocated to any category because there was no discernible audience. This category was not intended to be a dumping ground for cases where a decision was difficult. It was meant to include those cases where, for one reason or another, the writing had no audience direction. It should not be confused with category 1, 'child (or adolescent) to self' (see p. 66).

Notes and references

1   G. Campbell, *The Philosophy of Rhetoric*.
2   J. J. Gumperz, 'Types of linguistic community'.
3   See B. Malinowski, 'The problem of meaning in primitive languages'; J. R. Firth, 'The techniques of semantics'; M. A. K. Halliday, 'Language in a social perspective'. Firth (p. 27) gives the following description of context of situation:

> The central concept of the whole of semantics considered in this way is the context of situation. In that context are the human participant or participants, what they say, and what is going on. The phonetician can find his phonetic context and the grammarian and the lexicographer theirs. And if you want to bring in general cultural background, you have the contexts of experience of the participants. Every man carries his culture and much of his social reality about him wherever he goes. But even when phonetician, grammarian, and lexicographer have finished, there remains the bigger integration, making use of all their work, in semantic study. And it is for this situational and experimental study that I would reserve the term 'semantics'.

4   J. Lyons, *Structural Semantics*.
5   Dell Hymes, 'Competence and Performance in Linguistic Theory'.
6   Ibid., p. 22–3.
7   G. H. Mead, *Mind, Self and Society*.
8   J. Piaget and B. Inhelder, *The Psychology of the Child*.
9   E. J. Goodacre, *Teachers and Their Pupils' Home Background*.
10   H. S. Becker, 'Social Class Variations in the Teacher–Pupil Relationship'.
11   See A. McLeod, 'This is what came out'.

5 An approach to the function categories

We now turn to our second group of classifications, the *function* categories. These are an attempt to provide a framework within which to ask or answer the question 'Why are you writing?' in a specifically limited way.

To ask what reasons underlie any piece of human behaviour is usually to pose a very difficult question. Answers of many kinds seem admissible. Sanctions, or elements of *compulsion*, may enter in alongside aspects of *intention*, and the two may be interrelated in very complex ways. Intentions may be directed towards outcomes in the life of the doer or in the lives of other people. (A, let us say, marks examination scripts in order to earn money in order to take an expensive holiday; B does it for the experience that may make him a more efficient teacher; C does it to release a colleague who needs a holiday; D is forced to mark them by the conditions of his employment; E does it for a mixture of several of these reasons. All of which, of course, is a massive oversimplification of the problem at issue.)

If we then go on to ask what are the *consequences* of any piece of human behaviour we are likely to find them very variously related both to the intentions of the doer and to the sanctions of his situation (which may or may not include the intentions of other people).

When John Holloway[1] looked at the effects we set out to achieve in using language, his conclusion was 'that it is surprising, not if two utterances serve different purposes, but if they serve the same'. And he illustrated the multifariousness of the problem by cataloguing at considerable length some of the purposes served by language, including the following:

> to influence the actions or feelings or beliefs of other persons
> to influence our own feelings or beliefs
> to avoid awkward silences
> to pose questions, make promises, requests, bids, surrenders, bets
> to count and calculate
> to avoid or deflect questions
> to deceive, and to silence those who contradict us
> to enter pleas, give testimony, make confessions, take oaths
> to pray, to give thanks, to remit sins

to give commands, warnings, instructions, make requests, express wishes
to cause another to visualize our own states of feeling
to draw attention to gestures or our own location in space
to construct verbal complexes like poems, which conform to certain
   artistic requirements.[2]

There are many more items in his list, and he concludes it with, 'Doubtless it [language] is used in many other ways as well.' How then do we, for practical purposes, reduce this diversity to some order?

As indicated, our function categories are an attempt to provide a framework for the question 'Why are you writing?' We had in the early stages considerable difficulty in restricting the interpretation of this question so that a workable scheme of analysis might emerge. 'Intention', 'purpose', 'effect' and other such terms wove in and out of our discussions. A writer's intention, we saw, may be highly personal, unique, and sometimes hidden: he may, moreover, fail in his intention so that 'effect' and 'intention' are out of joint, and there will be cases where all trace of intention has been lost. Again, a piece of writing may create a different effect upon each of its readers, and some of these may be idiosyncratic and little related to the writer's intentions. Moreover (like the dropping of the whitewash bucket in the comedy act) the effect upon a reader may be a chain of outcomes, and who is to say where the analysis is to stop?

We came to the conclusion that we could settle neither entirely for the writer's intention nor entirely for the effect upon a reader: we had in fact to exclude those aspects of both which were idiosyncratic, peculiar to individuals and their particular situations, covert, or so deviously related to the writing that they might be declared irrelevant. And we needed to take, both from 'intention' and 'effect', those aspects that were customary, part of the expectations shared by writer and reader, *typical*.

At this point in our thinking we found our solution in John Lyons' description of 'context' as a term in linguistics:

. . . the situational context of an utterance cannot simply be identified with the non-verbal matrix of the 'speech-event', as some authors have suggested. A much wider and more abstract notion of context must be adopted; one that brings the verbal and non-verbal 'components' together under one head. The context of the utterance must be held to include, not only the relevant external objects and the actions taking place at the time, but the knowledge shared by hearer and speaker of all that has gone before. More 'abstractly', it must be held to comprehend all the conventions and presuppositions accepted in the society in which the participants live, insofar as these are relevant to the understanding of the utterance. In particular, the context of a sentence in a written work must be understood to include the conventions governing the literary genre of which the work in question is an example.

Part of what is meant here by context is covered by Urban's conception of the 'universe of discourse' . . . I consider that the idea of context as 'universe of discourse' (in Urban's sense) should be incorporated in any linguistic theory of meaning. Under this head I include the conventions and presuppositions maintained by 'the mutual acknowledgement of communicating subjects' in the particular type of linguistic behaviour (telling a story, philosophizing, buying and selling, praying, writing a novel, etc.).[3]

It will be evident, we believe, how admirably this spells out and clarifies the general notion that a range of intentions and effects of written utterances may be recognized as 'typical' by both writer and reader. It is the 'conventions and presuppositions maintained by "the mutual acknowledgement of communicating subjects" ' that provide a mature writer with a repertoire of known choices of function within our culture, and enable a mature reader to recognize which choice has been made. We must not imply, however, that choice will necessarily be a conscious or deliberate matter. A writer may well find himself applying a particular set of conventions without any sense of having made a choice, and what a reader does may often be described as 'getting on the right wavelength' without entertaining any alternative possibilities.

Oversimplifying for the moment, we might regard writer and reader as playing complementary roles in a range of games, each with its own rules: the games we are interested in here are those which embody different functions, i.e. a range of differing typical intentions and effects of writing. The ability of a writer or reader to take part in a variety of these functionally differentiated games will be an important aspect of his communicative competence. Since the 'rules' are 'conventions and presuppositions maintained by "the mutual acknowledgement of communicating subjects" ', they will have a degree of stability but be by no means immutable. They will be changed by a writer's initiative and by the degree to which his initiative is 'taken up' by his readers. New games, for example, may be devised and they will become part of the repertoire as and when, by the appropriate responses of readers, they are given currency among existing conventions. Thus, if advertisers persist in writing what appear to be autobiographical narratives, not for the purpose of sharing experience (as might be expected in accordance with existing conventions) but for the purpose of selling holidays abroad, additional 'rules' will come to be written in to distinguish such writings from fragments of autobiography.

We have finally to recognize, however, that the games metaphor is a misleading over-simplification, for the reason that our purposes in writing are seldom so unified, so well organized, so clearly defined as the outcome of a game. However clearly we may be able to define the conventions governing the achievement of particular purposes or functions, we are likely to find that a single utterance will apply in a partial way the rules of a variety of functions. A single piece of writing, in other words, may be serving many purposes.

This difficulty, we discovered, has been tackled in two ways, and we experimented with both of them. The first way is to segment the writing (say, to take it sentence by sentence) and attempt to allocate each segment to a category and so plot the functional flow and fluctuation throughout the utterance. We found this illustrated as one of the things that Charles Morris attempted in his *Signs, Language and Behaviour*. We noted also that, faced with a similar problem, Purves and Rippere[4] allocated each sentence in the writings they were analysing (written comments upon a piece of literature) to a category of 'style of response', and then attempted *to allocate the piece as a whole*. However, they found so much more agreement between the judges in carrying out the sentence ratings than in rating the piece as a whole that they abandoned this latter task.

Our experience with the categories of sense of audience predisposed us in fact towards the alternative solution: that of rating a piece as a whole. Many of the writings we classified for sense of audience had shown a good deal of wavering and uncertainty and our mode of classifying had to take into account writings in which the sense of audience changed in the course of the writing— those which seemed to hover on the borderline between, for example, the teacher in his teaching role and the teacher in his examining role, and those in which no consistent, perceptible sense of audience was developed at all. In discussing these problem scripts we had used the idea that among fluctuations in a writer's sense of audience we might perceive a *dominant* sense as a means of arriving at a verdict in cases where it would otherwise have been impossible.

We were prepared, therefore, when we came to these more complex categories of function to embrace the conception put forward by Jakobson (and developed by Dell Hymes) of *a hierarchy of functions*. This was, moreover, a discovery that supported and strengthened our notion of what we had set out to do in the first place: to identify kinds of writing in terms, not of linguistic items in a text, but of texts themselves—in terms of 'discourse', as linguists have defined it.

In Dell Hymes' words:

Even narrowing the perspective to that of a single participant in the situation, more than one function is usually present in a given speech event. Jakobson's way of handling this is to consider that all types of function are always compresent, and to see a given speech event as characterized by a particular hierarchy of functions.[5]

A schematic account of language functions

Clearly, any attempt to set out functional categories for utterances must rest upon a theory as to how language works: will constitute, in fact, a way of looking at language in operation. Our scheme derives from some important general ideas upon which scholars in many fields seem to have converged in the past fifty years or so.

Ernst Cassirer[6] pointed out in 1944 that, of all the animals, man alone responds with systematic *indirectness* to the signals he receives from the world around him. All creatures have systems of nerves bringing in such signals, and other systems carrying out their responses. In man, however, there is as it were a third system shunted across those two—the 'symbolic system'. From the incoming signals man *represents to himself*, cumulatively, what his world is like, and his responses are thereafter mediated by that world-representation. Thus what is from one point of view a storehouse of past experience for the individual is from another point of view a body of expectations regarding his future. Accumulating a 'retrospect', he projects also a 'prospect'. His response to signals from his immediate environment is to generate a hypothesis, from past experience, and put that hypothesis to the test.

Susanne Langer's *Philosophy in a New Key* sets the theory out in detail. Her 'new key' is the notion that man possesses a new need, over and above the biological needs he shares with the other creatures—the need to symbolize. Sapir makes the point again, and places language among the means by which man represents experience to himself:

It is best to admit that language is primarily a vocal actualization of the tendency to see realities symbolically . . . an actualization in terms of vocal expression of the tendency to master reality not by direct and *ad hoc* handling of this element but by the reduction of experience to familiar form.[7]

And Georges Gusdorf[8] has epitomized the idea as follows: 'Man interposes a network of words between the world and himself and thereby becomes the master of the world.'

Bruner,[9] taking up the work of Piaget, sets out the three principal systems of representation, genetically developed in this order: *enactive*—a representation in terms of movement-cum-perception; *iconic*—a representation in terms of perception freed from movement; and *symbolic*—linguistic representation.

Language, then, is only one way of representing experience, but plays a key role as a means of organizing and storing representations in other modes. Vygotsky's *Thought and Language* is a brilliant exposition of this idea.

The American psychologist, George Kelly,[10] making his own approach, takes the scientist as his model for man and sees learning, not as a special kind of human behaviour, but as behaviour at its most typically human. Man is born a predictor, forever framing his hypotheses from past experience, submitting them to the test of actuality, and modifying his predictive apparatus in the light of what happens. A man's 'personal construct system', to use Kelly's term, is his world representation.

In recent years, sociologists have arrived at similar conclusions and in doing

so enriched our understanding of what is involved. Their emphasis, necessarily, is upon interactions between people and the co-operative building of a
common world. Where the psychologist has looked at an individual successively
construing his confrontations with the world, the sociologist focuses upon
situations, encounters between people, and looks at the way individual representations fit into the jigsaw of a social reality. Thus, for example, Berger and
Luckmann:

> The most important vehicle of reality maintenance is conversation. One may
> view the individual's everyday life in terms of the working away of a conver-
> sational apparatus that ongoingly maintains, modifies and reconstructs his sub-
> jective reality.[11]

The effect of this convergence of thinking has been enormously powerful.
One general effect is to set up, alongside a sense of the importance of language
as a means of communication, a sense of its value *to the user*. With a communicative incentive, that of sharing experience, the speaker *shapes* experience,
makes it available to himself, incorporates it, so shaped, into the corpus of his
experience. Children using language in school are busy structuring their own
experience and weaving into its fabric the experience of others.

The role of participant and the role of spectator

It is an essential feature of this idea that in successively representing to ourselves our contacts with the world we are not simply making ourself into recep-
tacles for past experience, but are actively concerned to maintain an ever-
improving predictive apparatus. Our orientation is to the future rather than to
the past. Behaviour, as George Kelly has shown, is experimental, and our past
experiences provide the hypotheses. Thus every new experience must be
taken as a challenge to the established order of our past experience: and every
experience must be followed by modification or reinforcement of that order.
In general, we make the necessary adjustments as we proceed: if, on the other
hand, what happens is too unlike our expectations, we shall not be able to adjust
in our stride. We participate as best we can, but after the event we are left
with the adjustment still to make. And this we ordinarily do by going back over
the experience—in mind, in talk, or (if we are young enough) in make-believe
play. Our re-enactments are likely in some degree to distort the experience in
the direction of what is acceptable to us, or what is intelligible to us.

This process of re-enactment in order to 'come to terms' is essentially
similar to the process by which we enter into imagined experiences, either in
day-dreaming or in reading fiction. In terms of an abstract model we might
put it this way: given that man constructs a representation of the world as he
has experienced it *in order to operate in it*, an alternative kind of behaviour is
then open to him: he may manipulate the representation *without seeking out-*

comes in the actual world. The first of these two kinds of behaviour (operating in actuality via the representation) we would call behaviour *in the role of participant*, and the second (working upon the representation without seeking outcomes in actuality) we want to call behaviour *in the role of spectator*. To be in the role of spectator is, in one sense, to generate hypotheses without the present intention of putting them to the test.

D. W. Harding, the British psychologist, made a distinction of this kind as long ago as 1937.[12] He took first the example of an actual spectator looking at a building site or a street accident. The spectator takes up this role, Harding suggested, because what he sees 'discloses or makes more vivid to him some of the possibilities of his surroundings'. He is not concerned simply to perceive and understand, for what he sees engages his feelings and invites him to apply his sense of values. Of course, when we participate in events we evaluate in order to act, but 'it is as onlookers that we can most readily endure the penetration of general principles among our sentiments.' Harding is saying, we suggest, that 'the onlooker sees most of the game' *because* he is not called upon to meet the demands made upon the players. It is not simply that the spectator situation offers him an opportunity to try out his evaluations of 'the possibilities of his surroundings', but that a prior need to work upon the evaluative aspects of his world-representation encourages him to seek out those opportunities in which, because he is not committed to any action *vis-à-vis* the situation he is observing, he may do so with single-minded attention to principles—ethical, moral, social, aesthetic or any other. It is for some such reasons as these that Harding defines a spectator's response to events as a 'detached evaluative response', and goes on to claim that 'if we could obliterate the effects on a man of all the occasions when he was "merely a spectator" it would be profoundly to alter his character and outlook.'

But the claim does not rest solely upon occasions in which we are onlookers in a literal sense. Harding goes on to see day-dreaming and fantasying as 'imaginary spectatorship', and neighbourly gossip about events as 'social imaginary spectatorship', and suggests that what is afoot is essentially a traffic in values. In telling his tale, the speaker offers (both in what he selects and the way he recounts it) his own evaluation of the events narrated, and invites in return the evaluation of his listeners. Such a testing-out or sanctioning of our value systems provides what Harding has elsewhere called a 'basic social satisfaction'.[13]

Our final step, for which Harding also prepares us, is to bring into the category of 'social imaginary spectatorship' the work of the novelist, playwright and poet. Literature constitutes one kind of 'written language in the role of spectator' and presents in a highly developed form our social traffic in values. We have suggested so far that the spectator, being freed from the practical and social demands made of a participant, uses that freedom to focus upon evaluating the possibilities of experience. We must now add another use

[handwritten margin note: social traffic in values]

to which we believe he puts his freedom: he *pays attention to forms* in a way he is not able to as a participant: the forms of the language used, the pattern of events in a narrative, the dance-like movement of thought and, in particular, the pattern of feelings expressed. As participants, our feelings will tend to be sparked off in action; as spectators we are able to savour their quality *as feelings*. As participants we are caught up in a kaleidoscope of emotions; as spectators we have these emotions in perspective. This is a point we shall return to shortly.

In a very general way the distinction between the roles of participant and spectator is the distinction between work and play: between language as a *means* (to buy and sell, to inform, instruct, persuade and so on) and an utterance for its own sake, no means but an *end*: a voluntary activity that occupies us for no other reason than that it *preoccupies*.

The function categories

On the distinction between participant and spectator we have based our scheme for distinguishing the principal functions of written utterances. The scheme has three main categories, which are shown in diagrammatic form in Figure 2.

Fig. 2   The three main function categories

As mentioned earlier (p. 10), 'expressive', the central term in the model, is taken from Edward Sapir, who pointed out that ordinary face-to-face speech is directly expressive and carries out its referential function in close and complex interrelationship with that expressive function.

It is because it is learned early and piecemeal, in constant association with the colour and the requirements of actual contexts, that language, in spite of its quasi-mathematical form, is rarely a purely referential organization. It tends to be so only in scientific discourse, and even there it may be seriously doubted whether the ideal of pure reference is ever attained by language. Ordinary speech is directly expressive and the purely formal pattern of sounds, words, grammatical forms, phrases and sentences are always to be thought of as compounded by intended or unintended symbolisms of expression, if they are to be understood fully from the standpoint of behavior.[14]

An expressive utterance, for our purposes, is one in which the expressive function is *dominant*—whether we have in mind Sapir's 'patterns of reference and patterns of expression', or the whole hierarchy of functions set out by Jakobson (see p. 14). We would describe it as an utterance that 'stays close to the speaker' and hence is fully comprehensible only to one who knows the speaker and shares his context. It is a verbalization of the speaker's immediate preoccupations and his mood of the moment. Centrally (that is, in its purest form, for the horizontal lines in the diagram are intended to represent a continuum), it is utterance at its most relaxed and intimate, as free as possible from outside demands, whether those of a task or of an audience. It is, at this central point, free to move easily from participant role into spectator and *vice versa*: mutual exploration, the pursuit of 'togetherness', may proceed equally by the pleasurable reconstruction of past experiences—a traffic in values—or by the exchange of opinions about the world and information with auto-biographical relevance, and the borderline between the two modes will be a shadowy one.

It must be admitted that the more we worked on this idea of the expressive function, the more important we felt it to be. Not only is it the mode in which we approach and relate to each other in speech, but it is also the mode in which, generally speaking, we frame the tentative first drafts of new ideas: and the mode in which, in times of family or national crisis, we talk with our own people and attempt to work our way towards some kind of a resolution. By analogy with these roles in speech it seemed likely to us that expressive writing might play a key role in a child's learning. It must surely be the most accessible form in which to write, since family conversation will have provided him with a familiar model. Furthermore, a writer who envisages his reader as someone with whom he is on *intimate* terms must surely have very favourable conditions for using the process of writing as a means of exploration and discovery.

It is certainly not the case that every child's first attempts at writing are expressive according to our definition of the term, and to suggest that it is a 'natural' way to start probably raises more questions than it answers. But it must be true that until a child does write expressively he is failing to feed into the writing process the fullness of his linguistic resources—the knowledge of words and structures he has built up in speech—and that it will take him longer to arrive at the point where writing can serve a range of his purposes as broad and diverse as the purposes for which he uses speech.

This, at all events, provided us with a major hypothesis regarding the development of writing ability in school: that what children write in the early stages should be a form of written-down expressive speech, and what they read should also be, generally speaking, expressive. As their writing and reading progress side by side, they will move from this starting point into the three broadly differentiated kinds of writing—our major categories—and, in favourable circumstances, their mode of doing so will be by a kind of shuttling between their speech resources on the one hand and the written forms they meet on the other. Thus, in developmental terms, the expressive is a kind of matrix from which differentiated forms of mature writing are developed—see Figure 3.

use

Fig. 3   The expressive as a matrix for the development of other forms of writing

The more fully an utterance meets the demands of some kind of participation in the world's affairs, the nearer will it approach the transactional end of the scale: the more fully it satisfies the spectator-role demands, the nearer it will move to the poetic end. The move in both cases is from an intimate to a more public audience (and this change should be reflected in our classification by sense of audience).

In all other ways, however, the two moves are very different in character. Let us take 'informing' as an example of a typical task for language, a way of participating, a type of transaction. As expressive writing changes to meet the demands of this task, it will become more explicit: that is, it will supply more of the context, will reflect a concern for accurate and specific reference; it will seek the kind of organization that most effectively carries out such a task, and will exclude the personal, self-revealing features that might interfere with it.

To move in the other direction, however—to satisfy in full the demands of the spectator role—an utterance must become a 'verbal object', a construct. Language forms and *the forms of whatever is represented* become, as we have *poetic* suggested, the objects of attention and contribute to the 'import' of the work. What is afoot is evaluation, so that the embodiment by the writer of feelings and beliefs becomes paramount, and what is included in the utterance may be highly personal. It will be made accessible to an audience of strangers through the complex and subtle internal structure of the artefact: inner experience is, so to speak, given 'resonance' within the structure, and the whole becomes *an experience of order*. A poetic utterance may be said to be a special kind of self-presentation: not so much the embodiment of local or particular feelings as a glimpse into a 'lifetime of feeling', to use Susanne Langer's phrase.[15]

We have been describing the poetic 'pole', the verbal object as work of art; what we need above all to develop is a recognition of writings along the whole spectrum from expressive to poetic—a recognition of the principles upon which the work of literature is constructed, and the application of those principles to less highly organized kinds of writing, the 'art-like'. The work of Susanne Langer is pioneering the way.

Clearly, a mature writer does not 'grow out of' his need for expressive language: its interpersonal and exploratory functions continue to operate, and he develops mature forms of expressive writing to fulfill them—forms very different from the multi-purpose expressive writing of a young child. Here, for example, is part of a letter from Keats, away touring Scotland, to his brother Tom at home in Hampstead:

Have you heard in any way of George? I should think by this time he must have landed. I in my carelessness never thought of knowing where a letter would find him on the other side—I think Baltimore, but I am afraid of directing it to the wrong place. I shall begin some chequer work for him directly, and it will be ripe for the post by the time I hear from you next after this. I assure you I often long for a seat and a Cup 'o tea at Well Walk, especially now that mountains, castles and Lakes are becoming common to me. Yet I would rather summer it out, for on the whole I am happier than when I have time to be glum—perhaps it may cure me. Immediately on my return I shall begin studying hard, with a peep at the theatre now and then—and depend upon it I shall be very luxurious. With respect to Women I think I shall be able to conquer my passions hereafter better than I have yet done. You will help me to talk of George next winter, and we will go now and then to see Fanny. Let me hear a good account of your health and comfort, telling me truly how you do alone. Remember me to all including Mr. and Mrs. Bently.

Your most affectionate Brother
John.[16]

And here, transparent upon a very different mood, is part of his last letter, written to his friend, Charles Brown:

I cannot answer anything in your letter, which followed me from Naples to Rome, because I am afraid to look it over again. I am so weak (in mind) that I cannot bear the sight of any handwriting of a friend I love so much as I do you. Yet I ride the little horse, and at my worst even in quarantine, summoned up more puns, in a sort of desperation, in one week than in any year of my life . . . I am well disappointed in hearing good news from George, for it runs in my head we shall all die young. I have not written to Reynolds yet, which he must think very neglectful; being anxious to send him a good account of my health, I have delayed it from week to week. If I recover, I will do all in my power to correct the mistakes made during sickness; and if I should not, all my faults will be forgiven. Severn is very well, though he leads so dull a life with me. Remember me to all my friends, and tell Haslam I should not have left London without taking leave of him, but from being so low in body and mind. Write to George as soon as you receive this, and tell him how I am, as far as you can guess; and also a note to my sister—who walks about my imagination like a ghost—she is so like Tom. I can scarcely bid you good-bye, even in a letter. I always made an awkward bow.
   God bless you!

John Keats.[17]

This, then, is the broad picture, and we will leave it on a note of speculation. Taking the view currently being put forward[18] that linguistic competence embraces rules of two very different kinds, grammatical rules and 'rules of use', we suggest that the expressive function may mark out an area in which the rules of use are at their least demanding, an area of comparative freedom in this respect.[19] Thus, it may be that, as a writer moves from the expressive into the transactional, he increasingly takes over responsibility for rules of use that, in sum total, constitute one kind of order, one mode of organization by which we encode experience. It is a familiar order, at that—the 'cognitive order' described by psychologists and codified into laws of logic by philosophers. And it may be that, as a writer moves from the expressive into the poetic, he takes on responsibility for rules of use that represent, in sum, a different kind of organization: one that we can recognize in a work of art, while at the same time we know little about the general principles that govern it.

All this has obvious bearings upon our developmental hypothesis. From the area of least demand as far as rules of use are concerned, the learner-writer progresses by increasingly recognizing and attempting to meet the demands of both transactional and poetic tasks, and by increasingly internalizing forms and strategies appropriate to these tasks from what he reads and incorporating them into the pool of his resources: thus in the course of time he may acquire mastery of both varieties of rules of use.

There exists always, of course, an alternative hypothesis: that if you limp about long enough in somebody's else's language, you may eventually learn to walk in it.

SUB-CATEGORIES

Our transactional category clearly needed to be broken down in terms of the kind of transaction undertaken. We have proposed two main sub-categories, the *informative* and the *conative*. The latter we have divided further into *regulative* (where compliance is assumed) and *persuasive*—a function that has been of major interest to classical rhetoricians. The informative we have subdivided by applying from the work of James Moffett[20] his scale of abstraction in the relation of a writer to his topic. Moffett sees four categories—*recording, reporting, generalizing* and *theorizing*—the first most closely resembling the structure of external reality, the fourth most closely resembling the structure of man's mind. We have suggested a finer subdivision for practical purposes, using seven categories for his four (see Table 15, p. 149).

We spent many sessions debating the question of the subdivision of the poetic category* and finally arrived at what must be regarded as a partial solution to the problem. It must first be noted that transactional utterances

* At several of these sessions we had Professor Wayne Booth of the University of Chicago with us and we gratefully acknowledge his valuable assistance.

are 'contextualized'—made our own—in *piecemeal* fashion. We take what fragments interest us (from such an utterance as this chapter, for example), reject the rest maybe, build new connexions for ourselves between and around the fragments. But the poetic writer must resist such piecemeal contextualization. His 'verbal object' is a thing deliberately isolated from the rest of reality: to respond, the reader must contextualize only *after* he has reconstructed the object in accordance with its internal complexity. From this conception of *global contextualization* we derived sub-categories of poetic utterances. Novelists, may for example, put over 'a message' and that message may be classified in accordance with the kind of transaction involved. But to operate the conventions of the poetic, a message must be communicated in and through the total verbal construct, the artefact. The first thing to record about the poetic work, therefore, is to classify it as poetic; however, we may then go on, if we wish, and allot it to a second category in accordance with the participant function that seems appropriate to its global contextualization. We might, for example, call Orwell's *Nineteen Eighty-Four* 'poetic (conative)', Patrick White's *Tree of Man*, 'poetic (informative)', and perhaps Malcolm Lowry's *Under the Volcano*, 'poetic (expressive)'.

While these subdivisions of the poetic are a useful addition to our theoretical model, they would not appear to add very much information to our classification of writings in school, and they were not included in our briefing instructions to assessors of scripts.

ADDITIONAL CATEGORIES

Our principal concern in this work was to provide a set of function categories that would cover the range of writings in general use in our society; a developmental aspect was added in the notion that immature expressive writing might be a common starting point for the mature uses. It seemed important, in addition, that when we came to allocate the scripts we should make allowance for the existence of function categories that might represent either a child's purposes that had no counterpart in mature writing, or a category peculiar to the school situation—and, again, without counterpart in adult uses. The additional categories were intended to cover both these possibilities. As will be seen from Chapter 6, p. 103, our instructions to assessors for these categories constituted more of an invitation than a specification: it was not until we came to consider the findings that we were able to gather any very clear picture as to how important these 'transitional' or special functions were.

The next chapter defines the function categories in greater detail.

Notes and references

1   J. Holloway, *Language and Intelligence*.
2   Ibid., pp. 124–5.

3 J. Lyons, *Structural Semantics*, pp. 82–4.

4 A. C. Purves and V. Rippere, *Elements of Writing about a Literary Work: A Study of Response to Literature*.

5 Dell Hymes, 'The Ethnography of Speaking' in J. A. Fishman (ed.), *Readings in the Sociology of Language* p. 120. (We should point out that, in developing Jakobson's theory, Dell Hymes indicates the shortcomings for his purposes of an analysis that assigns one function to an utterance on the grounds of the dominance of that function in a hierarchy. For our broader purposes, however, we have stayed closer to Jakobson's original formulation.)

6 Ernst Cassirer, *An Essay on Man*.

7 E. Sapir, *Culture, Language and Personality*, pp. 14–15.

8 G. Gusdorf, *Speaking*, p. 7.

9 J. S. Bruner *et al.*, *Studies in Cognitive Growth*.

10 G. Kelly, *The Psychology of Personal Constructs*.

11 P. L. Berger and T. Luckmann, *The Social Construction of Reality*, p. 172.

12 D. W. Harding, 'The Role of the Onlooker'.

13 D. W. Harding, *Social Psychology and Individual Values*.

14 Sapir, *Culture, Language and Personality*, p. 10.

15 S. K. Langer, *Mind: An Essay on Human Feeling*, p. 112.

16 Letters to Thomas Keats, 23 July 1818, in *Letters of John Keats* (ed. Sidney Colvin), pp. 152–3. Of the Keats family, John was the eldest; George, the second son, had sailed with his bride to America in 1817; Tom, the third son, died of consumption in the December of 1818; Fanny, the youngest was fifteen at that time.

17 Letter to Charles Brown, 30 November 1820, in *Letters of John Keats*, pp. 376–7.

18 See J. Searle, *Chomsky's Revolution in Linguistics*, and J. Habermas, 'Towards a Theory of Communicative Competence'.

19 If the expressive function represents, as one aspect, the pursuit of intimacy, it may appear that we underestimate the difficulties of achieving such a relationship. This is not the case, however. What we suggest is that the conditions to be met, perhaps with considerable difficulty, are not codified into conventional rules of use, but lie in the more or less unique psychological intricacies of the personalities concerned.

20 J. Moffett, *Teaching the Universe of Discourse*.

6 Defining the function categories

Transactional
Expressive
Poetic

This chapter is based on the function categories briefing document used by our research team. The purpose of the document was to give the assessors who were allocating scripts a clear sense of those categories, which had evolved from a prolonged period of discussion. We were very conscious of the fact that what had become entirely familiar to our thinking might have appeared outlandish or obscure to those first encountering it, hence the length of the document. We were also aware of the need to keep the length down to a workable minimum and so, to aid assessors, included a summary of the category system, a version of which is given in chart form in the fold-out sheet which follows the index. (Details of our procedural instructions to assessors working on the function categories are reproduced in Appendix I.)

Our three main function categories for mature writing—*transactional, expressive* and *poetic*—are defined in the next three sections.

I TRANSACTIONAL

This is language to get things done: to inform people (telling them what they need or want to know or what we think they ought to know), to advise or persuade or instruct people. Thus the transactional is used for example to record facts, exchange opinions, explain and explore ideas, construct theories; to transact business, conduct campaigns, change public opinion. Where the transaction (whatever it is we want to do with language) demands accurate and specific reference to what is known about reality, this need constitutes a demand for the use of language in the transactional category.

We shall need to subdivide this category in various ways, but before going into this we shall describe the other two main categories.

2 EXPRESSIVE

Speech includes a wider range of uses of the expressive than does written language. We shall therefore list first examples of the expressive in *spoken* language:

> (a) Exclamations—expressions of fear, joy, pain, anger, surprise etc.— made when there is no one there to hear them.

(b) More extended remarks we may make to ourselves to express our feelings, put into words our immediate consciousness.

(c) Exclamations, as in (a) above, spoken in the presence of a listener. (In these circumstances exclamations will often be given and received as in part an appeal for help, sympathy, some kind of response. To interpret them fully the listener must know the speaker and see the predicament: the proper response to the boy who continually cried 'wolf' would be to ignore it, unless we could see the beast.)

(d) More extended speech addressed to a listener with whom the speaker has a common understanding (i.e. a listener who shares experience in common and whose context for the utterance will largely coincide with the speaker's), and constituting an expression of the speaker's feelings, mood, opinions, immediate preoccupations; thus, what is said reveals as much about the personality and state of mind of the speaker as it does about the events spoken about.

(e) Interpersonal expressive—we have referred to a speaker and a listener: to complete the account we must extend this concept, firstly, to include examples where there is an audience of more than two people and, secondly, to provide for the fact that any listener may become a speaker.

Similar criteria may be applied to the written language to give the following categories of expressive *writing*:

(a) The kind of writing that might be called 'thinking aloud on paper'. Intended for the writer's own use, it might be interpreted by a reader who had shared much of the earlier thinking, but it could not be understood by one who was not 'in the context'.

(b) The kind of diary entry that attempts to record and explore the writer's feelings, mood, opinions, preoccupations of the moment.

(c) Personal letters written to friends or relations for the purpose of maintaining contact with them (as a substitute, so to speak, for being with them). Where the writer deals with his own affairs and preoccupations, the letter may read very like the diary entry, and a close relationship with the reader is claimed or assumed by regarding him as a 'second self'. At other times the writer may more actively invoke a close relationship with his reader, firstly by importing references to shared experiences in highly *implicit* terms and, secondly, by implying strongly held shared opinions and values in the way he refers to people and events in general.

Some writing of the following kinds may also, on balance, be said to have an expressive function:

(d) Writing addressed to a limited public audience assumed to share much of the writer's context and many of his values and opinions and interests (e.g. topical newspaper commentary in a conversational manner, some editorials, 'interest' articles in specialist journals, gossip columns).

(e) Writing, intended to be read by a public audience, in which the writer chooses to approach his reader as though he were a personal friend, hence revealing much about himself by implication in the course of dealing with his topic (e.g. some autobiography).

From these examples of both speech and writing we can make three generalizations about the expressive function. *Firstly*, expressive language is language close to the self. It has the functions of revealing the speaker, verbalizing his consciousness, and displaying his close relation with a listener or reader. *Secondly*, much expressive language is not made explicit, because the speaker/writer relies upon his listener/reader to interpret what is said in the light of a common understanding (that is, a shared general context of the past), and to interpret their immediate situation (what is happening around them) in a way similar to his own. It follows that the meaning of an expressive utterance may vary in accordance with the situation: compare the meaning of 'So, you're home at last' said by a wife in the small hours and by a mother at the airport. *Thirdly*, since expressive language submits itself to the free flow of ideas and feelings, it is relatively unstructured.

3 POETIC

Poetic writing uses language as an art medium. A piece of poetic writing is a verbal construct, an 'object' made out of language. The words themselves, and all they refer to, are selected to make an arrangement, a formal pattern.

This pattern is made up of a number of different elements. To begin with, in all poetic writings the *phonic substance of language itself* is arranged (though the effect of the arrangement is generally more prominent, more sharply felt, in a lyric than it is in a novel). In addition, the *writer's feelings* (about himself, about his topic, towards his reader, about the human condition), which would be expressed naturally or casually in a piece of expressive writing, are in poetic writing ordered, arranged to create a pattern. Where there is a narrative, the *events* referred to also make up or are part of a pattern. Finally there is a pattern of *ideas*, a formal 'movement of thought', which adds a characteristically poetic dimension to the writer's thinking. These are not independent systems of arrangement, of course, but elements in a single significant design. Consonance and dissonance between formal elements bind the writing into a complete whole, a single construct whether it be a sonnet or a novel, an epic or a curtain-raiser.

The phonetic, syntactic, lexical and semantic aspects of the utterance itself are the objects of attention, by the writer and the reader, in a way that does not hold of non-poetic writing: we might roughly compare the two response processes with those of 'taking in' a painting and studying a map. The function of a piece of poetic writing is to be an object that pleases or satisfies the writer: and the reader's response is to share that satisfaction. In this sense, poetic writing constitutes language that exists *for its own sake* and not as a means of achieving something else. (Perhaps it should be added that the nature and degree of the author's satisfaction must vary very much from one piece to another. The more complex the construct, the greater, probably, the area of his experience that is lit by this satisfaction.)

A digression on the role of participant and the role of spectator

To make clearer our three-fold division of function categories, we shall outline a basic theoretical position which underlies them, to which we have already referred briefly (see pp. 79–81).

Suppose we recount an interesting experience to a friend—for his entertainment and our pleasure in doing so. We shall continue to breathe, stand up, sit down, drink maybe, or eat, attend occasionally to what is going on around us—offer him another drink, move nearer the fire if it's cold, answer a child's question, and so on. But mentally we are 'living in the past'—these other things are seen as unattended background to, or interruptions of, what we are principally concerned to do, which is to rehearse in mind an experience that is *not now going on*, but has been experienced in the past. Participating in ongoing experiences is thus a different process from 'reliving the past', which is one form of a process we are referring to as taking up *the role of spectator*.

What we feel as background or as interruption to our spectator role activity is likely to be similarly felt by our listener. In other words, in sharing this past experience with him we induce him also to take up the spectator role. But it is an experience we had, he did not. It follows that we may similarly take up the role of spectator of experiences *we* have never had—as when we read a novel or watch a film or a play, or as when we enter into a possible future experience in our day-dreaming.

However, we may recount past experiences in another way—and here the relationship between the past and the ongoing experience is a different one. If we describe a past experience in a doctor's consulting room it will be as a contribution to what is now going on—a diagnosis. If we tell a hard-luck story as prelude to trying to raise a loan, that again is pursuing our own ends—and our own ends are, as it were, a part of the world's ongoing affairs. In such cases, then, we are in the role of participants and not spectators. Only when we recount the past, or imagine a future or a conceivable experience—past, present or future—for the pleasure of doing so and for no further end, are we taking up the role of spectator.

To sum up: when we use language to recount or recreate real or imagined experience for no other reason than to enjoy it or present it for enjoyment, we are using language in the role of spectator; when we use language to get things done, we are in the role of participants (participants in 'the world's affairs'). The latter role includes the use of language to recount or recreate real or imagined experience in order to inform or teach, or to make plans or solicit help or to achieve any other practical outcome.

It should be noted that 'spectator' does not suggest any lack of involvement in the experiences being recounted: we may indeed enter imaginatively into them very fully and actively, but since the events are not ones *now going on*, we cannot (literally) participate in them.

THE ROLES OF PARTICIPANT AND SPECTATOR IN RELATION TO THE MAIN FUNCTION CATEGORIES

Thus we see the two roles of participant and spectator as two distinct relationships between what is being said (or written or thought) and what is being done: and as covering between them all uses of language. We see the main function categories—transactional, expressive, poetic—as representing a continuum related to the two roles, as set out in Figure 2 (p. 81). Expressive language straddles the participant/spectator distinction: that is to say, expressive language is able to move freely from one role to the other, across a boundary which is, at this central point, a shadowy one. Our function categories do not, therefore, try to make any distinction between the two roles *within the expressive*.

Nevertheless, to illustrate further what the two roles mean in principle, let us consider how they might operate within the expressive. Imagine a conversation in which you describe to a friend the holiday you have just had, in order to enjoy it in retrospect and entertain him. You are, in other words, taking up the role of spectator of your own past experience, and inviting him to do so. But in the course of listening the idea might strike him that he should take his next holiday in the place you visited. Planning his holiday is a participant activity, not a spectator one. He may begin asking questions which interrupt your retrospect: such things as, 'How far did you say it was from the sea?' 'Is it a rocky coast?' 'What's the swimming like?' and so on. In idle conversation this may be a minor interruption: in other words the expressive speech, as we have seen, moves easily from one role to the other. But if your listener is really taken with his idea, he may pursue his planning seriously, and the talk may move firmly into the participant role, changing (as we shall see) from the expressive to the transactional.

Dell Hymes describes a similar situation, a switch from what we should probably have called spectator-role speech to participant, and from expressive function to transactional:

A group of wives may be chatting about personal experiences with children. If another woman insists on exact information, she is failing to perceive dominance of expressive or phatic function in the situation. Polite enquiry is appropriate, but not persistent challenge as to fact. Or a group of wives may be discussing children in behavioural science terms. If another woman interposes purely associative and biographical comments about her own children, she is failing to perceive the dominance of a referential function. Evidence is appropriate, but not anecdotes irrelevant to the views and theory being exchanged. In either case, the offender may be excluded from communication, or avoided under similar circumstances later. ('The Ethnography of Speaking', in J. A. Fishman, ed., *Readings in the Sociology of Language*, p. 116.)

Of course, finding out things we do not know—about the speaker or about the people, places etc. in his story—is always likely to be a *part* of our concern as we listen to talk in the spectator role: it is only when such concerns become dominant that they cause a switch into participant role.

Finally, we would make one distinction between the expressive function and the poetic and transactional functions. Expressive speech is relaxed: half an hour's chat with a friend is likely to leave us less fatigued than half an hour spent briefing him for some undertaking, or urging him to do something we want done. Expressive writing is relaxed in a similar way. This amounts to saying that in expressive writing the demands made on the writer (demands from *outside*, by the reader, by the nature of the task) are at a minimum. What we are suggesting is that the demands which begin to affect expressive writing (so tending to change it into something else) are of two kinds. On the one hand, the demands of a *task*, the need to *do* something by means of language, will, if taken far enough, change the expressive into the transactional. On the other hand, the demands of the *construct*, the urge to *make* something in language and the intricacies of doing so, will, if taken far enough, change the expressive into the poetic.

Contrasting the extremes: transactional and poetic

It may be helpful to bear in mind the following pairs of contrasting characteristics:

Transactional (Participant role)	*Poetic (Spectator role)*
The writing is an immediate means to an end outside itself.	The writing is an immediate end in itself, and not a means: it is a verbal artifact, a construct.
The form it takes, the way it is organized, is dictated primarily by the desire to achieve that end efficiently.	The arrangement *is* the construct: the way items are formally disposed is an inseparable part of the meaning of the piece.
Attention to the forms of the language is incidental to understanding, and will often be minimal.	Attention to the forms of the language is an essential part of a reader's response.

Transactional (Participant role)	*Poetic (Spectator role)*
The writer is concerned in his writing to enmesh with his reader's relevant knowledge, experience, interests; and the reader is at liberty to contextualize what he finds relevant, selectively. This 'piecemeal contextualization' we consider to be a part of the conventions governing transactional writing.	The writer is concerned to create relations internal to the work, and achieve a unity, a construct discrete from actuality. Thus he resists piecemeal contextualization: the conventions holding between writer and reader in poetic writing call for *global* contextualization.

Subdivisions of the transactional: informative (1.1) and conative (1.2)

We transact all sorts of different tasks by means of language, and the language varies according to the demands of the transaction or task. In classifying these variations according to function the first broad distinction is between the *informative* and the *conative.* Informative language is used to make information available; conative language is an instrument of the writer's intention to influence the reader.

The informative is used to record and report, to classify and compare, to infer and deduce and hypothesize, to ask and answer questions, to assert, to explain and to evaluate. The conventions governing its use presuppose that facts should be right, assertions true, comments relevant, arguments consistent: in short, that its information may be used *if the reader so chooses.*

The conative, on the other hand, is used to order, instruct, advise or persuade someone (though it does not follow that he should, in fact, carry out the instruction or be persuaded). Although nearly all language can be thought of as to some degree an attempt to persuade, we have deliberately defined the conative as a fairly narrow category so that it will only include cases where an attempt to change someone's behaviour, attitude or opinion can be easily discerned.

SUBDIVISIONS OF THE INFORMATIVE

1.1.1 Record

A writer may attempt to record what is immediately present in his environment, the events, the appearance of things. He is saying what his world is like at that moment. This is the written form of the kind of language we encounter in the spoken sports commentary. We would expect this kind of informative writing to be rare. It has its counterpart in expressive writing (for example, it might occur in a personal letter), and in poetic writing (such as Auden's 'Look Stranger'), but this category of *record* is applied only to informative writing.

Perhaps the commonest use of this category of writing is by reporters, who are frequently obliged to record what is going on while it is going on. They may then edit their work so that the reader is presented with a text which refers to the past (which would then be *report*—see below) or they may preserve, in spite of editing, the immediacy of their original 'record' version. Thus we find the 'eye-witness account'. (It would be of some interest to know whether the increased use in many schools of inquiry and out-of-class investigation and observation has meant that there is much more of this kind of writing tucked away in pupils' notebooks.)

1.1.2 Report

In report, the writer takes up a retrospective stance (a stance which gives him a basis of selection denied to the writer in the previous category). He no longer appears as an observer who sees what is to be seen around him and what is happening as he writes: he may draw upon his own past observations (in a particular time and place) or he may write as one who by some means or another knows about the past (i.e. about particular occasions and scenes in the past) and is a reliable informant. In either case his stance is that of someone reporting past observations and not recording what is being observed. Narratives usually reflect this stance by using the past tense; descriptive passages may not do so since, obviously, the particulars of the scene observed in the past may well exist unchanged in the present.

It is important to note that report deals with particular observable events and scenes and does not cover generalizations drawn from scattered observations or from observations over a period of time.

1.1.3 Generalized narrative or descriptive information

It is possible for the one-time-one-place report of the past to be expressed in more general terms and yet not to constitute true generalization. By taking a few similar occasions or places the writer, usually by a mere shift of tense ('I *asked* the old man who sells newspapers' to 'I *ask*' etc.), suggests that events or appearances have recurred. Thus we reserved this category for the writer who is taking only the first step away from report, who remains very tied to particular events and places but is detecting a pattern of repetition in them. In order to do this he may well give to precise elements a more general quality than they actually have since there is a contradiction between the concreteness and the generalization ('My mother always comes upstairs and trips over the carpet, swears and gives me a cup of tea, half of which is, of course, swilling around in the saucer'). Moreover, the writer, whether by choice or necessity, makes no use of abstraction which could lift him out of the immediateness of the detail. It should be stressed that these are not value judgements, since a generalized narrative may for various valid reasons be the chosen form of the writer who wishes to strike a specific balance between the general and the particular. On the other hand it may be a category which represents the first efforts of an immature writer to break away from the particular. To put it most generally, we may say that the writer arranges classes of events on a chronological principle, or classes of appearances on a spatial principle.

We include in this category a great deal of everyday informational discourse: discourse in which the speaker generalizes from a number of events or procedures or situations in order to tell us in a concrete way how things occur, what things are like or how things are done, for example, 'Hydrogen sulphide is usually obtained from iron sulphide and dilute hydrochloric acid, using a Kipps apparatus.' Note that this is a generalization from observable repeatable processes involving concrete phenomena. However, a writer concerned to tell us how things occur may draw explicitly upon *principles* (rationally established relationships), and in this case his writing would move to a category higher up the scale of abstraction, such as the low-level analogic or the analogic (see next two categories): for example, 'Hydrogen and oxygen may be obtained by electrolysis of water to which a few drops of sulphuric acid have been added to increase the rate of ionization.' Similarly, a writer who is making his own generalizations from observable concrete phenomena may take his generalizations to a point of abstraction where the writing must be classified as low-level analogic or analogic.

It follows from what we said above that instructions for carrying out practical processes (e.g. recipes) are likely in spite of their form (see p. 99) to appear in the category of generalized narrative.

1.1.4 Analogic, low level of generalization

In this category we would place that writing which constitutes genuine generalization but of which the organization is very loose. The generalization is, moreover, at a low level. It is a further step away from report but, having cast off the link with the organizing principle of narrative/description which is retained in generalized narrative, it has not yet taken over the organizing principle of analogic writing (see next category). At this low level of generalization, a writer offering a geographical description of the industries of Scotland presents generalization after generalization. The relationship between one and the next, or amongst groups of them or a developing relationship running through the whole, is not only not made explicit but may well have not been in the mind of the writer in the first place. While it is true that the cohesion of a text may be signalled in very subtle ways, there are also texts which are in the tradition of the basic-facts-rather-than-their-significance and which do not set out to present a coherently organized view. Thus we may say once again that the writer may choose to limit himself in this way or be obliged to use this category because he can use no other for this kind of transaction. In the latter case his selection of generalizations may be so arbitrary that he presents a mere agglomeration or possibly a concatenation: one thing leads to another.

1.1.5 Analogic

In 1.1.4 (low level analogic) the writer has increased the distance between himself and his material. By classifying phenomena (i.e. selecting out shared features of many events and combining them in such a way that he is no longer tied to the events themselves) he has been able not only to handle classificatory concepts embodied in single words but to make classificatory statements, and to present a sequence of related classificatory statements. However, we have stated that in low-level analogic writing the relationship is a loose one. In 1.1.5 (analogic), then, we would place writing which has related its generalizations hierarchically or logically. Much scientific writing is of this kind. Thus it will not concern itself so much with what *happened* to, let us say, a particular object when treated in a particular way but rather with what *happens* to substances of such-and-such a kind when treated in such-and-such a way. Though some scientific writing constitutes a particularly obvious example of this category, there is no reason why analogic writing should not be drawn from personal experience. A writer may well present to us his ideas about the way men and things behave without reference to systematized scholarship. Thus an eleven-year-old writes, 'People get mad very easy.' Again, a great deal of historical writing deals in generalized statements about events rather than particular events, and must then be classified as analogic (see below p. 101).

Finally, we can say that analogic writing may or may not be supported by reference to particulars, rich or sparse. If it is, these particulars are seen as playing a subordinate role within the analogic function.

1.1.6 Analogic–tautologic (speculative)

In the three previous categories we have been dealing with different levels of generalization. A new element enters writing when the writer begins to inspect his generalizations and to make them the very subject of his discourse. One form of this is speculation. Here the writer begins to consider alternative possibilities and perhaps to weigh them. This speculation is for the most part open-ended in the sense that it can lead anywhere, any possibility might be sounded out, any analogic hare may be started. It is, so to speak, a thinking ploy in which the writer proposes to himself a potentially valid analogic utterance without feeling that he must push it to a firm conclusion or relate it to a closed logical system, though it may only be possible because of other firm conclusions or his access to a system.

We may speculate in all sorts of ways ('I wonder if it will rain?' 'It may be because they are heavier'). To qualify for this category (or the next, 1.1.7), the speculation would have to be of a theoretical kind—i.e. one that uses a formulation as a basis for prediction and extrapolation.

1.1.7 Tautologic

This is writing which concerns itself with *theory* and therefore with making propositions about propositions, or propositions about the relationships between propositions. It will produce hypotheses and make deductions from them. Generalizations are transformed into other generalizations in such a way that new assertions become possible, such as, 'The social life of man is characterized not by virtue of his being a tool-using animal but by virtue of his being a language-generating animal.' A great deal of impersonal logical argument (argument from principles or theory) would be placed in this category.

What distinguishes the tautologic from 1.1.6 (analogic–tautologic) is that it is *highly ordered* and consistent, and the free play of speculative ideas is disciplined and given the conventional shape which has evolved for this kind of discourse.

1.2   CONATIVE

The transactional function's second major subdivision is *conative*, which includes orders, instructions, advice and persuasion.

It is possible, of course, to regard almost all language as persuasive or partly persuasive. For example, a piece of writing which sets out what happened, or one which elaborates a principle or puts forward a hypothesis, carries with it the notion that the writer would like his reader to believe that what has been written is true, and he may be at some pains to produce evidence and explanations, and to provide good reasons why it is true; and generally the reader accepts that his knowledge or understanding is being influenced. In poetic writing, the author's way of looking at the world is, to some extent, shared with the reader, so there is an element of persuasion here also, using the word in its widest sense. (Some literary genres—satire, propaganda novel—make, or appear to make, persuasion their central function; the problems raised by such writing will be discussed later.)

This view of language—a view which is implicit in theories of language as social control—is not one with which we would want to argue, but in our system of classification we have found it more helpful to define the conative more narrowly, so as to include only writing where the attempt to instruct or persuade is much more explicit, where there is a deliberate and recognizable assault on other people's behaviour or attitudes or opinions, or where the assault, although deliberate, is disguised so that the reader may be all the more effectively persuaded without knowing it.

The reader is not necessarily persuaded: orders are not always carried out; people may fail to respond to the most logical arguments or the most subtle blandishments. They may even do the opposite to what was expected of them. Nevertheless, the essential characteristics of the conative—its conventions and presuppositions—are the use of an acknowledged means of commanding or urging or persuading, and the acknowledgement by the reader of the means being used (but see *Disguises of the conative*, p. 99).

1.2.1 Regulative

This first subdivision of the conative is writing which gives instructions, tells what is to be done or what should be done. The attempt to influence is direct, and it is therefore more likely to be concerned with actions and behaviour than with attitudes and beliefs. It is concerned with making demands, issuing instructions where there is an obligation to obey them and making recommendations which carry the weight of authority or the force of the speaker's wishes. (It is not concerned with giving information or putting forward reasons.)

Regulative writing is fairly rare in school tasks, because the rationale of most school subjects demands explanation and justification. When a pupil sets out to write about how to do something (how to mend a puncture, how to prepare oxygen, how to make a curry—i.e. technological discourse) the function is *informative* rather than conative because the writer is in no way inciting the reader to do whatever it is, he is merely letting him know how to do it, supposing he wants to. Thus, while rules are conative (regulative) because anyone who comes within their jurisdiction must obey them or endure the consequences of not doing so, recipes are informative, because the writer is in no way concerned with whether the reader makes use of the information; he provides it to be used by anyone who wants it.

1.2.2 Persuasive

In persuasive writing the reader is seen as someone whose behaviour, attitudes or opinions can be changed or influenced by reason, argument or strategy, rather than someone for whom a course of action can be prescribed and elaborated. As soon as the regulative is backed by argument, acknowledging potential resistance, it moves towards the persuasive. It is in the nature of the persuasive that it enters controversy, and may well attempt to foresee and counter all possible objections. The writer is, in effect, saying 'This is what I want you to do, and I'm telling you why' or 'This is a point of view that you ought to hold, and these are my reasons for saying so.'

FURTHER NOTES ON THE CONATIVE

Disguises of the conative

Conative writing may sometimes depend on concealment of its function in order to fulfil that function more effectively. This may occur in advertising and in some kinds of propaganda, and it can arise in children's writing. There is then a difficulty in relation to our *definition* of function (see p. 76). If a reader is in fact persuaded, but does not consciously realize what is happening, we cannot call this 'the mutual acknowledgement of communicating subjects'. Such a reader is persuaded because he lacks the subtlety and sophistication of the writer, but other readers, who do share that subtlety and sophistication, will recognize the persuasive function, and the requirements of our definition are fulfilled as far as the writer and his equals are concerned. The persuasive function, however, is concealed from the unsophisticated reader, hence our phrase 'disguised conative'.

Distinguishing the expressive and the conative

It is the function of the expressive not only to verbalize—to reveal the personality (feelings, preoccupations) of the writer—but also to set up a close personal bond between himself and his reader. The sort of situation and relationship in which this takes place would allow also for a different function— that in which the writer deliberately seeks to influence the attitudes or behaviour of his reader and *to do so in his role of intimate associate*. The language employed will in both cases bear the stamp of the close personal relationship; however, the first must be classified as expressive and the second as conative.

Distinguishing the informative and the conative

A writer in the process of informing his reader about a matter on which he has strong feelings may move towards, or into, the conative function if the expression of strong feelings is employed, within the convention, to arouse its counterpart in the readers.

Conative writing, propaganda, 'committed' literature and satire

It is easy to find examples of literature which have, as part of their function, the influencing of the judgement, beliefs and attitudes of the reader. Frequently this literature has a strong appeal for young people, and pupils often want to 'commit' themselves in their own writing in the poetic or expressive–poetic area. It is therefore necessary to distinguish conative transactional writing from poetic writing which also has a conative function. In the first, the conative function is the transaction itself, but in the second the relationship of the two functions is more complicated. A play or a poem or a story which has a conative function as well as a poetic one can have it only if the writer and reader both accept the poetic construct first. If this is not possible—if the poetic function is made subservient to the conative one—we should have no hesitation in putting the script into the transactional conative category, even though the writer may have set out to write a poem or a story and thought he had done so. It is not altogether a matter of deciding on which is the dominant function, as is the case in making judgements of other writing which has some of the characteristics of two functions. Satire functions as satire only because the poetic construct is established beyond all doubt; the same is true of a novel like Zola's *Germinal*, or a poem like Yevtushenko's 'Babi Yar'. Pupils often succeed in achieving this degree of commitment in their writing and expressing it within a poetic construct; this writing is not necessarily less conative because its poetic function is clearly established, but we would classify it as poetic.

Notes on applying the categories to school writing

HISTORICAL WRITING

It might seem that the presentation of a chronological sequence of historical events must inevitably be classified as report, but report as we define it (see p. 95) should be limited to events as they might have been observed by an onlooker. Such a statement as 'Charles I stepped on to the scaffold' is of a different order from 'Britain went to war with Germany', since the latter requires that the writer generalize from many possible statements of the order of the former (in much the same way as does the statement, 'Metals expand when heated'). In other words a statement of the latter kind is by its nature analogic, classificatory.

A sentence such as 'Britain went to war with Germany' might well be in a context of such sentences as 'Hitler refused to see the British envoy' and 'A British ship was torpedoed in the North Atlantic'. In this case, of course, the writing would be classified as report. It might equally well be in a context such as the following: 'Germany attempted a blockade of British seaports and, when this proved inconclusive, made preparations for an invasion by sea and air.' In this case the writing would be classified as analogic (see p. 97).

WRITING ABOUT LITERATURE (AND OTHER ART FORMS)

Writing about literature (or about other works of art) commonly takes one of two forms: *either* the interpretation of a particular text (or picture etc.), *or* the elaboration or application of a critical theory. Scripts of the first type may be classified under various categories, as follows:

(a) *Record* (though this turned out to be rare). E.g. (of a picture): 'The scene is a picture of looking through an old broken window. The window looks as if it used to be part of a church. Through the window you can see a mountain in the distance. At the bottom of the mountain there is a grassy slope.'

(b) *Report.* 'In the town of Hamelin there had been rats and the Pied Piper had got rid of them for the people. After this the people and children played about. But the only thing was that the town council wouldn't pay the Piper for getting rid of the rats.'

(c) *Analogic* (where particular references may be made in support of classificatory generalization). 'The images and diction of the poem are solid and give a feeling almost of earthiness. He talks of the brain growing, compares himself to a tree, a symbol of immobility and steadiness, yet still having life.'

(d) *Speculative* or *tautologic.* 'The art of the novel, wrote Thackeray, is to represent nature. In Vanity Fair therefore his purpose is to create a realistic portrayal of the manner of society around him. His method of achieving this is not to narrate a story dealing with the life of one individual character, observing society through his eyes and recording his responses, but to take a broader view of social activities describing a large number of figures in a succession of varying situations and commenting on the action himself as he goes along.' (There may be some difficulty in deciding whether a script of this kind is speculative or tautologic; but it should be noted, firstly, that the quotation invokes a *theory*—and, secondly, that it states a definition of art and draws inferences from that definition—i.e. it is tautologic in the sense of making statements about statements. Therefore we would call it tautologic.)

The second type of writing about literature—that which elaborates or applies a critical theory—will normally be tautologic; however, where the ideas suggest something more tentative and fragmentary (less organized than 'a theory'), the writing is likely to be in the intermediate analogic–tautologic or speculative category.

STORIES

Fictional narratives may have a *transactional* function. Just as you may appear to take up the role of spectator of your own experiences when in fact you are a participant who is trying to get something done (spinning a hard-luck story in order to go on and raise a loan), so a writer may appear to take up the role of spectator (imagine he is an Eskimo) for the real purpose of conveying information about Eskimos. Conversely, we cannot assume that a task set for a transactional purpose will necessarily produce transactional writing. The writer may enter into the fiction as into a daydream and write *expressively*, or shape it into a *poetic* narrative.

Fictional narratives, then, may have an *expressive* function. Just as you may give an account of your actual experiences in the spectator role in chatting to a friend—inviting his interest in the events and yourself—so a writer may take up a fictional role, or tell fictional anecdotes about other people, with the same purpose of inviting interest in his yarns and himself. The expressive fictional narrative does not take up all the presuppositions of the poetic narrative. The writer invites the reader to share the ongoing satisfaction of his fictional world, and what it reveals to himself, without the additional satisfaction of the highly selective shaping of that world. Thus the writer could stop at almost any point or go on, in a somewhat similar manner to the way in which the stream of fantasy-in-the-head can continue or break off.

The following rough and ready distinctions were used to help us to arrive at a decision when classifying fictional scripts:

(a) To qualify as *transactional* (*informative*), the piece had to seem concerned to satisfy the reader (or teacher) seeking information, while at the same time it maintained the framework of a fictional narrative. (As we have seen on p. 100, stories may be *conative* as well as informative.)

(*b*) To qualify as *expressive*, it had above all to seem to satisfy the writer's desire to verbalize his thought and feelings to someone willing to be interested in them and him.

(*c*) To qualify as *poetic*, it had to seem of value as a verbal construct made for the pleasure of making it and sharing it, and not as a means to some other end.

Additional categories (4.1 and 4.2)

We did not wish to assume that all children's writing could satisfactorily be allocated to the set of functions we had devised for mature writing. We had to allow for the following two possibilities: firstly, immature categories which were peculiar to children's writing (perhaps at particular stages) and which, having served a developmental purpose, disappeared when the writers matured; and, secondly, special categories created by the special contexts of education—a special set of presuppositions and conventions, not holding between people in general, but operating only within the relationship set up in those contexts.

It must be stressed that, in allocating scripts to 'immature' or 'special' categories, we were not looking for scripts which betrayed any or most of the signs of immaturity which occur frequently in the writing of younger or weaker pupils. We were concerned here solely with function and with the scripts which could not satisfactorily be placed in our set of (mature) categories. Markers were therefore asked to resist the temptation to use these additional categories as a dumping ground for pieces which they considered poor or inadequate.

4.1   IMMATURE CATEGORIES

We felt it was important for assessors to be on the look-out for these categories, for although we had some evidence that they existed in younger children's writing, we had not been able to establish any clear categories in our limited look at the sample of school work by eleven to eighteen-year-olds. We therefore only suggested the kind of criteria that might describe them, giving two possible examples, as follows.

Firstly, it was felt to be conceivable that a child who was not capable of taking into account the needs of an inquirer might write in a form which was neither informative nor expressive but undifferentiated 'informative-cum-expressive'. Such *undifferentiated* categories (and there could be other varieties) would constitute one kind of immature category. (A function tends to reveal itself over a stretch of writing rather than attach itself to a single sentence: a continuous shuttling between, for example, informative and expressive and a failure to build up either consistently would therefore be characteristic of writing in an undifferentiated category.)

Secondly, we thought there might be an immature category of a kind we could call 'practice-play', where a child amuses himself by playing at some kind of writing that has taken his fancy—with no evident transactional function, nor, in the terms in which we have described them, any clearly expressive or poetic function. Ought we, for example, to put the following script by a nine-year-old girl in such a category?

The Roski is a cat-like animal, living in the trees. When full-grown it is black, with a sandy coloured tip to its tail, and this is ringed with ginger. Its eyes are golden, and shine in the dark. Its pointed ears are edged with white. It has 4 orange claws on each foot, which help it to climb. The young, or raskis as they are called are light brown marked with lighter stripes. The ears are like an adult roski . . .

4.2   SPECIAL CATEGORIES

4.2.1 Pseudo-informative

Much school writing is functionally complicated by its double focus. On the one hand it appears to be normal transactional writing; on the other hand, behind the apparent transaction (for example, informing the uninformed) there lies another, that of showing the teacher that what he has taught has been learned. Much writing with this double focus caused us no difficulty, since where the writer was able to take up the presumed relations (i.e. between informer and informed) the piece could be allocated to the appropriate transactional category. If, however, the writer could not or would not take up these relations, but instead concentrated on satisfying the teacher-as-examiner *at the expense of* the apparent informative function, we called the writing pseudo-informative. The kind of script which would be placed in this category would be, for example, a history essay in which facts which had been arbitrarily selected were strung together to earn marks, but which could not genuinely inform an inquirer. Such 'random information retrieval' is far removed from a genuine informational transaction.

4.2.2 Pseudo-conative

The process just described can be seen at work when a pupil undertakes conative writing with a double focus, satisfying the teacher-cum-examiner that he has learnt a conative routine but is following it *at the expense of* the apparent conative function.

(It should be stressed that that writing which falls into the 'pupil to examiner' *audience* category will by no means necessarily be allocated to one of these 'special categories' of function.)

4.2.3. Dummy run

When within the school situation a pupil is called upon to perform a writing task in order (*a*) to exercise his capacity to perform that kind of task, and/or (*b*) to demonstrate to the teacher his proficiency in performing it, a special context of 'apprentice to master' has been created. As in category 4.2.1. (pseudo-informative) the writer may be able to take up the presumed relations which are appropriate to the task, but when he does not do so, the resulting writing would be put into the 'dummy run' category. A class which has been set the task of writing ballads in order to show that it can write ballads is likely to produce many 'dummy run' ballads.

7 Introducing the results

Faced with these long and complicated briefing documents—for audience categories and for function—what did our assessors manage to do? It will be recalled that each script was assessed by three people independently, at least one of the three in each case being a member of the research team. The seven* members of the team took part in the work and so did twenty-two other people (six on audience, fifteen on function and one on both). The only initiation these additional assessors had had was that which happened at the one-day briefing session to launch each of the two tasks. Thus, what was at issue was in part the question of whether our categories could be used by, and be of use to, teachers. The principal intention, however, was to secure a 'verdict', a description in terms of our categories that could with reasonable confidence be attached to any script.

The most direct answer to our opening question is, therefore, that on 1046 out of the total of 2122 scripts all three assessors gave the same audience category, and on 694 of them all gave the same function category. As will become clear later, the difference between the two totals reflects a difference in the nature of the tasks (there were in any case more function categories than audience categories in the 'blueprint'); but more to the point is the fact that two audience categories attracted very large numbers of scripts whereas there was a much more even distribution over many categories in the case of the function set.

So far, so good: an encouragingly large number of scripts had been given a clear designation—but of course we could not afford to leave it at that. We made an arbitrary decision to accept as verdicts any set of judgements that showed the equivalent of two-thirds agreement. This would include such cases as the following:

Individual assessments: A generalized narrative
B generalized narrative
C low-level analogic
Final verdict: generalized narrative

* Seven by this time, including the second research officer and the secretary.

Individual assessments : A generalized narrative
                          B generalized narrative/low level analogic
                          c generalized narrative/expressive
Final verdict : generalized narrative

Individual assessments : A generalized narrative
                          B generalized narrative/low-level analogic
                          c low-level analogic
Final verdict : generalized narrative/low-level analogic

On this basis, our teams of three assessors gave us verdicts on all but 126 scripts for audience and all but 384 scripts for function. For these, we had a fresh assessment made by three members of the team and reduced the 'no-verdicts' to 18 for audience and 130 for function. (It was interesting to note how effectively our original assessors identified the 'problem scripts', particularly in the function task: what the team members had to work on was a collection of those eccentric examples which seem designed to defeat any kind of classificatory intention.) Fuller details of these arrangements and an attempt to estimate the reliability of the verdicts will be found in Appendix II.

What sort of conclusions, then, are the category verdicts likely to lead to? Perhaps the first thing to say is that the distributions do throw light on what was going on in the schools in our sample. Differences between subjects in the curriculum, and changes from year to year over the secondary school age-range, provide an interesting and sometimes surprising picture—and in general these differences are statistically significant. In other words, as ways of describing written tasks, the categories yield information which promises to be useful in our attempts to understand and evaluate what goes on in secondary schools.

We are not, of course, in a position to make broad generalizations. Another sample drawn by another method at another time would be likely to show different results. Our collectors were volunteers—that is to say they selected themselves, no doubt for a variety of reasons of which we have taken no account. The writings were produced under a variety of circumstances, related to a variety of teaching objectives and methods which, again, we have no means of accounting for.

We are confirmed in our belief that the two factors, sense of audience and function, are important ways of differentiating one piece of school writing from another, yet we are in no position to claim that other factors, equally important ways of describing difference and development, do not exist to be discovered. Some possibilities we have indeed suggested in the course of our account (see p. 16).

We are clear about one thing: the work we have classified cannot be taken as a sample of what young writers *can do*. It is a sample of what they *have done* under the constraints of a school situation, a curriculum, a teacher's expectations, and a system of public examinations which itself may constrain both teacher and writer. Our results may be useful in suggesting the nature of some of these constraints and their relative pressures.

What the computer gave us were print-outs of the distribution of the scripts in the sample by audience categories and function categories according to the verdicts arrived at by our assessors. The verdicts were also cross-tabulated by sex, by type of school, by year (first, third, fifth and seventh years in the secondary school) and by curriculum subjects. Here, because of the limited numbers of scripts in many of the subjects, we have been able to examine only English, history, geography, science and religious education independently: all the other subjects have had to be grouped, so that there remains nothing very useful we can say about them. Finally, cross-tabulations were produced for audience categories by function categories. Chapter 8 below will examine in detail the results of the audience classification, Chapter 9 that of the function classification, and Chapter 10 will look at the interrelationships between the two. Meanwhile, in the rest of this chapter we shall take up one or two matters that can conveniently be reported at this stage.

Split categories

What our assessors were attempting to do was to classify pieces of writing *as a whole*. Where a writer consistently held in mind a single reader or category of readers the assessors were likely to have no problem in classifying for sense of audience. Where this was not the case, they were asked to look for the *dominant* sense of audience, and naturally enough this is where problems might begin to arise. Inconsistency might show itself as a *change* of dominance in the course of the writing, or as a *fluctuation* from one audience to another throughout; and in this latter case the effect might sometimes be a kind of uncertainty, a hovering midway between one category and another. Each of these cases was likely to be classified as a split category; for example, 'pupil to teacher/expert to known layman', or 'child to peer group/group member to working group'.

Such complications arose even more frequently in the case of the function categories, where the idea of 'dominance' is an integral part of the way we have defined function. Following Jakobson and Dell Hymes we have assumed that most functions are co-present in any utterance, but hierarchically arranged: a category is assigned in accordance with the function to which other functions seem to be subservient. A glance at our function assessment sheets indicates how often a two-thirds agreement (hence a verdict) was lost through the refinement of using split categories. As an example, a short run of consecutive items from our record sheets is reproduced in Table 3.

Table 3 Sample run of consecutive items from record sheets (function categories)

Assessor A	Assessor B	Assessor C	Verdict
Expressive/report	Expressive/poetic	Expressive	Expressive
Report	Report	Report	Report
Pseudo-informative	Report	Low-level analogic	No verdict
Analogic	Speculative	Analogic	Analogic
Pseudo-informative	Low-level analogic	Generalized narrative/low- level analogic	No verdict
Poetic	Poetic	Poetic	Poetic
Analogic/report	Report	Low-level analogic	No verdict
Report	Report	Expressive/poetic	Report
Generalized narrative	Low-level analogic	Generalized narrative/low- level analogic	Generalized narrative/low- level analogic

Our categories and the school situation

Had the distribution of scripts in our categories proved to be unrelated to the sex of the writer, the type of school, progress from year to year, and curriculum subjects, it would have been very difficult to claim, as we have claimed, that the categories provide a meaningful way of describing what goes on in schools. In fact, we have worked out a series of very general measures of the degree of association that exists between the distributions by categories and these factors as they apply to our sample. These figures are shown in Table 4 below. It has to be borne in mind that these measures (called 'contingency coefficients') are not as straightforward as the more familiar correlation co-efficients. Since the categories in our sets cannot be assigned numerical values—like marks in a test—correlation coefficients were not appropriate. The main difference lies in the fact that the upper limit of a contingency co-efficient depends upon the number of categories entering into the calculation. Thus, whereas the upper limit of a correlation coefficient is always 1·0, the closest possible association between two sets of data in our tables might in some cases be represented by a figure little above ·75. For this reason also, comparisons between the various coefficients must be taken as a rough indi-cation of interrelationships rather than an exact one.

It would seem that variations in school circumstances in our sample have rather more to do with the way different functions are taken up in writing than they have with the way a sense of audience varies in the writing. This sug-gests, amongst other possibilities, that the teachers in the sample differed from each other more in terms of the kind of writing tasks they set than in the roles they were prepared to take up as readers.

Table 4   Contingency coefficients* relating audience and function categories to school factors

	Audience categories	Function categories
Sex of pupil	0·09†	0·16
Type of school	0·24	0·41
Year in school (1st, 3rd, 5th, 7th)	0·32	0·57
Curriculum subject	0·54	0·65

* The contingency coefficient used was $c = \sqrt{\dfrac{\chi^2}{n+\chi^2}}$. See S. Siegel, *Nonparametric Statistics for the Behavioral Sciences*, p. 197.
† This coefficient is only just significant, as measured by chi square ($P<0·1$). All the others in this table are highly significant ($P<0·001$).

In Table 5 we move in a little closer. The coefficients represent the relationships between our categories and progress through the school in individual subjects. Clearly, one year's work in science differs from another far more in terms of the kind of task set (or, more accurately, the kind of function produced) than in the kind of audience the writers address themselves to: in English and history, by contrast, both factors are important ways of differentiating between one year's work and another.

Table 5   Contingency coefficients relating audience and function categories to year in school by individual subjects

	Audience categories	Function categories
English	0·44	0·59
History	0·43	0·60
Geography	0·21*	0·44
Religious education	0·38	0·48
Science	0·29	0·60

(Since numbers in the sample for seventh year work in geography and religious education were disproportionately small, the calculations for these subjects are based on years 1, 3 and 5.)
* Significance, as measured by chi square, is $P<0·01$ for geography: for the rest it is $P<0·001$.

The coefficients we have been considering here do no more than indicate whether meaningful relationships exist. To discover the nature of the relationships we must go beyond the coefficients to the detail of the distributions. This we shall do in Chapters 8 and 9 below.

Sex differences

Having included 'sex of pupil' as a factor in the school situation, we must now see whether we can draw from our findings any institutional implications. The straight comparison of the boys with the girls in the sample yields little of interest; the girls favour audience category 2.1 ('child to trusted adult') and function category 2 (expressive), whereas the boys provide more than their share of the scripts in audience category 2.4 ('teacher as examiner') and function category 4.2.1 (the pseudo-informative).*

However, even these differences begin to disappear when we compare boys and girls in coeducational schools; and they are correspondingly sharpened when we compare boys' schools with girls' schools in the sample, as Table 6

Table 6 Contingency coefficients for sex differences in audience and funtion categories by single-sex and coeducational schools

	Audience categories	Function categories
Boys/girls (single-sex schools)	0·124 ($P<0·1$)	0·196 ($P<0·001$)
Boys/girls (coed. schools)	0·086 ($P<0·2$)	0·146 ($P<0·2$)
All boys/all girls	0·090 ($P<0·1$)	0·155 ($P<0·001$)

suggests. The separate analyses raise only one fresh distinguishing feature, the fact that boys in boys' schools in the sample do not use function category 4.1 (immature), while all the other groups (i.e. girls in girls' schools and boys and girls in coeducational schools) do so.

Categories of writing and types of school

The 65 schools represented in our sample were allocated to types of school as follows: secondary (16 schools, 513 scripts); comprehensive (15 schools, 331 scripts); grammar (20 schools, 722 scripts); direct grant (5 schools, 257 scripts); independent (7 schools, 254 scripts); colleges of further education (2 colleges, 45 scripts).

Distinctive profiles emerge, both for audience and for function categories, and the main features of these are plotted in simplified form in Tables 7 and 8. A plus sign is used to indicate strength in a category (i.e. total of scripts markedly above the mean), a minus sign to indicate weakness; and in the most marked cases the sign is doubled.

Clearly, for audience categories secondary and comprehensive schools are very similar in profile and stand in contrast to the rest. The function categories throw up more distinguishing features, but the general pattern is similar. In

* Details of these and all other distributions are given in Appendix III.

Table 7 Types of schools: audience category profiles

	'Child to trusted adult'	'Pupil to teacher' (general)	'Pupil to teacher' (partic. relation.)	'Pupil to examiner'	'Writer to his readers'
Secondary	+	+ +	−	−	− −
Comprehensive	+ +	+ +			− −
Grammar	−	− −		+ +	+ +
Direct grant		−	+	+ +	+ +
Independent					+ +
Further educ.		−		+ +	

Table 8 Types of schools: function category profiles

	Report	Generalized narrative	Low-level analogic	Analogic	Speculative/ tautologic	Persuasive	Expressive	Poetic	Additional categories
Secondary	+	+ +	+	− −	−	− −			+ +
Comprehensive	+	+		− −	−	− −	+		+
Grammar		− −	−	+ +		+ +	−		−
Direct grant	−	− −	−	+ +	+ +	+			−
Independent	−		−	+ +	+ +	−	−		−
Further educ.	−	−	+	+ +				−	

Table 8, a steady movement from secondary schools through to direct grant schools appears in the use made of the transactional informative categories (see first five columns)—a movement, it will be recalled, along what James Moffett called an 'abstractive scale'. It is difficult to see why persuasive writing should be a near monopoly of the grammar schools; though it is conceivable that such schools might be more formal in their approach and that in other cases, where a degree of informality was not discouraged, the persuasive function might (particularly by younger writers) be carried out in expressive writing.

Since the 'additional categories' (see right-hand column of Table 8) represent immaturity of writing in some form or other, we should expect to find them occurring with younger and with less able writers, as the table suggests. It is to the general distribution of these additional categories that we now turn our attention.

Additional categories (function)

The allocation of scripts to these categories presents, once again, a not unexpected picture. As Table 9 shows, the categories feature mainly in the first

Table 9 Distribution of scripts to additional categories by years

	Immature category	Special categories: Pseudo-informative	Dummy run	Totals
Year 1	46	48	16	110
Year 3	7	20	14	41
Year 5	0	3	14	17
Year 7	0	0	3	3
TOTALS	53	71	47	171

year and have virtually disappeared by year 7. They fall into two divisions. Category 4.1 (see left-hand side of table) was intended as an 'immature' category in a direct sense, and it is clear that our assessors interpreted it as such. We thought of it as representing a stage before the writer has sorted out for himself the major function distinctions, when he is therefore using an 'all purpose' kind of writing—likely in our view to be expressive (as we have defined it). (On this point, however, we did not commit ourselves in the briefing notes, but hoped the assessors would come up with fresh evidence: looking back now at what they had to cope with, it does not seem surprising that they did not.) Table 10 indicates that fifty per cent of the scripts in the 'immature' category are in English work, the rest scattered throughout most other subjects. Their allocation to audience categories clearly relates them to a *teaching*

Table 10   Distribution of scripts to additional categories by subjects of the curriculum

	Immature category	Special categories: Pseudo-informative	Dummy run	Totals
English	27	3	41	71
History	6	16	2	24
Geography	0	17	0	17
Religious educ.	4	10	3	17
Science	2	16	0	18
Other subjects	14	9	1	24
TOTALS	53	71	47	171

and not a testing situation: 49 of the 53 scripts were put into audience categories 2.1 ('child to trusted adult') and 2.2 ('teacher–learner dialogue'). A reading of the scripts suggests that ambiguous assignments may account for some of them: assignments, for example, which left the inexperienced writer in doubt as to whether informative or fictional writing was expected. Thus, of the fourteen entries for the 'immature' category under 'Other subjects' in Table 10, eight came from a single assignment in social studies set to three first-year classes. Here it is:

Spoken instructions. 'The pupils were reminded of the work they had done on archaeology and anthropology over the months and told to note, particularly, contrasts in ways of living, especially the contrast provided by modern urban living in an advanced complex society.'
Written instructions. 'Imagine that you visit a primitive tribe. Describe your impressions of them and their life and, also, tell us of their reactions to you and the modern gadgets you have with you e.g. tape-recorder, cine-camera etc.'

And here is what one first-year girl made of it (classified 4.1—'immature'—by our assessors):

I aimed my canoe at a spare place by the river. There were some Natives welcoming me as I got out of the Canoe. They led me to their village. We had to go through the jungle. It was very weird and noisy, and I felt very frightened. The Natives did not feel frightened and carried on. In the jungle their was brightly-coloured birds, snakes and other creatures. The people or Natives or Eskimos, some were farming in the fields. Some were waiting by the river, for animals to come, then the Natives would through spears at them and eat them. For a snak they had some part of a strange animal to eat. I had a bit too it tasted nice. They made a fire by rubbing to bits of wood together, and succeeded. I made a tyape recording secretly. I took some photographs of things when they saw me taking photographs they were amased and atonished. I was shooked when I saw them eating slugs and worms. They even offered me some slugs and worms.

The two 'special categories' (those dependent upon circumstances peculiar to the teaching situation—see right-hand side of Tables 9 and 10) are in some senses complementary to each other. The pseudo-informative occurs, as one would suppose, mainly in subjects with a 'body of knowledge' curriculum; the 'dummy run' savours of a narrowly conceived apprentice–master relationship, and since the craft in question is that of writing, scripts in this category are virtually exclusive to work in English.

Of the seventy-one entries in the pseudo-informative, fifty-seven are in the audience category of 'pupil to examiner'. Those in the 'dummy run' category show an interesting change in this respect: from being principally in the audience category of the teacher–learner dialogue in years 1 and 3, in year 5 they fall largely in 'pupil to examiner'.

We were right in believing that the system we had devised to describe the functions taken up by mature writers would not cover all that came from the schools in our sample: these additional categories were useful, and used. However, it is perhaps worth noting that of the 1992 scripts our assessors succeeded in classifying for function, only five per cent had to be placed in categories peculiar to the school situation.

Now read on

In the three chapters that follow we shall be looking in detail at the light thrown upon work in school by the way audience and function categories relate to progress through the secondary school and to work in the various subjects of the curriculum. We shall have in mind as we do so a teacher's understanding of the written work he handles week by week; we shall hope therefore to penetrate beyond the figures to a realized sense of what the pupils in our sample put down on paper. If we succeed in providing some guidelines with which to explore the uncharted territory lying between what (for want of better terms) we have in the past referred to as 'personal' and 'impersonal' writing, we shall have achieved one of our principal objects.

A final chapter, Chapter 11, will present for discussion what seem to us to be the main implications of the study, its limitations, and hence what, in broad prospect, remains to be reported or to be done.

8 Results: the writer's sense of audience

Differentiation in the writer's sense of his audience was the first of the dimensions we looked at in our sample. As we have said, we envisaged that in any piece of writing the writer would *express a relationship with the reader in respect of the topic*; and that the writer's capacity to accommodate his audience—to predict and deal with his implied demands—would be one aspect of development. Beyond this broad formulation of our concern, we had also to recognize that audiences differ in kind—typically, that is, rather than merely as regards whom they happen to be—and that the demands made by one type of audience would be different from those made by another. Hence we might pose as a central hypothesis that development in the writer's sense of his audience was essentially a differentiated process, having as its complementary aspects the capacity both to recognize differences and to cope with the modification of utterance necessary to accommodate them. Inasmuch as there was a line to be drawn between, for example, the young child whose sense of the 'other' was insufficiently differentiated to 'see the problem' and the older writer who might see but be unable to accommodate, both aspects had to be entertained. But the central task was to construct a classification by which the total range of audiences which a child might encounter in school—or which he might propose to himself—could be accounted for.

An account of the audience classification itself and of the theoretical position behind it has been given earlier, in Chapter 4. Starting from a broad distinction between factors which affect the writer within his context of situation and those which derive from the context of culture, we may further recognize that much of the writing of our culture is public and formal, reflecting the institutional frameworks whose business it carries forward; but that for our purposes we needed to develop an account which was close to the experience of the young writer. Implied by this was a categorization which would be sensitive to the special educational features in the context of the writers of our sample. The audience categories within our scheme, accordingly, are grouped under the broad divisions of *self, teacher, wider audience (known)*, and *unknown audience* (for the individual categories see the fold-out sheet which follows the index). The purpose of this chapter, now, is to give examples of the writing in our sample allocated to these categories and to present the resulting patterns of distribution.

(It will be remembered that in the allocation of the scripts it was not the expectation that each script would reflect unambiguously a single audience, but that among competing audiences it would normally be possible to perceive a dominant sense.)

Self

Writing from one's own point of view without considering the intelligibility to others of that point of view; a written form of 'speech for oneself'

We have explained earlier that our broad understanding of the role played by audience in writing was derived from George Mead's conception of 'the internalized other'; hence, it seemed to us that development in the writer's sense of audience might be best elucidated in terms of the power to operate a more highly differentiated—and more general—internalized other. Clearly, though, not all writing needs to operate in this way: for while all worthwhile writing must be to some extent for the self, it is by no means true that all writing needs to be for some other audience as well—and this would apply at any level of development. In a range of possible situations, we may envisage writings taking a private, or anticipatory, form—some forms of diary entry, for example; or jottings for memory or towards a more sustained treatment at a later time.

It seems important to keep the distinction between writing which is specifically *for* the self and writing in which no particular sense of audience is discernible: the category of self as audience was reserved for writings of the former kind.

The range of such writing in our sample was, however, small—a proportion merely of 0·5%, the bulk of it formed by sixth form notes. The following history script is an example:

Hope of Byzantine unity came to nothing. Pope got credit, however—shown willing to discuss with Greeks, failure not his fault. Papal position strengthened by Eugenius. Conciliar movement ended at councils of Constance, Basle.

Hussite wars (cont.) News of Huss's death back to Bohemia, great hostility there to Germany; result—religious reformers developed into party, led by Nicholas Hussinitz, and John Zizka (soldier), which demanded receipt of cup by lay in mass and objected to indulgences. But divisions in party, though common hostility to Germany. Utraquists, moderate (Calixtines, Praguers) extremists (Taborites—Zizka fortified place in S.W. Bohemia, called it Mt. Tabor). Puritans, rejected real presence in the mass (Transubt.), belief in Purgatory, indulgences, use of images, veneration of virgin and saints, insisted on priesthood of all believers—essential beliefs of Puritans, ∴ first Protestants . . .

(seventh-year boy)

Teacher

In distinction from writing for the self as audience may be set the remaining range of writings which have some additional audience in mind. The distinguishing mark is the operation of the 'internalized other' in seeking to meet (or in expecting) an interest which is construed as from 'outside'; and we may make a first broad division, within our classification, centred on a teacher audience. In this broad division is included writing which differs from that for the self in having a definite 'other' audience in mind, but which does not seek to pass beyond the teacher to any form of wider audience, known or unknown. As might be expected, the bulk of the writing in our sample (about 95%—see Table 11) was allocated to the various sub-categories of this division; and it is at the level of these sub-categories that the writing is best illustrated.

'CHILD TO TRUSTED ADULT'

In the early stages, transference into writing of the talking relation with the mother—writing that accepts an invitation because it comes from this particular person; later the liberating sense that this particular adult wants to hear ANY-THING you have to say

Writing for a specifically 'educational' adult, whether as a fairly routine matter or with a more positive orientation, represents a relatively highly differentiated form of utterance. There remains, however, the possibility of writing which is for a teacher, but in which he is construed in a less differentiated way—as a sympathetic and interested adult, rather than specifically as a teacher. In this first subdivision of the teacher audience was envisaged writing ranging from, at the one end, scripts in touch with the egocentric speech of young children to, at the other, the scripts of relatively mature writers dependent on this relation in the circumstances of a particular piece of writing—one handling difficult or intimate material, for example. Outside the school context the normal communication of young people and adults—relatives and friends—is likely to be more or less of this kind. In that it is less highly differentiated than other teacher categories, we may add that the category of 'child to trusted adult' is also less demanding.

The last characteristic suggests that writing within this category is likely to be more like writing for the self than that in other categories. Here again, however, only a small proportion (two per cent) of the writing in the sample was allocated to it. The following English script is an example. (In this, and other examples, details of the teacher's instructions to the class, as supplied to our researchers with scripts, are also given.)

Spoken instructions. '"Write me something about insects or spiders. You might decide to be an insect yourself, or you might prefer to be a zoo-man or an insect collector. Or perhaps you are just an ordinary person who meets a strange insect in some way." (Preliminary ten minutes to describe emotionally rather than scientifically insects they were looking at. Stimulus for this came from a boy in class whose father is in charge of Insect House at Zoo. Brought transparencies of insects which were projected on to large screen.)'

INSECTS
My friend David had Just come running round the corner. I saw him and ran over to him and said what are you running for and he said there's a centipede coming down the road. I said what's wrong with that and he said nothing exept its about a hundered yards long. I said I don't believe you so I had a look for myself and when I came back I said now I believe you and then saw a bus go pass so we ran after it and got on it and went straight back home.

(first-year boy)

In reading this piece we may suggest that we are in touch with a writer who to some extent needs to operate with this sense of audience if he is to write at all—at any rate in a way rewarding to himself. In the following piece of writing (a geography script) the sense of a specifically educational audience is more strongly marked, but we may best regard the piece as transitional from the 'child to trusted adult' sense of audience and at the same time signalling something of the writer's difficulties in operating a more highly differentiated sense.

THE COUNTRYSIDE AROUND SCHOOL
The countryside around the school were I go is mainly farmed land. And at the school its self there is a playing field were the girls play hockey and the boys play rugby. There is a big swimming pool.

And also the countryside around school is grass and if it rains there is a lot of mud around. And going back to school there is a tuck shop and it is open every Thursday at 4 o'clock and on Tuesday at 4 o'clock.

This school is about 1 mile out of Wigton But I live at wooverton 1 mile from here. The places were I live has about the same countryside.

There is a railway that goes to Wigton and I pass it when I get off the bus. The school is bording school and about 30 children come to the school.

(first-year girl)

Finally we should add that, while the proportion of scripts in this category is low in our sample, the total reflects the response of our judges to scripts in which this sense of audience was positively marked. It may well be, however, that children sometimes write with this sense of audience in mind without its being very strongly marked in the issuing script. This, which is a caution against too rigid an interpretation of the results of allocation, leaves of course the theoretical distinction intact.

*

As well as the writing for 'teacher as trusted adult', we may envisage writing for the teacher which operates a more highly differentiated sense of audience. The remaining three teacher sub-categories share this general characteristic.

But we may also make two further distinctions—on the one hand, between a general sense of dialogue between teacher and pupil and that of a more specialist kind; on the other, between an active sense of dialogue, in which the teacher as audience features as a participant, and the sense of a terminal offering, where the teacher as audience features as an examiner. These interlocking distinctions serve to mark out the remaining teacher audiences.

'PUPIL TO TEACHER, GENERAL' (TEACHER–LEARNER DIALOGUE)

Writing for a specifically 'educational' adult, but as part of an ongoing interaction; and in expectation of reponse rather than formal evaluation

With the writing for 'pupil to teacher, general'—the teacher–learner dialogue—we reach one of the two major blocks of writing in the sample. In all, 817 scripts were allocated to this category—a proportion of about 39%, which was exceeded only by writing for the teacher as examiner. As we shall see, writing in the former category derived from all curriculum subjects, though most prominently from English and religious education. The following is an example from English, where the sense of dialogue—of the writing as an event within an ongoing interaction—is strongly marked.

Instructions. 'This work was an attempt to push the examination of personal privacy in story form, or writing about own wishes etc. as regards own room, out towards the whole question of environment in general and how important it is. This discussion was reached simply by listening to personal writing about "Privacy" and commenting. For homework, asked the class to pick up whatever aspect of the discussion had interested them most, and take it further for themselves. Several titles were suggested ("The Search for Individuality", "Does Environment Matter?" etc.) but they were free to alter or adapt the title as they saw fit.'

DOES ENVIRONMENT MATTER?

To a certain degree—yes. The world into which you are born, or rather, the home into which you are born, makes one, what one is. But some people, if they are born into unhappy surroundings, try hard to improve themselves, though perhaps they do not need to improve themselves. A bad environment makes some people ashamed of their standing, perhaps gives them an inferiority complex, and in this case, environment does matter to them.

If one grows up in a happy home, and there are no worries, the person may be happy too, accepting anything that crops up, dealing with it and then dismissing it, going on through life in this way. I think that people develop their own personalities, doing what they think is right, perhaps what others think is wrong. But if there are worries at home, for instance, these people carry them around and always they are at the back of their minds. They probably need to talk about it but know that they should not, and try to hide it, perhaps by putting on a show.

Work and school influence people too. I think that children that start off at mixed schools are much more relaxed and easy-going than those that go to an all girls or all boys school. Being able to be at ease as one gets older is very important and even more important, is being able to put others at their ease as well. At work, if you get in with a good crowd helps, not being the odd one out.

'Snobs' depend a great deal on their social position. To be able to have something that is better than anyone else's is everything to them. They are not happy unless they are rolling in money and would hate the idea of being 'one under'. To them money is important, so that they may have everything just so.

Environment does matter as a basis but I think that one builds up one's own personality and private views through experience.

(third year girl)

It is worth pausing for a moment, at this point, on the principles of allocation—not, that is, on the defining features of particular senses of audience, but on the general procedures involved. Viewing the above piece of writing from the simple perspective of saying what the audience is, a first point is that the sense of dialogue carried forward is unmistakable; also, the adult with whom the dialogue is entered into is a teacher. It may be remembered that the task before our judges was to work from an individual script, within a scrambled collection, towards its allocation to a single category. Intuitive decisions along the lines above proved to be sufficient to mark out the one audience and rule out the others. It was in this way that our allocators proceeded.

It has to be said that not all writing within the teacher–learner dialogue is marked by as positive a sense of the relationship as the script above; however, even a less striking example, such as the following biology script, still expects to be replied to rather than assessed. The sense of audience, fundamentally, is the same.

Instructions. 'The girls were asked to write a short account of everything they knew about leaves. The girls have studied leaf structure in great detail during this term.'

The first thing that I would like to mention about leaves is their colour. It is the first thing that really stands out, when you look at a leaf. The colour of a leaf can vary from a greeny yellow to a dark bronze. The colour can change by the different seasons they go through. For example in Spring the leaf is a lightish green, in Summer a full green, in Autumn, any colour varying from orange to dark brown, and in Winter there are no leaves at all. Of course it all depends on what sort of tree it is. Anyway the colour of the leaf can make a great difference.

(first-year girl)

As has been said, writing within the teacher–learner dialogue represents that kind of writing most closely enmeshed with the ongoing business of teaching and learning in school; yet its proportion of the sample, while high, is considerably lower than that taken by writing for the teacher as examiner and (as we shall also see) undergoes a steady decline after the first year in the secondary school. We shall return to such matters in more detail when considering the distributions of audience in the sample.

'PUPIL TO TEACHER, PARTICULAR RELATIONSHIP'

Writing for a specifically 'educational' adult; a personal relationship but also a professional one, based upon a shared interest and expertise, an accumulating shared context

This category is in essence a second, but more finely distinguished, form of teacher–learner dialogue. Writing was allocated to it where a special relation appeared to operate between writer and reader, based on a shared interest in a common subject matter. Only twenty-one scripts in all were allocated to this category—a proportion of approximately one per cent. The majority of these, such as the following English example, derived from the specialist sixth form.

Instructions. 'Appreciation of "Here" by R. S. Thomas.'

'HERE' BY R. S. THOMAS
This poem is a self-examination of himself by a man. He is looking into himself to see what has happened to him and he comes to the conclusion that his environment has changed—not him. He feels lost in the change that has taken place and his quiet bewilderment changes to despair. He is standing out against 'Progress' but he knows that there is nothing he can do, he knows that 'Progress' has happened and is happening. As a result he knows that he has lost his fight against it before he ever begins. This is the cause of his final despair. This is a cry from the heart not from the brain, he has tried to be rational but has failed and his last refuge is this soul-searching cry. He introduces also the idea of the guilt of all men for this state of affairs despite the fact that men were born with the facilities to avoid it. Basically, the poem is concerned with Modern Man's dilemma. Is 'Progress' really progress?

(seventh-year boy)

We may add that, while the writing in our sample allocated to this category was largely confined to specialist sixth form level, it is not impossible to conceive of an analogous relationship operating in other parts of the school.

'PUPIL TO EXAMINER'

Writing for a specifically 'educational' adult, but as a demonstration of material mastered or as evidence of ability to take up a certain kind of style; a culminating point rather than a stage in a process of interaction and with the expectation of assessment rather than response

It is in fact the audience of the teacher as examiner which, at nearly forty-nine per cent of the total sample, is the most prominently represented category of all. Given the distinction made by most teachers between teaching (initiating learning) and the more practical matter of examining or training in examinations, the high proportion must cause some surprise. On the other hand, writing, by its nature as a record and in its openness to inspection, may often become in school the principal means of testing, playing its predominant part in closing a learning situation rather than opening it to further exploration. Looking at the distinction from the pupil's point of view we have represented it as a difference between writing which seeks to *explore* one's learning and writing which seeks to *show* it. Much writing in school seems to be used, broadly speaking, to show. This, in part at any rate, underlies the high incidence of writing indicative of a test situation in our sample.

There is also the possibility that situations not specifically intended as testing ones by the teacher may be interpreted as such by the pupil. Theoretically it seems worth recalling that the categories of audience depict the *relation* which the writer takes up with his reader, not the formal (or intended) situation in which the writing takes place. The relation is construed by the writer— though in many cases he will not be aware that he is doing so—and the sense of audience which he in fact operates may only imperfectly correlate with the role normally taken up by the teacher in the classroom, or with the role as reader that the teacher would like to take up. We may expect, then, that where the writer, in operating his sense of teacher audience, loses touch with the positive sense of dialogue he is likely to express a relationship which is merely one of examinee to examiner; and it is clear that a range of factors may underlie this. Many of the scripts allocated to the 'pupil to examiner' category appear to conform to this less definite specification—a point confirmed by reference to the observable gap in such cases between the instructions given by the teacher and the way in which the task was interpreted. Writing of this kind is witness less to the intention of much educational practice than to its drift.

The following three pieces of writing, for example, were written by one third-year boy in history, geography and science respectively. Their similarity catches a thread common to much of the writing allocated to the category of teacher as examiner.

Instructions. 'Write an account of some English seamen of the 16th century; mention the lands they sailed to, the trading they were involved in, the hazards they encountered, and the character of the men themselves.'

SOME ENGLISH SEAMEN OF THE 16TH CENTURY
John Hawkins
In 1568 John Hawkins sail the atlantic selling slaves to America. This slaves were captored in africa and take often to america to be sold as cotton workers. Most of then died on the way to there distenation the ones that did not die. Did not last very long the climate was hot and thay were not well fed. The pope realised how monterous this was and band it But John Hawkins being a protistant toke no notice and carried on his trading, this was not to last long for the spanish sunk his ship because of his unloyaty to the pope.

Sir W. Raliagh
Started up a settlement in Virginia in 1620 the pilgrim farthers fled to Virginia to escape persiation becorce thay were puritanes.

★

Instructions. 'Children had to use text books and information learned in class to write about industries of California.'

Aircraft
The biggest Aircraft company in america is the Northrop corporation trade name Beoing it is based at Beverly hills, California, perhaps the most famous plane thay have built is the 707 which was sold to many leading Airlines encluding, Saudi Arabian Airlines, Etheopian Airways, Arance, Continental Western, El Al, Northwest Orient, Lofthansa, PIA and pan am, Also beoing have had great sucesses with there 720, 727, 737 and 170 And now there is the 747 Gumbo Jet and the first to carry 500 passengers.

Gold
California was the first gold prodising State in North America and produces one third of Americas gold the mines are around the foothills of Siera Nevada.

Oil
The oil wells are at the upper end of San Joaqin Valley by Los Angeles. It is pumped to refineries on the coast such as San Francisco, Nolney, Portland, Harford, Santa Monica and Wilmington. This oil is exported all over the world.

Filming
California has proved a most convenient place for filming because of the clear skys well lit from the sun [*not finished*]

★

Instructions. 'Blackboard summary—"Combination of Oxygen and Hydrogen. Plastic Bottle—water, $\frac{1}{3}$ full oxygen cylinder, $\frac{2}{3}$ full hydrogen—Kipps apparatus, water formed." Class told to write as they would normally write an experiment in their books. This piece was written immediately after seeing a demonstration of the experiment.'

COBINATION OF OXEGEN AND HYDROGEN

Method
A plastic bottile was filled to the top with water then imersed in a tank of water (tap water) then one third of the bottle was filled with hydrogen which was obtained from a cylinder of hydrogen then the next two thirds were filled with Oxegen got from a Kip which was made by passing Sylevric acid over zinc which forms Oxegen then a lited splint was put to it.

Result
A vilent flame and bang aperd.

Conclusion
Oxegen and hydrogen explode when a flame is put to it.

(*third-year boy*)

We may suspect perhaps that we are in the presence of a writer who, never entirely at ease with the written word, is here further impeded by the sense of an examining audience, derived most notably from having to make manifest in his writing the acquisition of various set contents. But it should be added that it is not in informative writing alone that the slide towards interpreting one's audience as an examiner is possible. The writer of a story or poem, too, may end by interpreting his audience as requiring no more than a demonstration of his ability, as the following examples of English scripts illustrate.

Instructions. 'Lesson based on Chapter 8 of "English through Experience" Book I. Class discussed some "moments" which remained vivid in their memory. I looked at the work and did not think it very successful, so two days later I offered the class 4 alternatives: (a) copy out the work for you if they liked, (b) rewrite it if they felt they could improve it, (c) select a *sad moment* from their experience rather than a happy one, (d) write out a moment in the form of a poem instead of prose.'

PIRATES

One year I went to Skeggness,
I had a happy week.
On Wednsday night I walked two miles
Along the sandy beach to Skeggness
When I got there,
I did what I wanted to do.
I hired a canoo for half an hour.
I cast it of I ramed a boat.
I grounded once again.
I cast it of I got the hang of it.
I ramed a pile of boats
And then I lerned to Stear
I speed along like a big dolfin.
I went around a small island
And pulled into the side
but as I was just climbling in I fell back
       In my boat.
A whistle went my time was up.
Home I had to go
But I always rember I am a hazard to the sea.

(*first-year boy*)

Instructions. 'A few minutes in class devoted to the importance of choosing the best subject for each individual. Choice taken from "O" level paper—400 words approximately.'

BEING INTERVIEWED

George Peabody embrassed his wife Anna and with a perfunctory nod, began his journey to Norfolk House and the interview. For fourteen years, George had prayed for the position of a Chief Clerk, now it was within his grasp, if only he could contain his weaknesses.

Arriving at Norfolk House, George was directed by the porter to the green-room, which was ten floors up. George preceded with a brisk and athletic movement, that is until the tenth floor, then for no reason at all, his legs collapsed to sticks of rubber. Before entering the waiting-room, George examined his appearance and feeling satisfied, with a sudden jerk swung open the door of the room, releasing it to crash agaist the wall. Immediately, all eyes were upon him. George gave a weak smile and seeing through the corner of his eye a vacant seat, advanced towards it. Once seated George was at liberty to examine the room and its contents. The room, itself was pleasantly decorated with pastel shades, which soothed his eyes if not his nerves. Apart from a few chairs the only other articles in the room were three gentlemen of identical dress, a little older than himself and all having an air of experience. George clutched his umbrella for support, but seeing a pile of magazines, released it and with a rather ungainly movement lurched out and grabbed the nearest book, to his dismay the pile collapsed before his eyes. As George was in the process of re-organizing the pile, his name was called over the loud speaker to enter the green-room.

On entering, George was beckoned to a seat in the centre of the room, methodically he removed, his bowler, gloves and various other articles, which might release him of the feeling of a roast-chicken. After mopping his brow, George's eyes beheld four portulent gentleman sitting behind a large oak table. The gentleman in the centre rose and gazing at George through his monocle, began to address his colleagues. George sat in a daze, his hands were hot and his knees wouldn't stop jumping, for they still had not recovered from the stairs. Hearing his name, George awoke with a jerk, to find all four gentleman standing up and examining him. Apart from asking him general questions concerning his salary his previous situation and his age, they appeared to be more interested in his physical structure and one gentleman even went as far as to advice him in doing knee-bends every morning. George nodded meakly and reseated himself upon his chair from which he had nearly fallen. After a further twenty minutes of whispering and arguing, George was presented with papers, which he christened with his signiture and a few blots. Then with a humble smile George made his exit, bowing at each gentleman in turn.

Once outside, new life returned to George, no longer did his heart thump or his knees wobble for he was a new man with a new body, if not a new job. Now the only thing he had to do was to go home and tell Anna all about the ridiculous interview.

(fifth-year girl)

The last piece reminds us of a further point: that not all writing for the teacher as examiner need necessarily be incompetent. A piece such as the following history script—a quality A level performance—makes the point strikingly.

Spoken instructions. 'I warned them 2 days in advance that they would be set a "Time Question" on this subject next lesson, so they had some time to think about it. The actual writing was done in class under exam conditions—they were able to consult notes for facts and details while writing if they wished.'

WHAT WAS THE ORIGIN OF THE CONGRESS SYSTEM AND WHY DID IT FAIL TO SETTLE EUROPEAN PROBLEMS?

The Congress System was a new way of approaching the problems of Europe. The idea was for the powers to meet and discuss the main issues which had arisen in Europe. It was set up in 1815 after the end of the Napoleonic wars. Europe had been ravaged by Bonaparte and no one wanted it to happen again so the idea was conceived that if discussions occured early in any situation, the situation would not develope and get out of hand as France had done. Naturally the powers had to meet after the wars to decide the best future for the confused members of Europe. The idea of future meetings was introduced when the chaos left by Napolean was sorted out. So that the first congress was only for the discussion of the divisions and resettlement of Europe. The most important point to remember however here, is that only representatives of the four main powers attended. The minor countries, who were affected mostly, were not consulted as to their opinions of the way their life should lead . . .

(seventh-year girl)

Here the writer has coped with the 'pupil to examiner' audience by adopting the posture of public discourse. As a performance, the script depends, perhaps, on sufficient awareness of the published mode of discourse to interpret the testing situation as calling for display both of the relevant information and of the ability to take up the role of the practising writer of history. Less specifically it is a reminder of the degree to which the dimension of audience is entwined with other dimensions in the development of the writer—here notably that of his developing resources. None the less the correspondence here between public discourse and an examining audience should not disguise the real distinction which is to be made between them: that between choosing what sort of writer you want to be on the one hand, and on the other demonstrating that you can cope, in however sophisticated a way, with what is mandated from outside. We may add that—like the clothes in the fashion window—any virtue there may be to the display will depend upon how such clothes are worn in the street.

The more powerful point is that the conventions of this particular audience category may be a severe restriction upon a young writer. The mere allocation by our judges of scripts to the category of 'pupil to examiner' distinguishes neither between those scripts which are there because of an explicitly testing situation, and those which have got there 'by default'; nor between scripts which have 'mastered' the relationship, and those (such as the writing by the third-year boy), where we may speak of mastery more hesitantly. Such distinctions are, in the end, not those of audience alone. But it means that, as we shall see, the block of scripts in the examiner audience—virtually half the total example—tell us little that is positive about development. They speak much more strongly of the possibilities of development which writing in school may inhibit.

Wider audience (known)

Expert to known laymen; child (or adolescent) to peer group; group member to working group

It is to be expected that much of the writing in school will have the teacher as its audience and we may recognize that unless the situation is actively varied it is likely that the teacher's response and opinion will be the most valued element in it; further, that nobody else, after all, is going to maintain quite the same quality of interest and of nobody else has a learner the same right to demand it. On the other hand, writing for the teacher, of whatever kind, involves the operation of the 'internalized other' in the shape of a single reader, while we must also envisage the possibility of wider audiences—either within the known context of the school or beyond it. With the partial exception of the 'unknown audience'—see next section—these were but slenderly represented in our sample. Most of our knowledge of them comes in fact from our follow-up study, where, among other lines of inquiry, we were able to experiment more systematically, particularly with writing for a peer group audience. At the present stage, all we can say is that the evidence of our sample suggests that little use is made in school of such 'wider known audiences' as the interested layman, the peer group, the working group. It may, however, be worth making the point that there are strengths within the school context which are available to be used and which might be genuine alternatives to a teacher audience in the provision of more open contexts for the exercise of informative writing in particular—and facilitating for all writing, perhaps, the transition from a known and immediate audience to a wider public. In our sample, writing of this intermediate kind, even when all three categories are taken together, occupied a proportion of only 0·3% of the total.

Unknown audience

Writer to his readers, marked by a sense of the general value or validity of what he has to say, of a need to supply a context wide enough to bring in readers whose sophistication, interests, experience he can only estimate and by a desire to conform with and contribute to some cultural norm or trend

There seem grounds for thinking that to seek to pass beyond an immediate and known audience to a wider public is an ability which marks the maturity of the writer and indicates, if not necessarily his skill, at any rate his ambition within a particular kind of discourse. We may recognize too that the resources which make it possible are not to be easily won: a pupil's speech resources, with their relative dependence on an immediate context, must be shaped anew in the altogether different element of written language and its evolved cultural forms. Then in reaching beyond the immediate context the writer may contemplate a different kind of permanence, and with it a greater degree of freedom to choose, or make of himself, the sort of writer he wants to be. We therefore regard the ability to operate this sense of audience as a mark of the pupil's growing independence from the teacher and the most complex level of differentiation in his sense of the internalized other. It is a note to be heard fairly early on in some of the stories that children write; in informative writing, on the evidence of our sample, its achievement is less accessible. Writing of this kind occupied a significant, if low, proportion of our sample (1·8%), largely concentrated in the two higher age levels. The following two scripts (science and English) may serve by way of example.

Both the motives and methods of scientific research have undergone a profound change. Today, they bear little resemblance to those of the previous half century, still less to those of the previous two centuries.

For centuries, scientific research has been the concern of men with an almost eccentric curiosity. The researchers of the past were often amateurs who had had no scientific training, for example the Dutch microscopist Leeuwenhoek. Leeuwenhoek was obsessed with the visual powers that a lens could give him. He knew nothing of lens manufacture and had to learn this trade, starting at the beginning. When he mounted his carefully ground lenses in metal, Leeuwenhoek had first had to learn from alchemists, the business of metal extraction and fashioning. He was part of no vast research laboratory and was a layman. He was merely a man with no idle curiosity and a desire to find out more about the structure of the organisms, by which he was surrounded.

During this period which lasted approximately to the beginning of the 18th century, there was no government help for these researches, no public fund from which they could draw money for their researches and much prejudice against new ideas . . .

(seventh-year girl)

Spoken instructions. 'Consider the effect of ordinary lawn weed killer. Write a story entitled "Weedkiller too Strong", or "Something nasty on the Compost Heap".'

WEEDKILLER TOO STRONG

Growth of plants in the Palace grounds just haven't been the same since Tom, the absent minded gardener, forgot to add ten pints of water to each pound of weedkiller. The grass, well, for a few weeks the soil had a scorched appearance, then suddenly blades of grass the thickness of water rushes grew, from nothing. The life cycle of each blade was approximately twenty four hours. This meant that the whole episode lasted about a week, at the end of this time, it all died down again; now the soil was back to its normal colour. All the inhabitants of the palace were very relieved.

Drooping of some roses was put down to the fact that there had been some weeks with no rain, but when we finally did get it, water flowed in torrents, even still the roses drooped. One morning, Tom came running in, and breathlessly he announced that: 'Thems roses has got forns six inches long!' He has always been known to exagerate, but this time he was right. The actual plants had remained there normal sizes, but all the leaves had vanished, in their places, sets of five tentacles had appeared. This was the most strange occurance since Tom's mistake, and it must have been caused by the weedkiller, as no-one else in the neighbourhood had experianced such forthcomings. . .

(fifth-year girl)

The patterns of distribution

THE GENERAL TENDENCIES OF THE SAMPLE

Turning to the figures yielded by our sample in more detail, we may begin by confirming the balance, already noted in passing, of the proportions of writing within the various categories of audience. Table 11 sets out the distributions

Table 11 Distribution of audience categories ($n = 2104$)

Categories	%
Child to self	0·5
Child to trusted adult	1·6
Teacher–learner dialogue	38·8
Pupil to teacher, particular relationship	1·0
Pupil to examiner	48·7
Expert to known laymen	0·0
Child to peer group	0·1
Group member to working group	0·2
Writer to his readers	1·8
Child to trusted adult/teacher–learner dialogue	0·6
Teacher–learner dialogue/pupil to examiner	4·0
Teacher–learner dialogue/writer to his readers	1·0
Miscellaneous	1·7

Handwritten margin notes: Self — 5%; Teacher — 95%; Wider Audience (known) — 3%; Unknown — 1–8%

within the sample as a whole, represented as percentages of the overall total. Inspection of these figures demonstrates the overall predominance of the 'teacher audience' categories, and in particular those of 'pupil to examiner' and (secondarily) the teacher–learner dialogue.

As will be seen from Table 11 only a small proportion of the scripts (roughly 5%) fall in categories other than the four teacher subdivisions. Overwhelmingly, the majority of the writing in our sample (about 95%) was for the teacher audience; and within those teacher subdivisions, writing for the teacher–learner dialogue and for the teacher as examiner taken together constitute something around 88–92%. The overall predominance of the teacher audience is certainly striking, but the main questions raised by the findings must concern that proportion of scripts in the category of 'pupil to examiner'.

THE PATTERN YEAR-BY-YEAR

Striking though the figures above may be, it might be misleading to describe the general tendencies of the overall sample, without considering the pattern given by exploration of the subtotals at the four age levels of the sample. In turning to these figures, we shall find, however, that it is still the convergence of the totals which is of most interest. In none of the four years of the sample did the proportion of writing for an examining audience fall below 40% and in no year but the seventh did the writing for the teacher, taking the four sub-categories together, fall below 90%. That the picture is this common to *all* age levels in our sample is significant. Table 12 sets out the proportions. (In order to bring out the broad picture, we have grouped borderline category

Table 12 Distribution of audience categories by years

| Categories | Percentages of year totals | | | |
	Year 1 (*n* = 619)	Year 3 (*n* = 552)	Year 5 (*n* = 462)	Year 7 (*n* = 471)
Child to self	0	0	0	2
Child to trusted adult, and child to trusted adult/teacher–learner dialogue	2	3	2	1
Teacher–learner dialogue	51	45	36	19
Teacher–learner dialogue/pupil to examiner	6	5	1	3
Pupil to examiner	40	45	52	61
Pupil to teacher, particular relationship	0	0	1	3
Writer to his readers, and teacher-learner dialogue/ writer to his readers	0	1	5	6
Miscellaneous	1	0	3	5

Note: Percentages have been rounded so that in this and some subsequent tables figures do not always add to exactly 100.

'child to trusted adult/teacher–learner dialogue' with 'child to trusted adult', and 'teacher–learner dialogue/writer to his readers' with 'writer to his readers': that is to say, we have maximized the two minor categories at the expense of the teacher–learner dialogue elements. Again, the distribution of scripts in the three categories 'expert to known laymen', 'child to peer group' and 'group member to working group'—a total of seven scripts—is not shown, but is conflated with 'miscellaneous'. In this table, percentages are given to the nearest whole number.)

Inspection of these figures suggests the following:

(a) A cumulative increase in writing for the teacher as examiner.
(b) A corresponding decline in writing for the teacher–learner dialogue.
(c) Note also the rise, in the fifth and seventh years, in writing for 'pupil to teacher, particular relationship' and 'writer to his readers'.

A sense of the overall range of change is best brought out by comparing the figures at their point of sharpest contrast in the first and seventh years. Thus in the first year only 1% of the writing was for an audience other than a teacher, whereas by the seventh year this figure has risen to 13%. Also the first year is the only year in the sample where the proportion of writing for the teacher–learner dialogue in fact exceeds the proportion of writing for the teacher as examiner. As will be seen in the table, in the first year 51% of the writing was placed in the former category, where by the seventh this has dropped to 19%. Part of the movement away from the teacher–learner dialogue is to be explained by the increases in writing for audiences other than the teacher, already noted. On the other hand the increase in variety suggested by that development is more than counterbalanced by the increase in writing for the teacher as examiner. At 40% this proportion is at its lowest in the first year; by the seventh it has risen to 61%.

All in all, the pattern which emerges year by year is not one which markedly qualifies the first impression gained from looking at the sample as a whole. In the first and third years the writing is totally dominated by the teacher audiences, to the exclusion of other audiences. There is little indication of change between the first and third years. The proportion of writing for the teacher as examiner increases somewhat in the third, while writing for the teacher–learner dialogue correspondingly declines; but the shift is not great. A more marked change comes with the fifth year, when writing both for an examiner audience and for audiences other than the teacher (an unknown public audience in particular) increases, while writing for the teacher–learner dialogue decreases sharply. The pattern is continued through into the seventh year, the decrease in writing for the teacher–learner dialogue becoming even more marked. Looking at the pattern of figures as a whole, we may note the step-by-step consistency in the rise and fall of the two dominating teacher categories; though we would recognize, too, that the pattern of writing for the teacher as examiner is already strongly marked in the first year. In the end the lack of development is as significant as its presence. For the evidence of the sample suggests that the pupil in his first year in secondary school would appear to join a situation where little writing outside the teacher audience is posed as a possibility and where a great deal of that is marked by a testing relationship; further that thereafter, while there are indications of the possibility of posing audiences other than the teacher, these possibilities remain unexploited. The weight of the writing becomes yet more concentrated on the teacher as examiner.

THE ROLE OF CURRICULUM SUBJECTS

Consideration, then, of the general tendencies of the total sample and of the pattern year-by-year tends to focus, above all, on the role of the teacher as examiner. We may now look at the contribution of the different curriculum subjects within this pattern. In what follows, however (and the same qualification will need to be entered at a similar point when we come to consider function categories), it should be borne in mind that in order to arrive at workable totals it was necessary to combine some subject totals and to omit others; reducing, in sum, a range of twenty-one different curriculum subjects —itself perhaps a comment on some of the factors influencing the writing of the secondary school pupil—to the following five: English, history, geography, religious education and science. The details for those subjects not included in the text here may be found in Appendix III (G). It may be added that, even after this consolidation, the proportions of writing were not evenly distributed between subjects and varied somewhat from year to year. The effect of this will be allowed for in the interpretation.

Tables 13 and 14 set out in broad terms the proportions of writing for different audiences in the various curriculum subjects. Inspection of these figures suggests the following:

(a) English is characterized by its predominant use of the teacher–learner dialogue, together with a significant but relatively low proportion of scripts allocated to the teacher as examiner category. We may notice also the relatively wide spread of writing across the various audience categories, in particular the virtual monopoly of 'child to trusted adult' and 'writer to his readers'. Note, too, though, the change of pattern in the seventh year observable in Table 14.

(b) History, geography and science are each characterized by the predominance of writing in the 'teacher as examiner' category together with a relatively low proportion of scripts allocated to the teacher–learner dialogue—a common pattern, in contrast to that of English and religious education.

(c) Religious education conforms to the same pattern as English, with the qualification that few scripts were allocated to 'writer to his readers' —a reflection in part perhaps of the very small number of scripts (four) in this subject in the seventh year of our sample.

We may note then from Table 14 the contrast in our sample between the pattern of audience in English and religious education, and that in history, geography and science. Thus in the first and third year of the sample the proportion of writing for the teacher–learner dialogue within English remains constant at rather over 80% of the total for that subject. Correspondingly, writing for the teacher as examiner does not rise above 6%. This is markedly different, of course, from the overall pattern presented by the figures above. Thereafter, while the pattern changes for English in the fifth and seventh years, the change does not involve a shift to one audience (the teacher as examiner) so marked as that which occurs in the sample as a whole. In the fifth year, the proportion of writing for the teacher as examiner rises to 17%, while that for the teacher–learner dialogue falls to 62%. At the same time, writing for audiences other than the teacher also increases. By the seventh year the proportion of writing for the teacher as examiner has increased to 41%

Table 13 Distribution of audience categories by subjects

| Categories | Percentages of subject totals | | | | |
	English ($n = 868$)	History ($n = 287$)	Geo-graphy ($n = 230$)	R.E. ($n = 156$)	Science ($n = 340$
Child to self	0	2	0	0	0
Child to trusted adult, and child to trusted adult/teacher–learner dialogue	4	0	0	4	0
Teacher–learner dialogue	65	17	13	64	7
Teacher–learner dialogue/pupil to examiner	3	8	5	5	2
Pupil to examiner	18	69	81	22	87
Pupil to teacher, particular relationship	1	2	0	0	1
Writer to his readers, and teacher–learner dialogue/writer to his readers	6	0	0	1	1
Miscellaneous	3	2	1	4	2

Table 14 Distribution of audience categories by subjects by years (percentages of subject-year totals)

Subject and year	Self	Trusted adult & trusted adult/ teacher–learner	Teacher– learner	Teacher– learner/ examiner	Examiner	Particular relationship	Public aud. & teacher–learner/ public aud.	Misc.	n
English:									
Y.1	0	5	83	3	6	0	1	2	229
Y.3	0	6	82	2	6	0	3	1	212
Y.5	0	4	62	2	17	0	10	5	2C5
Y.7	0	3	34	4	41	4	9	5	222
History:									
Y.1	0	1	39	14	46	0	0	0	87
Y.3	0	0	8	13	80	0	0	0	80
Y.5	0	0	6	1	90	3	0	0	73
Y.7	7	0	10	2	57	7	0	7	42
Geography:									
Y.1	0	0	20	5	75	0	0	C	85
Y.3	0	0	15	8	77	0	0	C	88
Y.5	0	0	0	0	98	0	0	2	4
Y.7	0	0	0	0	94	0	0	6	15
Relig. Educ.:									
Y.1	0	0	52	8	39	0	0	2	62
Y.3	0	8	73	6	11	2	0	0	52
Y.5	0	5	79	0	0	0	5	11	3E
Science									
Y.1	0	0	16	5	77	0	0	2	113
Y.3	0	0	7	1	92	0	0	0	76
Y.5	0	0	0	0	97	2	0	2	65
Y.7	0	0	1	1	88	2	2	6	86

(For full names of categories see Table 13.)

Notes / ✗

of the total for that subject; but the proportion of writing for the teacher–learner dialogue is still, at approximately 34%, relatively high, and writing for audiences other than the teacher has also increased. The writing in English, then, as might be expected perhaps in this curriculum subject, is characterized by relatively greater variety—but more significantly still, perhaps, by its low proportion, at all the age levels of the sample, of writing for the teacher as examiner. Only religious education exhibits a similar pattern.

By contrast, in geography, history and science the variety is less and the proportion of writing for the teacher as examiner higher. Moreover, this is consistently so. While there are significant amounts of writing in the first year in history within the teacher–learner dialogue, the proportions are not repeated; and at no other point do the proportions of writing in curriculum subjects other than English and religious education rise above 15% for the teacher–learner dialogue or fall below 57% for the teacher as examiner.

We may also confirm in more detail the changes from year to year which were noted above (Table 12). Thus the increase in writing for the teacher as examiner between the first year and the third, together with the decline in writing for the teacher–learner dialogue, derives substantially from changes in the pattern of writing for history; and while a similar movement in science may help to reinforce the pattern, it is much less marked. We remember that the overall changes between the first and the third year are not great, the point being (as may be confirmed from the figures here) that writing for the teacher as examiner is already, by the first year of the secondary school, the established audience for many curriculum subjects. In the fifth and seventh years it is in effect the changes in the pattern of English and religious education which underlie the broader changes in the yearly subtotals. In interpreting these, we need to allow for the increased proportion of the total sample (47% by the seventh year) which the English scripts came to contribute and also for the disappearance of writing from religious education in the seventh year—factors in the drawing of our sample which may have helped to swell the totals in the 'teacher as examiner' category. But the point remains that it is only within English that change by the fifth and seventh years is apparent; further, that it is as the pattern of audience in the writing for English becomes more like the pattern for the other curriculum subjects that the proportion of writing for the 'pupil to examiner' audience increases so decisively. Even then, of the 19% of writing for the teacher–learner dialogue in the seventh year, the share of English (34% of the seventh-year English writing) is 83%; and of the 13% of writing for an audience other than a teacher, the share of English is 74%. Within the broad contrast, then, between the curriculum subjects in our sample, it is the pattern of writing in English which underlies the sample's overall variety and movement.

Looking back over the distributions in sense of audience as a whole, we may add that the overall convergence of the pattern which emerges neither wholly establishes nor falsifies the central hypothesis of the research that development as a writer is a process of differentiation—despite some suggestive indications. The distribution of figures for 'child to trusted adult' is in fact quite evenly spread through the year groups, whereas a higher concentration in the earlier levels of the sample might have been expected. Moreover, since forty-five of the forty-six scripts in this category are divided between English and religious education, it seems best to regard the evenness of dispersal as in part a product of the pattern of audience in curriculum subjects. The figures for the categories of 'pupil to teacher, particular relationship' and 'writer to his readers' are more concentrated in the fifth and seventh years. The former result might be expected, since a specialist relationship is characteristic of work in the sixth form. On the other hand we may treat with some caution the relatively late emergence in our sample of writing for an unknown public audience. It seems likely that the low figure for it is again partly due to the very heavy convergence of the sample as a whole on the category of 'teacher as examiner'. If we are right to regard writing for an unknown public audience as a measure of the writer's ability to penetrate through his immediate context, then it is not surprising that such writing appears in our sample at a relatively late stage. But to draw the conclusion from that that the ability need be as restricted to the fifth and seventh years as would appear from our sample would probably be unjustified.

Further implications of our findings will be the subject of a later chapter. We may also add now that the allocation of at any rate some scripts to all of the categories of audience within our scheme provides some measure of confirmation for the workability of the classification. By way of conclusion of this chapter the following outline of our findings in respect of the writer's sense of audience, as evidenced in our sample, may be helpful.

Summary

The overall tendencies of the sample suggest the dominance of the teacher audiences, and in particular those of the teacher as examiner and (secondarily) the teacher–learner dialogue. Analysis of the subtotals in the four age levels represented confirms this pattern, revealing a cumulative increase in writing for the teacher as examiner together with a decline in writing for the teacher–learner dialogue. While there is some evidence of a movement towards a wider public (the category of 'writer to his readers') in the fifth and seventh years, the proportion of such writing is low; moreover it is virtually monopolized by English as a curriculum subject. Finally, analysis of the various subtotals by curriculum subject suggests a major contrast between the pattern of writing in history, geography and science, and that in religious education and English.

9 Results: function

Use of the functions which writing may serve was the second of our dimensions of the writer's development which we looked at in our sample. In effect this is a second picture—to be added to that of audience. Naturally it concerns the same writing. Also, if it is right that certain broad constraints within the educational context may be hypothesized as lying behind the way in which the pattern of audience was realized, then these we are likely to meet again. None the less it seems best to approach the picture provided by the investigation of function independently. Consideration of the interplay between the two dimensions will be left till later.

Our interest in function we have already explained. One feature of this interest, as distinct in some ways from audience, is that the problem which is its starting point is nothing new. On the whole, despite considerable debate about the ways in which writing should be received in school, systematic consideration of the part which audience plays in writing has been relatively scarce. But that writing is of different kinds and that this fact constitutes a substantial part of the difficulties facing young writers—this is more familiar ground. We found it unsatisfactory, certainly, that studies of development could be undertaken which paid no attention to differences in writing tasks; or that examination papers could be set which assessed the performance of writers without distinguishing between the framing of an argument or the recounting of an anecdote. But this is out of symmetry with much that is currently being explored in classroom and research alike. Scarcely a secondary school pupil cannot (or does not) say that what he writes for history is different from science and different again from English; or alternatively that he has to be more personal here and more impersonal there; here he must use his imagination, there he mustn't . . . and so on. The starting points were all about us.

There are landmines as well as landmarks. Differences in writing are not merely widely accepted, but felt as intimately bound up with the objectives of different subject-teaching. Thus it is that grenades, deriving from one corner, marked 'They spend all their time on personal writing' meet and shatter in transit against those marked 'They never let them write personally about anything', which are lobbed from another. The dangers are well known. Different departments may be working not merely in different ways, but in contradictory ones. As for the pupil if it is not always all cries and confusion, it is sometimes a bit like a tug of war.

Attempts to interpret such dilemmas are going to involve a more general perspective. Debate turns from what should be done in the context of different subject-teaching to more general questions about the perspectives under which such decisions should be taken. These perspectives are a part of our concerns, though a part only. But it seems worth acknowledging, by way of orientation, that in the aspect of our investigation concerning function—in distinction in some ways from audience—it is less a new interpretation that we are offering than the argument that fairly familiar issues may be looked at in this way.

The problem is to give some account of the diversity. We have explained our difficulties earlier and to some extent the conditions we felt our theory had to meet. The broad dichotomy between, for example, personal and impersonal writing seemed too general for our purposes. On examination, anyway, it is a distinction which leaves much confused. Similarly, differentiation of writing by curriculum subject poses obvious difficulties of classification: one sort of informing in history may be very like another sort of informing in science, for example, while within the same subject a report of a scientific experiment may involve quite different operations from the proposal of a theory to explain its outcomes. Such problems point to larger theoretical difficulties; and two especially seemed important for our theory to meet. Since the key to our concerns—and, as we saw it, to those of the classroom too—lay in an account of development, it seemed important that our categories be psycholinguistic in nature. They had to be related to what writers have to do and ultimately to the part played by language and thought in the individual's mental life. Secondly, and for the same reason, it seemed important that our categories be interrelated categories. To oversimplify—it was not so much the differences between various kinds of writing which we wanted to explore as the way those differences related to each other in defining the developing complexity of the tasks which young writers could accomplish.

Another way of putting the same sort of points would be to reassert that our classification presupposes what has been called an operational view of language—one, that is, which gives weight to the fact that language is something which is put to use; further, that in being used it is not turned on like the electric light but goes on all the time, interpenetrating and continuous with consciousness. The overall theory of 'representation', which underlies the way we have classified function, starts from this point. For our belief is that different kinds of writing, whatever may be specific to them, have their roots in the general processes of the individual's ongoing use of language. In particular, the central hypothesis we wanted to test is that the ability to cope with the various functions of language involves a differentiation from—more exactly a differentiation of—expressive language. There is also an attempt, then, to pose a model which is adequate to the dynamic of development.

This much is largely repetition. Inasmuch, though, as classifications tend to lose touch with the theory which begets and informs them—it happens sometimes, as we shall see, to writing in schools too—perhaps the detour was necessary. More sense can be gained of what the theory explains in practice by turning to the expressive writing in the sample.

The expressive function

If we are right in the fundamentals of our approach, it will be possible to see the dynamic of processes which the model attempts to articulate reflected in the writing of our sample. The focus of our analysis is the pattern of function in the writing. As we have explained, this is not to expect that all writing will be marked unambiguously by a single function, but that in the application within a single utterance or script of the rules of a variety of functions it may be possible to perceive a dominant sense. We may clarify this starting point as we proceed.

The points of substance about *expressive* writing in particular may be approached by considering the nature of informal talk. Many have expressed the truth that learning to talk is the most universally successful piece of language learning—not that it is the place here to enter the arguments about the implications of this for cognitive psychology. More central for our purposes is the descriptive point that children learn to talk in a context; the family is at its centre, which is essentially intimate. Some, then, who have stressed the importance of the mother's role in the child's early learning, have been divided as to whether to give principal emphasis to the mother's adaptation of her language to that of the child, or to the importance of the sympathetic adult who enters into the child's meaning and gives him encouragement. For the point may be less that the mother is the *de facto* teacher at the linguistic level—important though that may be—than that in penetrating through language to the nature of the child's attempts to formulate meaning for himself she lends point and purpose to the impetus from which language is developed. If this is so, it is a reminder of a number of broad themes. We may recognize that the talk of the young child, in following very closely the contours of his thinking, depends very considerably on the intuitive understanding of his listener; and—in the confirmation to be derived from this that the primary impetus behind development in language is to put it to work in interpreting one's own world—suggest further that the intimate context, for the young child, may be necessarily the matrix of his language development. It might not be merely empirically difficult, but in point of fact logically too, to envisage any other starting point.

It would be a mistake to direct attention like this to the talk of the very young child if the impression were left that the intimate—perhaps 'supportive' might be a better word—talk of adults is in all ways markedly different. Clearly it is not. In such 'intimate' situations adults, just as much as young children, will allow talk to follow the contours of their thinking, posing in individual ways the issues and experiences which interest them. This is one sense of what we mean by personal: not necessarily that the content of utterance is intimate or private nor that it is actual experience which is being related, but the sense rather that the language and posture of the speaker invites the listener to enter into his world and respond to him as a person. Such language is revealing of self inasmuch as, being informal, and leaving much implicit, it is closer to the way the individual thinks when he thinks by himself than more developed or more mediated utterance. It is this function of language which we have called *expressive*.

If it be accepted that much of the talk of adult and child alike is of this nature, it is reasonable, at least, to explore the inference that some writing too may serve the same purposes. And just as the child's talk develops to include the possibility of less intimate utterance (as an extension of course rather than a replacement), so we might expect his use of the written system to develop in a similar way. It is unlikely that development will be exactly the same, if only because children learn to write at a point when their spoken language is already developed, and in the context too of making acquaintance with the forms of the written language in their reading. Learning to write is not learning to speak again but learning to adapt the resources of language which have been gathered from many points into a second more abstract mode. But in anticipating a predominant role for expressive writing, no more is suggested than that the written language, as it is put to use, may also be used to follow the ebb and flow of the writer's consciousness, to articulate the concerns and interests of the writer, free of external demands, in the same informal and implicit way as is characteristic of supportive talk.

Thus we have defined *expressive* writing as writing close to the self, carrying forward the informal presuppositions of informal talk and revealing as much about the writer as about his matter. In the opinion of our judges such writing constituted 5·5% of our sample (109 scripts). Much of this writing, as we shall see, derived from English as a curriculum subject, dealing, on the whole, with matters of primary experience, though we would regard it as equally possible to handle difficult or abstract ideas in expressive writing. Thus, while the following examples are intended to give some idea of the range of expressive writing in our sample, the limited quantity overall, together with the absence of expressive uses outside English (and to some extent religious education), imposes some restrictions on the degree to which the total possible range can be explored here. This again was a matter we were able to take further in our follow-up study.

As has been said, one hypothesis of our research was that expressive writing, in carrying forward the expectations and resources of expressive talk, is likely to be both the most accessible mode for younger writers and the key to developing confidence and range in using written language. Here then, firstly, are three examples from among the writing of the younger members of our sample. (The first and third examples are English scripts; the second is a needlework script.)

Spoken instructions. 'Work in disappointment written after hearing "The Music Book" by M. Whitaker (BBC).'

A GREAT DISAPPOINTMENT

At three years old I was given a dog, we named it chummy. I took him for walks and trained him.

When I was nine chummy was having ear trouble as he was getting old. I knew he would soon have to be distroyed but I hoped it would be a long time.

Then during the summer holidays I was told he had to be distroyed. This was a great shock to me. Saturday came and he was distroyed.

I was very sad, but new it was the best thing, because he was old and sick.

(*first-year boy*)

Spoken instructions. 'Describe, as fully as you can an outfit which you would enjoy wearing for a party. Collect a picture of garments which specially appeal to you.'

I would enjoy wearing this dress [accompanying picture] for partys, dances & outings. The colour I would choose would be blue and I would like it in crimpleen material, white for the collar. With it I would wear a gold watch like this [picture].

I would enjoy wearing these shoes [picture] with the dress and watch. They have got a nice shape front. I like the style very much and I would like them in white black bointant.

(*first-year girl*)

Spoken instructions. 'A choice of seven subjects given. General instructions concerning type of composition and choice—to think of ideas concerning subject chosen—and to jot these ideas down and sort into order before starting the actual writing.'

PETS I ENJOY KEEPING

I have four pets altogether, a cat, a fish, a rabbit and a hammster. The gold fish we keep in a bowel outside on top of the coal bunker, for four years we have had it out there cleaning it out once a week or once every two weeks and feeding it every day with fish food and now and then chopped worms.

Last tusday a ginger cat which we have never seen before knocked over the bowel and all the weed and gravel and of course water was all over the top of the coal bunker. Soon after my father found the fish on the floor but it was still living.

Harry the Hammster is kept in the shed usualy we keep it there but as it is very cold in the snow and frost we brought it down to the house. You don't see much of Harry as he sleeps in day and plays on this wheel at night. He is fed on any greens and mixted grane which contans nuts, of different kinds and sunflower seed with lots of other things. Harry belongs to my sister.

Kept at the top of our garden is the rabbit called twink and he is black all over. Every day we let it out of its hutch into a pen about five yards square where he runs about all day. I feed him on oats and greens and almost anything. Twink is two years old and we have it since it was a baby.

Judy is the oldest out of all our pets she is seven or in cats age 42. Judy is all black with a white bib lasting right across her belly and about an inch of white on each frount paws and two inches on the back paws. We feed Judy on fish or tiny tim cat food.

(first-year girl)

In these examples we are in touch with the anecdotal talk and ready opinion of younger children. The following English piece, by a third-year girl, gives some indication of development in expressive writing. The piece opens introspectively, recalling some of the games of the primary playground.

Instructions. 'I read them an extract from an old copy of the *TES* about a teacher's reflections on games played in the playground in his day—including a violent game of leapfrog. We talked about it and then they had about twenty minutes to write.'

THE PLAYGROUND 1958–1967
Before I went to primary schools the only games I knew were hopscotch, tiddlywinks, skipping and snakes and ladders. After I had been in primary school for a year I had become corrupted and knew how to play games like kiss chase or spot the boy. Spot the boy was played with three boys and nine girls. The girls had to find the boys and take their shoes. The boys to get the shoes back had to pay a forfeit by giving the girls a kiss . . .

Towards the close of the piece, the writer moves on from recollection to sustain a more evaluative interest: the ease of transition between such modalities constitutes a further feature of expressive utterance.

But as I sit and talk with my friends about fashions, money, prices and boys, boys and more boys we are thankful that we aren't like D——School's new generation who cuddle and kiss each other. Play with puppets and themselves. Some evn last year who were wearing stockings and long Johns were playing handstands in full view of all. Ah well that's life its takes all sorts to make a world.

(third-year girl)

Taking such examples as a first rough and ready illustration of what expressive writing looks like, we may now look back on them from the point of view of allocation, and in doing so clarify further the operation of our approach. The focus of our concern, then, is less on the achieved effects of the product than on what the writer is using language to do; and our starting point is that it is open to us to interpret differences in writing as differences in function rather than of any other kind. To pursue the analysis—it may be accepted that one aspect of the functions of all of these writings has been to offer information. To say that is to make clear by contrast that none has sought to develop and integrate meaning in terms of a poetic construct. On the other hand, neither have the writers been concerned to sequence and simplify meaning in a way characteristic of attempts to inform one and all. What is dominant rather is the use, by each of these writers in their different ways, of language to follow the unfolding of experiences and thoughts in the head, close to their emergence and close to the contours of thinking—this in the expectation that the supportive reader will be able and willing to enter into such a use and such a purpose. Allocation, then, involves a series of discriminations of this kind concerned with the dominance of the function which the writing serves, sensitive to the underlying premises on which it is based. A more general point is that to classify writings in terms of function is to classify them in terms of the use which is displayed in them.

Behind expressive writing lie the resources of speech and the ongoing accomplishment of spontaneous informal talk, which occupies much of the lives of most of us and arguably informs more centrally than any other use of language our pupil's encounters with, and versions of, experience. To complete our illustration of it we need now to add the further hypothesis of our research that expressive writing may operate as the matrix from which differentiated forms of mature writing are developed. In the following English example we may note the way in which the sort of anecdote which forms the substance of much expressive talk has been worked on to form an independent poetic construct.

Instructions. 'I didn't instruct exactly—we discussed, sharing ideas and also considered writers' treatment of Fog, e.g. "The yellow fog that rubs its back against the window pane." We jotted ideas and phrases on the board but we did not make a communal plan.'

FOG

I felt inferior, but awed, as I wandered home on that stifling, airless night. The grey fog, inert yet moving, swirled round the orange lights, drawn to it as a huge moth is drawn to a candle.

Life seemed shrouded in unreality.

I was trapped in an enveloping curtain of evil feeling that should I emerge from my imaginary cage, I would be trampled by the rest of the ignorant world.

As I walked by the inn, even the sound of happy voices could not raise my spirits and I walked on while the swirling fog, dense and grim, rolled on like time itself.

I shuddered as the dank, sluggish atmosphere touched my throat, and as wisps of cold air sent shivers running down my back.

It is at times like that when one particularly appreciates the warm log fire, and the security of a happy home life.

(third-year girl)

Such an example illustrates the movement from expressive writing towards poetic writing in satisfying the demands of the spectator role. In the following two examples (English and religious education) the movement in a transactional direction may be observed. Here, while the writing remains open to the emergent flow of the writer's thinking and relatively free of external demands, essentially it is the 'traffic in ideas' which is taking place. Writing of this kind we might see as illustrative of the role of expressive language in developing a provisional first draft of ideas which at another time (or in other hands) might be open to a more explicit and calculated treatment. Here, though, the function remains dominantly expressive.

Instructions. 'Write a criticism of the film "The Day of the Triffids". After most of the class had read the book.'

THE DAY OF THE TRIFFIDS

After reading the book 'The Day of the Triffids' I found the film different in many ways. The flash back in the book which told the story of how Bill had been stung by a Triffid, when he was a boy and how he then went on to work with Triffids might have taken some time if it had been contained in the film. However I think this part of the story is very important as it shows why Bill did not die from the Triffid sting and in later years how he became practically immune to it.

Bill in the film was a sailor, after removing his bandages he left the hospital, no mention of Coker was made at this point. But Susan the girl which appears near the end of the book makes an entrance at this point. The two of them now travel to the dockyard and take a boat over to France. Here they meet up with an organization which is helping the blind people and the appearance of a Miss Durant makes up for the absence of Josilla ...

(fifth-year girl)

Spoken instructions. 'I asked them to put down on paper "What do you think is wrong with the Church and its services ... how do you think it could be improved, particularly to attract more young people?" Much of this work was done anonymously, as some find it easier to express their views really freely like this.'

HOW THE CHURCH COULD ATTRACT MORE YOUNG PEOPLE

I feel that the Church does not need to be 'swinging' as so many people seem to think. Pop groups singing hymns does not seem to me personally to be such a good thing. I think many young people laugh at the Church trying to be modern. However there is much which can be said in favour of livening up Church music ie the hymns and getting rid of the boring chanting of the psalms.

I think that young people could be attracted to the church by youth clubs and so on, where they can meet Christians. These Christians should show by their example what Christian life really is like.

The Church should be more of a family willing to welcome new members, rather than the 'holier than thou' attitude which seems to prevail in some churches . . .

(fifth-year girl)

In both of these two examples, then, the writing is moving in a transactional direction, specifically towards *informing*, under the demands of the participant role. We may now turn to the transactional writing in the sample.

The transactional function

Within the term transactional are classified those uses of language where the writer, operating in a participant role, seeks, in his writing, outcomes in the actual world: to inform or to persuade. As we have suggested before, we may regard such writing as one end of a continuum—centred on expressive writing —whose other end is constituted by the poetic function. In the opinion of our judges, transactional writing formed a proportion of 63·4% of the total sample. As such it may be regarded, by a considerable measure, as the dominant use of writing evidenced in our sample. The contributory proportions of the various sub-categories within that overall proportion will concern us in more detail later. (Definitions of sub-categories may be found in the fold-out chart which follows the index). For the time being it will be enough to illustrate something of the range of transactional writing in the sample.

Of the two main subdivisions of the transactional, we may begin with the conative, since there is less to say about it. This category is further subdivided into *regulative* (where compliance is assumed) and *persuasive* (where compliance is not so much assumed as, one might say, worked for).

CONATIVE WRITING: INSTRUCTION AND PERSUASION

Regulative: language which lays down a course of action to be followed, makes demands, issues instructions where there is an obligation to obey them and makes recommendations which carry the weight of authority or the force of the speaker's wishes

No writing in the sample was allocated to the regulative category.

Persuasive: action, behaviour, attitude and belief are influenced by reason, argument and strategy; potential resistance is acknowledged, and an attempt is made to overcome it

A small proportion (1·6%) was allocated to the persuasive category. Such writing is often close to writing of an informative kind, as reflected of course in the ambiguity of our ordinary sense of what constitutes an 'argument'. In allocation, the crucial distinction concerned whether the argument presented was of a 'take it or leave it' kind or whether it sought actively to enrol the reader's compliance with the writer's view. In the following two examples the first piece (an English script) was judged to be closer to the former case and therefore to be more properly allocated to an informative category, while the second (religious education) was judged persuasive. Comparison of the two may help to clarify the distinction.

Spoken instructions. '" Use of English" specimen test. Worked as trial for exam.'

When I heard that you were looking for accommodation in this area I made some enquiries amongst my friends and found four places that might be suitable for you.

The first is a two roomed flat owned by a middle-aged widow. It has central heating and hot and cold water in the bedroom. Included in the price of five pounds are breakfast and dinner. The owner does not allow cooking in the rooms so the evening meal would have to be obtained from a restaurant. The house is situated about two miles from the town and four miles from the college that you will be attending. Buses to the college run quite regularly but the fare is quite expensive. This flat, I consider, would be very expensive when bus-fares and meals are taken into consideration although there would be plenty of opportunity for studying.

The second place is a second floor bed-sitter situated about fifty yards from the town centre. It is quiet with no traffic outside making ideal for studying. The bed-sitter consists of an old panelled room with an electric fire, which has its own meter, and you have the use of bath and gas ring. The room costs three pounds and that does not include any meals. This will not be very suitable for you as you have not fended for yourself before and taking this flat would entail you doing all your own cooking.

The third place is a boarding house in a quiet square. Breakfast and an evening meal are provided and there is a gas fire, with a meter, in the bedroom. Other facilities include a lounge, television room and reading room. This room costs seven pounds a week. The price together with the fact that there are many old people in residence there leads me to believe that it would not be very suitable for you.

The fourth place is a small bedroom in a house owned by a young couple with three children. The cost is one pound a week for the use of the bedroom alone or with breakfast and evening meal on weekdays and full board at week-ends they charge four pounds. The house is situated close to the college so that transport is no problem.

In my opinion the last house is the best of the four. At four pounds a week you only have to provide yourself with a mid-day meal during the week and this I should imagine could be obtained quite cheaply at the college. The couple have three children but they should not stop your work as they will be in bed when the greater part of your work is to be done. The owners are also willing to treat the lodger as one of the family which counts for a lot when you are away from home and not used to fending for yourself.

(*seventh-year boy*)

IS CHRISTIANITY FIGHTING A LOSING BATTLE AGAINST
POP-GROUPS?

The question of numbers is the first thing to turn to in any discussion of popularity. Obviously it cannot be denied that those who follow the fortunes of the raucous singers are more in number than the more sober-minded fellows who try to live a Christ-like life. Indeed, it appears that the foremost 'Beatle' John Lennon quite admitted (some sources suggest that he was dismayed) that some of the worship which ordinarily would be attributed to God is being wholeheartedly proffered to otherwise untalented pop-groups. This can only result in harm both for the worshipped and worshippers. The former is bound to decline in the popular view, and he becomes disillusioned, thinking that the adulation afforded him is all he will ever need; the latter may become too enthusiastic in the belief that their 'idol' is an infallible 'God', and thus their world collapses when the career of their 'idol' crashes, as it is bound to do.

Now, the Bible itself has condemned the worship of idols, since it presumably takes away the worship due to the creator. But even in the Christian Church itself, this can happen. In a Church, the central theme is Christ. But are there not those within the church who idolize their own eloquence in committee meetings, or their skill in playing, singing, or accompanying? Indeed, some worship is accorded to the vicar or minister himself.

But in all these adversities, the true Christian knows one thing: if the all-powerful God exists and supports his church, then the church cannot fail; and that, while everyone should make an almost superhuman effort in seeing that good and right have a clear way in the world, God will even make use of tragic circumstances and (in this case) loss of priority, to bend and fabricate these wrong things into instruments by which the world may be saved.

(fifth-year boy)

It may be added that writing which takes up a persuasive function may be of many different kinds, for there are many different ways in which we may seek to persuade, including often enough an apparent show of having no such purpose.

INFORMATIVE WRITING

It will be remembered that the subdivision of the informative category was developed from an abstractive scale originally proposed by James Moffett (see page 85). Before proceeding, it may be helpful to set out briefly the resulting sub-categorization—see Table 15. By way of reminder, and also of indication of the basic structure of the scale, which we have subdivided more finely, the original Moffett levels are also included in this table.

Record : eye-witness account or running commentary
The lowest level of abstraction from experience is constituted by direct *recording*, a running commentary (or fictionalized as such) on events at the moment of perception. Only a relatively small proportion (0·8%) of writing in

Table 15   Subdivisions of the informative, with corresponding
values on Moffett's abstractive scale

Subdivisions of the informative (category 1.1)	Moffett scale
1.1.1 Record	Record
1.1.2 Report........................	Report
1.1.3 Generalized narrative	
1.1.4 Low-level analogic	
1.1.5. Analogic	Classificatory
1.1.6 Speculative	
1.1.7 Tautologic	Theoretical

the sample was allocated to this category. The following English script is an
example.

Instructions. 'Follow-up on *Great Expectations* (Pip and convict) or imaginative
writing from stimulus of any illustration in "Listening and Writing" pamphlet.'

DESCRIPTION OF THE COTTAGES

In the foreground is a old building, with attached roof and only one leval. In
the background are some more modern houses with tiled roofs and two levals.

The picture may have been meant to show the contrast between the old and
the new.

Also in the picture is a rough road. On either side of the road is a rough wall
with no signs of reinforcment.

There is no road lighting.

(first-year boy)

*Report: the writer gives an account of a particular series of events or the
appearance of a particular place (i.e. narrative)*

At a stage further removed than that of record the writer may *report* on events
already passed: here the ongoing principle of the record is exchanged for the
narrative principle of report. Writing of this kind derived from a number of
sources in our sample and formed a substantial proportion ($12 \cdot 1\%$) of the
writing in it. Amongst the most prominent of these sources was the writing in
science, where preparation and results of an experiment were being written
up—as follows, for example:

Instructions. 'Write up the experiment as briefly and precisely as possible. (Pupils
do not normally write original notes but make them from points arrived at orally
and then put on the board for accuracy.)'

EXPT TO SHOW THE EXTENSION OF A SPRING (COPPER) IN
PROPORTION TO THE FORCE APPLIED

The apparatus was assembled. We made sure that the metre stick was perfectly
vertical. To make the copper spring we bound some cotton covered copper wire

round a pencil leaving about three inches unbound on each end. We hung the wire. After this different weights were added from ½lbs to 3½lbs as the spring strethed we put the readings in our books.

(first-year boy)

It should be added that where report of an experiment also drew conclusions from results as evidence of a general scientific finding, then a classificatory principle was also involved—often (functionally) by way of separate coda to the dominant function of the writing. Such scripts were usually classified by our judges as moving from report to an analogic level.

The writing of report also featured prominently in our sample from history. We have mentioned in Chapter 6 (p. 101) some of the ambiguities surrounding the term historical 'narrative'. In the following, the writing stays close enough to a strictly narrative (rather than to a classificatory) principle to be allocated to report; this should be contrasted with the example of historical narrative organized on a classificatory principle, which is given later (p. 155).

THE LIFE OF MARTIN LUTHER

Martin Luther's father was a German Stone-miner who worked very hard for his living has he was poor. Martin Luther was gifted for his intelligence and was a begging scholar.

Martin Luther being poor, gave up his live for the Roman Catholic Church here he worked in a monastery like the other monks did.

He went on a visit to Rome by himself and from his room in Rome he could see a man selling indulgences. These were being sold by the church as the Pope needed more money to build St Peters. Indulgences were little cards and it was said if the person who had done a wrong deed would be forgiven for their sins. Of course this was all a fiddle and only ignorent people bought these worthless cards.

Luther was angry at this and thought that the religion in Rome was wrong. He immediately wrote out thirty three of these on paper and nailed it to the Church door of Wittenburg in Germany. Soon people began to talk about these and they were soon printed all over Germany making Luther a popular man.

The Pope was outrageous as people now began to turn aside the indulgences and no-one at all would by them. In the square of Wittenburg the Pope had put up a Papal Bull. This was a parchment with a seal on wrote by the Bulla so this is how it got its name.

When Luther saw this he just tored it down and put it on the bonfire in the square. This was a foolish and a most extraordinary thing to do and the Pope was even more against him now than ever before.

The Pope wanted Martin Luther outlawed and to do this he invited Luther to the Diet of Worms which was the German Parliament. This lasted three days and Luther was sentenced guilty. Luther knew this was going to happen but he was brave and while journeying back from the Diet of Worms he was kidnapped by Prince Frederick who took him to his palace where here Luther stayed for the rest of his life with friends.

Martin Luther broke away from the Roman Catholic Church when he burnt the Papal Bull and it was said 'The Reformation began as the flames consumed the bull.'

(first-year boy)

Finally, a further matter which is raised in Chapter 6 concerns writing where a fictional role is taken up in the context of writing of a dominantly informative kind. Examples of such scripts derive principally from 'humanities' subjects such as history, religious education or social studies, where pupils are sometimes invited to take up a fictional role in order to enter imaginatively into an experience removed from their own in time and space. It seems important, however, to distinguish between those writings which respond to an invitation of this kind by developing an independent poetic construct (as in a historical novel) and those where the poetic possibilities are not developed and the adoption of a fictional stance is essentially a strategy within writing of which the dominant function remains that of informing. A number of scripts of the latter kind were allocated to the category of report. While they derived from various sources, an example from religious education—the third principal contributor of report-level writing in our sample—has been chosen by way of illustration.

JOSEPH'S JOURNEY

One night I had a dream. I dreamt that there were eleven sheaves in a circle and in the middle was a stronger one and the other seemed to bow down to it. The next day I told my brothers and they seemed cross. The next night I had another dream. I dreamt there were eleven stars in a circle, there was one bright star in the middle and there was the sun and the moon and they all bowed down to the one in the middle. The next day I was walking through some fields and I met my brothers. They asked me if I had had any dreams lately and I told them. They asked me if I would go with them. I said yes. They took me to a pit and through me down it and they sold me to be a slave in Egypt. I had to walk all the way there. When I got there they gave all the slaves a big dinner to build them up, and they gave some new clothes. The next day they took us to the slave market. I felt awful, then I had to be looked at. They kept on poking me, then I was sold to a captain. I got friendly with the captain and then I became the chief slave.

(first-year boy)

Such writing does not move outside the informative category, despite its fictional form, nor does it move beyond the abstractive level of report.

Generalized narrative or descriptive information: the writer is tied to particular events and places but he is detecting a pattern of repetition in them; and he expresses this in generalized form

A further level of abstraction is reached when the writer organizes a range of events or phenomena beneath generalizations. To take this step is to exchange a narrative principle for a classificatory one. In our scheme the most developed use of such a principle is reached with the analogic category; and in the original Moffett scale the level of classification follows directly from report (see Table 15). For our purposes, though, it seemed helpful to attempt to categorize more precisely writing which moved beyond report in its abstractive level without yet reaching the fully developed level which we reserved for allocation to the analogic category. Accordingly two further levels were introduced, intermediate between report and analogic writing.

The first of these we have described as generalized narrative, which occupied a proportion of 5·7% of the writing in our sample. Here, writing, while it remains close to events, is beginning to detect recurrences and regularities in them. One example is writing in science such as the following, where the principle of report of an experiment is exchanged for methodological generalizations about the way in which a particular experiment is to be conducted.

EXPERIMENT TO SEPARATE SALT FROM SALT WATER
1   [Drawing]
2   To separate salt from salt water you have to boil it. You can not decant it because the salt would have dissolved into the water. You can not filter it because of the same reason as above.
3   To boil salt water you need a bunsun burner on top of that you have a tripod stand. On the tripod stand you lay a sheet of wire gauze on top of the gauze you put a bowl made out of white porcelain as it shows above.
4   Then you put the salt water into the bowl. You then light the bunsun burner and wait untill all the water has all boiled away. Then you will be able to see all the salt crystals on the inside of the bowl.

(*first-year boy*)

Writing of this kind might be thought to be close to writing of a regulative order, where instructions are being given and compliance assumed. But it seemed to us important to distinguish, along the lines which have already been mentioned in connection with persuasive writing, between writing which offered instructions to any who might want to know and choose to follow them (take it or leave it) and writing whose purpose was to exact a compliance in the reader—the difference, in other words, between instructions in a telephone booth on how to make a call and the order to make one. Writing of the former kind seemed more properly allocated to this level of the abstractive scale of informative writing, as in the following example (an English script):

PREPARATIONS FOR A PICNIC
If you are packing up food for a picnic you have to decide what is and what is not needed in the way of food. You should think of food to take which does not need take up a lot of room and not take cakes which are made of cream or anything in that line that would squash. For a meal instead of having food that squashes, Cornish Pasties, sandwiches and sausage rolls would be ideal for the occasion as they would not easily squash. When taking the cakes it is best to have plain ordinary buns or any kind of biscuits as these fancy cakes whipped with cream

would squash and would not be at all pleasant to eat. When taking the drink it is dangerous to put pop into ordinary glass bottles as they easily brake and could be very dangerous in doing so.

For packing put the food like Cornish Pasties and so forth into plastic containers or wrap them in greaseproof paper. It is also wise to pack the biscuits and plain buns in the same manner as the Cornish Pasties. For the drink put it in a vacuum flask if it is tea or coffee and if it is pop you could use a vacuum flask or one of those long tupperware beakers would be very handy.

When packing the food into the basket it must not take up a lot of room as there are other things to put in also. The tablecloth must be neatly folded up and that way it will not take up much room in the basket.

Packing the right amount of cups, plates and saucers it would be best if they were made out of plastic so they would not easily brake when dropped or banged against one another.

When you arrive at your picnic spot it is best to choose a shady spot and where it is quiet and do not leave any litter where you have picnicked.   Good picnicking.

(third-year girl)

Mention should also be made, at this level, of writing where a fictional role is taken up in a context which remains dominantly informative. The following example (a Latin script) is similar to that considered earlier ('Joseph's journey'), except that here the writer is operating at a generalized-narrative level in depicting the recurrence and regularities of events.

Spoken instructions. 'You will remember our studying a passage in Latin about entertainment in Arles; I want you to write an essay: "If you were to go to a Roman amphitheatre for a day's entertainment, what would you expect to see?"'

If I went into the amphitheatre at Rome for a day's entertainment I would expect to see a lot of blood.

The day would start with a parade of gladiators filing into the arena. They would be dressed ready for battle and at the signal of the emporer they would file out again and await death or glory underneath the stands in the small cages provided.

Perhaps, to start the bloodshed, a few Christians would be herded into the sand ring and hungry lions would be let loose upon them. This would cause great delight among the crowd, they would be standing on their seats listening to every crunch of bone and ripping of sinews. After the lions were back in their cages the flies would swarm in and settle on the piled up bodies and feast on the blood.

Then a few gladiators would enter the ring, fighting in pairs. If one gladiator had his man on the ground the emporer would give the signal as to wether the man would die or not.

The gladiators would be armed with either a long tripointed spear and a net or a short sword and sheild.

There would be a short break after this while wild animals entered the ring and while the remains of bodies were thrown to the dogs. Soon people would get bored with this and there would be a cry for more blood.

In some great theatres a sea battle could be staged by filling the arena with water. These battles were few and far between but they were very popular.

In answer to the cry for blood slaves would be pushed into the ring and stalked by bears, lions, and wolves. This would be a source of great amusement as the slaves were always very weak.

In the afternoon there would be more gladiators, more christians, and more blood and then everyone would leave in the evening thoroughly satisfied.

(third-year boy)

Low level analogic : genuine generalization but organization is loose AND relationships between generalizations are not perceived and/or not made explicit
The second transitional category introduced between report writing and the analogic we have described as analogic with a low level of generalization. Here, while genuine generalizations are being made in the writing, they remain at a low or loosely related level. Writing of this kind derived from all curriculum subjects, constituting a proportion of approximately 14·7% (as we shall see, one of the features of development marked within the sample is the movement of the young writer beyond this level). But in particular much of the writing of geography was of this kind. One of the following examples is taken from geography, the other from science.
Spoken instructions. 'Write summary of geography of Scotland in few paragraphs, contents of each paragraph indicated as (1) Highlands, (2) Southern Uplands (3) Industry in Central Lowlands, (4) Settlements of Central Lowlands. Work needed for first two paragraphs already covered, but for Central Lowlands it was necessary for pupils to find their own information at this stage.'

SCOTLAND

Fishing and farming are the main occupations of the Highlanders. The oldest method of farming still survives and is called crofting. The crofter keeps sheep a few cows, some poultry, and perhaps some pigs, he also grows vegetables for himself and his family and winter feed for the animals he keeps, by hand cultivation. The crofters may sell hand woven cloth. 'Harris tweed' is made in this way. The spinning of 'Harris tweed' is done in factories now but at one time it was spun by hand, the cloth is still hand woven and the demand for this cloth is still strong. Many crafts are now abandoned. In the Southern uplands sheep are kept mainly for wool. This is the most important sheep rearing district in Britain. Most sheep are found in the upper basin of the River Tweed, this area has long been famous for its woollen cloth industry. Today the Tweed woollen towns specialise in high quality knitwear and the well known tweed suitings.

Many people live in and around the coal fields and work in the industres in the area. By the 1850's Scotland produced one quarter of all british iron. The many heavy industries include the making of cinders, steel tubes, Boilers, ships engines steam pumps, machine tools, mining equipment, sugar making machinery, heavy electrical machinery and ship building. On the clyde there are 20 miles of shipbuilding yards on each side and all belonging to some thirty firms and employing about 56000 men. This is the largest shipbuilding area in the world.

The main cities of the central lowlands are Glasgow, Edenburgh the capitol, Dundee and Perth. Glasgow prospered as a port because of the american trade and today one fifth of Britains trade is handled there Glasgow being the third largest city in Britain. As well as engineering and shipbuilding, Glasgo has many vast industres. Edinburgh industries are paper making, printing, Book binding, engineering, Brewing, distelling, confectionery and buiscuit making. Dundee makes linen, [illegible MS] also engenering shipbuilding, brewing, barley for malt is grown in the locality.

(fifth-year boy)

Instructions. 'This is a continuation of class work. We had done a series of experiments on the expansion and contraction of metals—followed by a discussion on the advantages and disadvantages of this fact—and the written work came out of this discussion.'

THE ADVANTAGES AND DISADVANTAGES OF METALS

Thermostats is one thing that is useful for expansion of metals. Thermostats are lights on ovens that are lit by a metal expanding. This keeps the oven at a set temperature. Some people have automatic fire alarms which are set off by the heat of the fire. Mercury is a liquid metal, which is put in thermometers. This is to find the heat of the body, and stops when it gets to the right temperature. A disadvantage of this is railway lines. A gap has to be left between rails for expansion, when trains pass over.

(first-year boy)

Analogic generalizations related hierarchically or logically by means of coherently presented classificatory utterances

In both of the examples above, the classification of particulars beneath generalizations remains relatively loose—in the example from geography, because the linking overall generalizations act as a way of grouping the data rather than being inherent in it; in that from science, because the writer has here tended to put down generalizations much as they 'come' without concern to connect them within a coherent order. We reserved for the category of analogic writing the operation of a relatively highly wrought system of generalizations. As we shall see, it is this level of writing which came to dominate the output evidenced in our sample (an overall proportion of 22·2%); and in consequence examples can be drawn from all curriculum subjects. Three examples, though, must suffice us here, the first taken from history, which will also allow comparison with the earlier example of report and so focus the nature of historical narrative; the second and third are taken from science and geography.

WHY WAS GREAT BRITAIN INVOLVED IN THE WAR OF THE SPANISH SUCCESSION, AND WHAT DID SHE GAIN BY IT?

When Charles I, King of Spain, died, Louis XIV of France ignored his obligations under the partition treaties of 1698 and 1699, and claimed the Spanish throne—which meant control over Spain—for his nephew, Philip of Anjou. Meanwhile, Emperor Leopold of Austria claimed the right of the Spanish throne for his son, Charles.

Unfortunately, at this time, France was by far the most powerful country in Europe. This, then, in itself, virtually supressed Charles's claim for the Spanish throne. Great Britain now was set firmly against France, because a Spanish–french alliance would upset the balance of power in Europe, i.e. that no country, or group of allied countries, should be able to dominate the rest. England was also concerned about Louis XIV's. Louis, instead of recognizing the protestant succession in England, recognized only the Old Pretender, James II, as legitimate King of England, and he threatened the Revolutionary Settlement. Another reason for England's dislike of France was that Britain wanted trading privileges in South America, but wanted to deny France similar privileges. When, consequently, Louis claimed control of the Spanish Netherlands, war was inevitable.

The victory of the allied forces of England, Holland, and Austria against Spain and France was followed by the Treaty of Utrecht in July 1713, drawn up by the collaboration of the Tories from England, and the French. The Treaty was drawn up secretly a year after the war had ended (1713). In it, England made several gains.

Firstly, Louis XIV of France recognized Queen Anne to be rightful monarch of England. Next, Gibraltar—which Rooke had captured in 1704—was given to the British, as well as Minorca—captured in 1708. Great Britain also gained the Asiento from Spain, and England had gained an overall victory. One section of the Treaty said that Philip V could have Spain, but with the promise that the French and Spanish thrones were not united. This helped England to regain her foreign policy of having a balance of power in Europe. England also drew up the Methuen Treaty with Portugal in 1703, which allowed Britain to keep a base in Portugal.

Britain, from the treaty, also ensured that Newfoundland was hers, and also secured trading rights in the Hudson Bay area. Hence Great Britain became involved in the war because she could see no other way of preventing French domination inside and outside Europe, and, thanks to the skill of Marlborough who was in charge of the English army, they gained by it.

(fifth-year boy)

Written instructions. 'Describe the main characteristics of the mammal with reference to the rabbit.'

A DESCRIPTION OF THE MAIN CHARACTERISTICS OF THE
MAMMAL WITH REFERENCE TO THE RABBIT

The rabbit has a bony internal skeleton preventing the body from sagging. The bones and muscles of the legs carry the whole weight of the body while the backbone or spinal column acts as a 'girder' between them. From this backbone the gut and other organs hang. The legs themselves are levers worked by the leg muscles, by the movement of these muscles the rabbit is able to move from one place to another. In the rabbit the hind legs are long and provide the power for hopping. The rib cage protects the lungs and heart.

The lungs and heart are separated from other organs in the abdomen by a thin sheet of muscle, the diaphragm. The diaphragm with the ribs and other muscles works to enlarge the chest, so drawing air into the lungs. By reducing the chest air is forced out. The diaphragm in the rabbit moves backwards and forwards.

The rabbit is warm blooded and has a body covering of hair which helps to prevent heat loss through the skin.

A rabbit eats plants almost entirely and this is digested in the caecum where there is much bacteria. Waste is passed out as faecal pellets through the anus.

The rabbit lives on land which is its natural habitat, they make burrows in the ground and live in colonies called warrens. Rabbits reproduce asexually and the gestation period is thirty-one days. There is much parental care during the early stages of a rabbits life.

(fifth-year boy)

Instructions. 'The written instruction was "Discuss the relative importance of each primary source of power in Great Britain." Each source of power i.e. coal, oil, hydro-electricity and nuclear energy has been dealt with individually, so that this will also be a test as to their ability to relate the individual topics under one heading.'

TO DISCUSS THE RELATIVE IMPORTANCE OF EACH PRIMARY SOURCE OF POWER IN GREAT BRITAIN

In Great Britain today, there are several sources of electricity, which is our main power. Hydro-electric, coal, and Neuclar energy. There is also gas and oil, but neither of these are very important, as a lot of people prefer electricity to gas and oil.

When coal is taken from the ground there is always an element of danger and it costs a lot of money. It takes up a lot of room, is dirty, and is difficult to transport, therefore taking up even more money. When it arrives at the power station it needs a lot of coal to keep the furnaces going at the required temperature, therefore costing even more money. But even now there are still many thermal-electricity power stations which are cheap to build but costly to run. One better way to produce electricity is by using water.

In Canada, from one river it makes as much electricity with a few Hydro-power stations as Britain's whole output is, and theres is only one sixth of our population. There are two different ways to produce Hydro-electricity, the Dam method and the diversion system. Both need carefull positioning and building and cost a large amount of money to build but the water to run them is free, and the system soon pays for itself. As in France, it would be a good idea to build a large dam across the wash which worked off the tides.

It has been stated that in about another fifty years the oil and coal resorces of the world will run out so another method of producing large amounts of electricity for areas of intensive industry such as Sheffield and Newcastle which use tremendous amounts of electricity is wanted. This is neuclar energy. I think that this will be the power of the future, as it has been made safe, from radio-activity.

In Great Britain the power is evenly distributed, such as coal in the Midlands and Wales, thermal electricity around London and Newcastle and some Hydro in Scotland.

In industry such as iron and steel, there would be nothing without electricity, most of all, and oil and gas, for what whould there be to drive their tools? Even in everyday life most things would stop. With all the power stations in Great Britain, there are still power cuts in winter so surely there is a need to explore in new ways to produce electricity, more cheaply, quickly and in greater amounts?

(third-year girl)

THEORETICAL WRITING

Analogic/tautologic (speculative): speculation about generalizations: the open-ended consideration of analogic possibilities
Tautologic: hypotheses and deductions from them; theory backed by logical argument

From analogic writing we may pass to theoretical writing—from the third principle of abstraction (the classification of particulars beneath generalizations) to a further possibility: writing where generalization itself is the substance of the discourse. This level of abstraction, described by Moffett as theoretical, while moving beyond the classification of particulars, incorporates the possibilities of analogic writing within a higher order. To put it epigrammatically, in theoretical writing particulars exist to substantiate generalization rather than generalizations to organize particulars. Meaning is carried by an interconnected web of generalizations, serving to advance a theory. Naturally the presence of theoretical elements is to be expected in some forms of analogic writing also: it is a question again of the point at which one level of abstraction rather than another becomes dominant.

In the original Moffet scale, the theoretical level of abstraction follows directly from the analogic (see Table 15). For our purposes, though, it seemed best to reserve, for the category which we called tautologic, writing where the web of generalization had been articulated to a high and finished order of interconnection. We had in mind that there also exists writing which seeks to pass beyond the classificatory level, but is on a stage towards the ordered marshalling of propositions of a formal theoretical exposition. Writing of this kind it seemed appropriate to think of as *speculative*. Such writing is theoretical in its seeking to pass beyond a classificatory level and to make of generalization the substance of its discourse, but is speculative in that generalization in it is entertained in an open-ended way rather than expounded. We might add that it seemed likely to us that writing of this kind—on the way towards theory—should have an important place in learning.

Theoretical writing, however, of either a speculative or a tautologic kind, occupied only a small proportion of our sample (4·1%). By way of illustration, the following two examples (from sixth form general studies and physics) may

be given—the first where the writing moves beyond the analogic to a speculative level, the second where it is marked by an ordered exposition of a
tautologic kind.

WHAT ARE THE LIMITS OF TOLERATION, IF ANY?

There should not be, ideally, any limits of toleration. Remember the Lord said
'seventy times seven' when a certain man asked him how many times he should
forgive his brother, meaning he should 'alway' tolerate him. However, were
the Holy Bible translated into practical English, instead of merely 'New
English', the answer, I'm sure, would be 'till you can forgive him no more,' that
is, until you reach the limits of your toleration. However, this is one of the major
problems of today—when to stop tolerating and to start acting.

So, practically, tolerance and its limits vary a great deal in different people,
according to how they answer the above question. It is most interesting to find
out in someone this particular aspect of his character, mostly this is done sub-
consciously. How many times have you thought: 'I wonder how much more I
can tease this chap before he turns nasty', or, 'How much more can I get out of
him before he stops giving?' These are both illustrations of testing tolerance;
and some of the sets of circumstances to which they can be applied are rather
eye-opening. Now, lots of people will stop 'giving' as soon as they know they are
being 'sucked', and others will never turn nasty; here where the expected pattern
shows traits of irregularity, like the cracks in the M.1., the system, breaks down;
the situation presents problems; and these problems get worse, as more remedies
are applied to them.

The colour problem is a matter of tolerance, or, more accurately its non-
existence in some quarters. What most people do not realise is that an equal
amount of tolerance is required on both sides. As the situation is at the moment
the greater amount of tolerance is shown by the coloureds, themselves; another
fact few people realise. This produces the impression given to the whites that
they can get away with it; the others never 'turn nasty' so the whites go on 'teasing' them; the whole situation is linked up.

So here is the answer to the question: there are always limits of tolerance, but
—and this is the whole point—they must be adjusted to fit the circumstances,
(obviously you cannot observe the same tolerance with a coloured immigrant as
with your son or daughter.) Above is an example of when tolerance should be
equal, but even that must not be fixed at equality, (it usually comes round to
that in the end); that equality must be adjusted to accord with the relationship,
whether it is judge to convicted, or plumber to plumber's mate. So, we must not
fix our tolerance at a certain rung, there must be many rungs, and movement up
and down the ladder must be easy.

This brings one more resultant realisation, which is important; and it is that
tolerance is a part of our daily, even hourly, life, and its maltreatment or the ignorance involved in deciding how much to have, is the cause of so many minor and
major problems. When this is realised, it is, at least, the beginning.

Compromise is the essence of cohabitation.

(seventh-year boy)

Written instructions. 'Describe and explain 2 methods of producing a beam of plane-polarised light. How would you demonstrate that the beam so produced differs in its properties from ordinary light? State, giving your reasons, whether or not it is possible to polarise (*a*) sound waves (*b*) radio waves.'

EXPLANATION

By using an analogy of rope waves which are transverse, the phenomenen may be explained. Suppose a rope is threaded through a type of grid, and a second grid through which it is threaded, is placed further along the rope. If both slits are parallel, the wave will pass all the way along the rope and emerge at the other side of the second slit. If however the second slit is placed perpendicular to the first, the wave is blocked or cut off.

In the rope wave before it reaches the first grid, transverse vibrations of the rope particles occur in every plane, but the vibrations are restricted to those moving up and down in a plane parallel to the grid, when the rope wave has passed through the first grid or slit. Hence if a second slit is placed parallel to the first, the wave due to these transverse vibrations in one plane will pass through. In the second case, where the next slit is placed perpendicular to the first the transverse vibrations cannot occur due to the position of the slit which cuts them off.

If the analogy is applied to light waves, which must now be assumed to be transverse, the polarisation phenomenen can be explained. The crystals must have the power of restricting light to one plane. Hence polarised light is obtained when the light is passed through the first crystal which is called the polariser and continues polarised through the second crystal—the analyser—if placed with axis parallel to the first. If placed so that it is perpendicular to the first, the polarised light is cut off & darkness is seen. This experiment shows how polarised light differs from ordinary light.

(seventh-year girl)

★

In transactional writing then—to return to the more general theory—the expressive language of the writer is modified, under the demands of the participant role, to perform a transaction which seeks outcomes in the real world. It is language to get things done. Making the comparison between the writing illustrated here, and that illustrated earlier as exemplifying the expressive function, we may note the concern in transactional writing for a greater explicitness and for the subordination of the personal, self-revealing features in the writer to the matter set out between him and reader. As has been said, it is a movement which is at once more public and more conditioned by external demands. One illustration of these distinctions can be gained by comparing the sense of audience here with that of expressive writing.

A further index—an indication only—is to compare the opening sentences of the two sets of scripts. If we read them not as isolated constructions, but as openings to the possibilities which are to follow, there is some contrast to be pointed between such opening lines as 'At three years old I was given a dog, we named him chummy', or 'I feel that the church does not need to be "swing-ing" as so many people seem to think'; and other lines such as 'To separate salt from water you have to boil it', or 'Fishing and farming are the main occupations of the Highlanders,' or 'Thermostats is one thing that is useful for expansion of metals'. The difference is one of explicitness—not, though, that it is being suggested that a single line is sufficient to indicate the dominant function of a piece. It might be added that we can only interpret the difference in the possibilities opened by such lines with reference to our sense of the underlying presuppositions by which they are potentially informed—a point, of course, which for us is close to being a starting-point.

The poetic function

The poetic writing in our sample may be considered fairly briefly—since it has already been illustrated earlier, and since our theoretical approach to it has been expounded fairly fully in chapters 5 and 6. In poetic writing the ex-pressive language of the writer moves under the demands of the spectator role towards the articulation of an independent verbal construct. In the opinion of our judges such writing constituted nearly 18% of the sample. This propor-tion, as we shall see, was drawn principally from English and religious edu-cation. The following example is taken from English.

Spoken instructions. 'The class was asked to write—a story, a piece of verse, whatever suggested itself to them—on the title—"For thine (or Thine) is the power and the glory", in which they would draw on their experience of liter-ature, painting and documentary of the 1st World War (with reference to the Oxford and Cambridge Board's current Related Set Books Paper).'

The wiring parties had returned and dawn was approaching. The dawn of another day—a day the same as yesterday, the same as the day before, and the same as tomorrow. Probably a day bringing rain into the already flooded trenches, in which we lived like rats in a hole, hemmed in by enemy fire, and only the escape that Death offers presents itself to us. While sitting in those trenches I often wonder why we are fighting. It was the politicians' war. Why couldn't they do something about it themselves insteading of sending us out here and telling us to blow the enemy off the face of the earth. They don't know what it is like to live here and fight and die. Have they no humanity as they sit back in their armchairs by their fires sticking flags into maps. If only they could understand. If only the Almighty could understand, and do something about this futility. I am sure that He must see that it is getting nobody anywhere.

I have seen people shoot themselves, taking one way out of the war. These soldiers are only too happy when they are wounded in the leg or arm, so that they can get out this slaughter.

The Germans have now started firing. I wonder if they know why they are fighting. I expect they too have been told the lies about it being brave and noble and a great thing to die for one's country.

Every now and then there was a 'crump' as the shells exploded. There was a yellow butterfly perched on the grey hand of a corpse. I had almost forgotten about butterflies, and the fact that Nature was all around us. I wonder if the insects know what is happening. They seem to live perfectly happily without any wars, but I suppose they do not have politicians to bundle the affairs of the country onto every single individual.

A man, shot through the face, falls back on to some cans, creating a new noise in the din of the battle-field. The butterfly has now flown away and the morning is bringing light to the land through a thick cloud cover. It begins to drizzle. The war goes on . . . Will man ever recover his senses? . . .

(fifth-year boy)

In interpreting such writing we may note that, analogously to the process of transactional writing, the writer has here proposed to himself a less intimate mode than that characteristic of expressive language—but for a very different purpose. Where transactional writing seeks outcomes in the real world—to inform someone or to persuade him—in poetic writing such concerns are subordinate to the attempt to create a 'world', a totally independent construct: not that a reader may not derive information from it or be persuaded by its cumulative effect towards a certain point of view—nor indeed that the writer may not have such purposes somewhere in mind—but that the overall undertaking is different in kind from one which seeks such outcomes directly.

From the point of view of allocating writing to the poetic category, we might add here the converse of the point raised in connection with the writing which takes up a fictional role within a dominantly informative function. Seen from the perspective here it is the concept of the spectator role which supplies the crucial key to such a distinction. For there does seem a distinction to be made—and it is in the light of the spectator role that we are helped to make it—between poetic writing, on the one hand, and on the other, writing which may take up a fictional form but whose concern is not *with* form, which deals with individual (or fictionally individual) experience and yet is not concerned with the achievement of a 'resonant' verbal construct; between writing which seeks an outcome in the actual world and that of which the function is 'to be' rather than 'to do'.

However, with this consideration of the third of the principal categories in our scheme, we may now turn in greater detail to the patterns of change and development in function as evidenced in our sample.

Development and changing demands

THE GENERAL TENDENCIES OF THE SAMPLE

The range of demands made on the young writer's use of writing in the secondary school and its changing pattern; the development in his ability to cope with certain functions rather than others; overall, a sense of the priorities and emphases in secondary school writing—these issues confront us when we turn in greater detail to the patterns reflected in the sample.

Provisionally, at any rate, we can simplify things for ourselves in two directions. If the total range of functions is as we have described them, we shall be concerned with *sequence*: with the order, that is, in which the writer comes to command that range. On the whole this will direct our attention, discretely, to certain functions rather than others: to those which, on the evidence of the sample, seem crucial in the process of school learning—or more exactly, to those with which, being crucial, the young writer seems most recurrently to engage. As we shall see, the overall drive of school learning seems to concentrate attention most prominently on the analogic level of the informative function: on the ability to classify particulars within a relatively highly wrought system of generalizations. But then to view the writer in school as apprentice, as it were, to certain more exacting functions of the written language is only one way to look at him. For the range of writing in our sample reflects not only this engagement with certain critical functions, but more generally the use of writing in the ongoing business of interpreting experience and mastering new ideas. Our interpretation, then, will need also to encompass this second, broader direction, concerned not merely with the acquisition of new functions—with what is successor to what—but with the *overall balance* in the uses to which writing is put. A sense of this larger pattern, and its altering definition within the school situation, will need to concern us. Sequence, then, and the overall configuration.

We may begin with the general tendencies of the sample as a whole, as some sort of benchmark. Table 16 sets out the proportions of writing in the principal categories in the sample as a whole, together with the proportions of writing in the subdivisions of the transactional function, represented as proportions of the total sample. Inspection of these figures suggests:

(a) the overall predominance of transactional writing within the general tendencies of the sample, and within that the predominance of informative writing:

(b) the overall predominance of the classificatory levels of informative writing, both as a proportion of informative writing and as a proportion of all the writing in the sample.

The greater part, then, of the writing in our sample was placed in the transactional function (63·4%). Of the other two principal functions within our scheme, the proportion occupied by expressive writing (5·5%) is low to the point of marginality, while that occupied by poetic writing, though more significant, is no more than 17·6%. As a rough and ready way of describing this overall configuration we can say that there is three times as much transactional writing as both of the other functions put together, and approximately thirteen times as much transactional writing as expressive. It is this very

Table 16   Distribution of function categories ($n = 1992$)

(a) *Distribution of main categories*

Main categories	%
Transactional	63·4
Expressive	5·5
Poetic	17·6
Additional categories	8·6
Miscellaneous	4·9

(b) *Subdivisions of the transactional category*

Sub-categories	%
Record	0·8
Report	12·1
Generalized narrative	5·7
Low-level analogic	14·7
Analogic	22·2
Speculative	2·4
Tautologic	1·7
Conative	1·6
Miscellaneous	2·2

general starting point, at any rate, that more detailed analysis will enable us to clarify.

Consideration of the proportions of writing within the subdivisions of the transactional function enables us to take the first further step. Most of the transactional writing, as can be seen from Table 16(b), is informative—only 1·6% being classified within the conative function (and all of that persuasive rather than regulative). The subdivisions within the informative function reflect the scale of abstraction from recording to tautologic theorizing. Here, while the pattern is fairly dispersed, it is clear that the classificatory level predominates. The greater part of the classificatory writing is what we have called analogic—greater by about half as much again as the amount of writing for the low-level analogic. Both categories, though, involve the classification of particulars under generalizations, and taking the totals in the two categories together makes clear the predominance of this level of abstraction within the informative writing in our sample. On the one hand, there is approximately twice as much writing in these two categories as in the three remaining levels of the abstractive scale below it. On the other, and in some ways more surprisingly, there is nine times as much as any theoretical writing in the two categories (speculative and tautologic) above it.

In point of fact, though, it is not merely the informative writing in the sample which is dominated by the classificatory level: it would be more exact to say that classificatory writing predominates in the sample as a whole.

THE PATTERN YEAR BY YEAR

Against the background of the general tendencies of the sample overall, we may turn to the patterns suggested by consideration of the proportions year by year. This next step confirms rather than markedly qualifies the overall picture, but adds some significant detail—to our concern with development,

Table 17   Distribution of function categories by years
(a) *Main categories*

| Categories | Percentages of year totals | | | |
	Year 1	Year 3	Year 5	Year 7
Transactional	54	57	62	84
Expressive	6	6	5	4
Poetic	17	23	24	7
Additional categories	19	8	4	1
Miscellaneous	4	6	5	4

(b) *Breakdown of subdivisions of the transactional category*

| Sub-categories | Percentages of year totals | | | |
	Year 1	Year 3	Year 5	Year 7
Record	2	1	0	0
Report	22	17	4	3
Generalized narrative	10	8	3	1
Low-level analogic	17	17	18	7
Analogic	2	11	28	55
Speculative	0	0	3	8
Tautologic	0	1	0	6
Conative	1	2	2	2
Miscellaneous	0	0	3	2

in particular. Table 17 sets out the percentages year by year both for the principal categories and for the subdivisions of the transactional, and notes some of the most significant implications. Inspection of these figures suggests the following:

(a) that the lower levels of informative writing give way to the higher levels after the third year;

(b) that the higher levels are broadly concentrated in classificatory writing (low-level analogic and analogic) and only minimally pass beyond classificatory writing to theoretical (speculative, tautologic);

(c) that what theoretical writing there is is developed during and after the fifth year;

(d) that while the proportion of expressive writing is consistently low, it remains broadly constant through all the years of the sample;

(e) that the proportion of poetic writing, increasing in the third year, remains broadly constant through to the fifth, but drops sharply in the seventh year;

(f) that while there is a marked decline in writing in the additional categories after the first year, it is not until the seventh year that a very low level is reached.

As can be seen from Table 17(a), the most marked change at the level of the principal categories concerns the steady and decisive increase in transactional writing over the four age levels of the sample (it is worth noticing, though, that the proportion is never less than 54% of the yearly total). However, the steadiness of the rise in transactional writing is accelerated at the end of the fifth year—a rise from 62% in year 5 to 84% in year 7, compared with a difference of only 8% between the figures for year 1 and year 5. Correspondingly, the proportion of poetic writing, which has in fact tended to rise during the early years of the sample (as we shall see, this is partly a reflection of the decline in 'additional' categories), drops decisively and suddenly in the seventh year. No doubt such changes mark, in part, the advent of the sixth form curriculum.

To be added to this, however, as can be seen from Table 17(b), is the similarly steady movement beyond the lower levels of abstraction in the subdivisions of the informative function. Both report and generalized narrative, which occupy a considerable proportion of the writing of the first two age levels, decline markedly after the third year. Similarly there is a sizeable decline in writing in the low-level analogic after the fifth year, at a time when the proportion of transactional writing—and within that the proportion of classificatory writing—is increasing. Given the marked rise in analogic writing in the seventh year (from 28% to 55% of the total sample), the significance of the decline in writing in low-level analogic seems beyond question: the ability to cope with a higher level in the ordering of particulars simply replaces it. Overall, then, examination of the pattern of subdivisions within the informative function year by year suggests a progress beyond the lower levels of the abstractive scale, coupled with a concentration of writing in the analogic subdivision. As one might expect, too, there is evidence of an increase in writing on a theoretical level (speculative, tautologic) in the seventh year. This is in tune with the general rise in abstractive level marked by the sample. But while there is evidence of the possibilities here, they remain relatively undeveloped. It seems likely that the concentration of writing in the analogic function is to some extent at the expense of higher-level writing. Equally it has to be added, as before, that the predominance of analogic writing (55% of all the writing in the seventh year) has to be seen not merely in the context of informative writing alone, but also in the context of the total range of possible uses to which writing can be put.

To return to a rough and ready way of illustrating this predominance, one can say that by the seventh year analogic writing occupies over half the total output of the sample: this is a proportion five times greater than all the lower levels of abstractive scale taken together and about four times greater than any theoretical writing. In addition to this, poetic writing has become by the seventh year, in common with expressive writing throughout the sample, no more than a very small proportion of the total output.

The implications of the increasing concentration of writing in the analogic subdivision of the informative scale can be seen in two ways. On the one hand, there is indication that the analogic function is something which young writers have to learn and which, on the evidence of the sample, is largely learnt during their time in secondary school. While no doubt it is not all quite as watertight as that, the pattern of figures here is still suggestive of development, the concentration of writing passing beyond the lower levels of the abstractive scale and beyond the lower level of analogic writing itself. But we may note, though, that possibilities close at the same time as new ones open. Use of the lower levels of the abstractive scale diminishes—jettisoned, presumably, in response to changing demands in the curriculum. Relatively little writing in the sample passes beyond analogic writing to either speculative or tautologic levels, while other functions of writing, such as poetic or expressive, seem either undeveloped or to pass out of the ambit of school learning with the coming of the seventh year.

THE ROLE OF CURRICULUM SUBJECTS

Having established that consideration of the general tendencies in the sample and of the pattern year by year tends to focus on the place of analogic writing, we may now turn to consider the demands of curriculum subjects in relation to this. Naturally there are divergences between particular subjects, as well as their overall contribution to the predominant pattern marked by the sample, and we must also keep a sense of these.

Table 18 sets out the proportions of writing in different functions for the various curriculum subjects. Inspection of these figures suggests the following:

(*a*) English is characterized by its under-use (comparatively speaking) of the informative (see first seven categories of table), with the exception of the speculative; and by its near-monopoly of the expressive, the poetic and the 'dummy run'.

(*b*) History shows a strong emphasis on analogic writing, and secondary emphases on report and low-level analogic.

(*c*) Geography is notable for its concentration on low-level analogic (but see also the generalized narrative category).

(*d*) Religious education puts an unexpected emphasis on report and makes little use of the analogic and low-level analogic; shows a similar pattern

Table 18   Distribution of function categories by subjects (*n* = 1992)

	Percentages* of subject totals					
	English (*n* = 822)	History (*n* = 266)	Geo-graphy (*n* = 218)	R.E. (*n* = 143)	Science (*n* = 327)	Other subjects (*n* = 216)
Record	1	—	—	—	—	—
Report	5	21	5	38	18	10
Generalized narrative	2	5	16	4	6	12
Low-level analogic	4	21	49	4	17	15
Analogic	12	39	18	5	42	27
Speculative	4	—	—	—	2	2
Tautologic	1	—	—	—	3	8
Conative	3	—	—	6	—	—
Miscellaneous informative	2	2	—	—	4	2
TOTAL TRANSACTIONAL	34	88	88	57	92	76
EXPRESSIVE	11	—	—	11	—	—
POETIC	39	2	—	12	—	—
Immature categories	3	2	—	—	—	7
Pseudo-informative	—	6	8	7	5	4
Dummy run	5	—	—	—	—	—
TOTAL ADDITIONAL CATEGORIES	8	8	8	7	5	11
MIXED CATEGORIES:						
Expressive/informative	2	—	—	—	—	—
Expressive/poetic	5	—	—	—	—	—
Miscellaneous	1	—	—	—	—	10

* Figures represent whole number percentages recording only cells of five or more

to English in the use made of the conative—which barely occurs anywhere else—and in taking a reasonable share of the expressive and poetic.

(e) Science stands out mainly for its frequent use of the analogic.

As can be seen from Table 18 a number of interesting divergences emerge,
some (such as history) which on reflection we might expect, others which are
more intriguing. It would be interesting for example to know what underlies
the concentration of much geography writing in the lower level of the analogic
or the common use made by both religious education and English of conative
writing. More generally, though, it seems worth remarking that something of
the same division as was observable in the pattern of audience is repeated here
between English and religious education on the one hand, and the remaining
curriculum subjects on the other. Thus, at the level of the major functions,
English and religious education are largely alone in making any extensive use
of functions other than the transactional. Between them they command the
total proportion of expressive writing in the sample and very nearly the total
proportion of poetic. The concentration of report writing in religious education is of course an interesting divergence from the pattern which the two subjects have otherwise in common. But in general the most striking feature, in
considering the use made by the various curriculum subjects of the principal
functions, is how little writing outside religious education and English is other
than transactional.

There is rather more divergence within the subdivisions of the informative
category. But, while both science and history (together with religious education) make significant use of report, the predominance of classificatory
writing, as of course might be expected from consideration of the sample overall, is on the whole reflected in the curriculum subjects outside religious education and English. Taking the two levels together (that is, analogic and low-
level analogic), classificatory writing comprises 60% or more of the total output
of history, geography and science alike. It is this general feature, shared by
these subjects, which of course underlies the predominance of classificatory
writing in the overall sample.

Consideration of the subtotals for function by curriculum subject at the
four age levels of the sample both confirms and refines this picture—see
Table 19. Inspection of these figures suggests the following:

(a) English is marked by its consistent pattern through the first three age
     levels of the sample, characterized by under-use (relatively) of in-
     formative, moderate use of expressive and extensive use of poetic
     writing. However, there is some increase in transactional writing in the
     fifth year, and a sharp change in the seventh marked by an increase in
     analogic writing and a decisive entry of writing at a theoretical (specu-
     lative/tautologic) level; also in the seventh year, poetic writing di-
     minishes radically.

Table 19 Distribution of function categories by subjects by years (percentages of subject-year totals)

(a) Main categories

Subject and year	Trans-actional	Trans-actional/ expressive	Expressive	Expressive/ poetic	Poetic	Immature categories	Pseudo-informative	Dummy run	Misc.	n
English:										
Y.1	16	3	14	7	43	9	1	6	1	217
Y.3	17	2	14	7	50	3	0	5	2	205
Y.5	28	2	8	2	52	0	0	7	1	191
Y.7	73	2	8	2	13	0	0	1	1	209
History:										
Y.1	76	0	1	0	1	8	12	1	1	73
Y.3	89	0	0	0	0	0	8	1	2	75
Y.5	95	0	0	0	3	0	1	0	1	76
Y.7	95	0	0	0	5	0	0	0	0	42
Geography:										
Y.1	86	0	0	0	0	0	14	0	0	81
Y.3	87	0	0	1	3	0	8	0	1	80
Y.5	100	0	0	0	0	0	0	0	0	41
Y.7	100	0	0	0	0	0	0	0	0	16
Relig. Educ.:										
Y.1	65	0	7	2	2	7	16	2	0	58
Y.3	55	6	10	0	24	0	2	4	0	51
Y.5	59	0	20	3	13	0	0	0	3	30
Science:										
Y.1	85	0	0	0	0	2	11	0	2	105
Y.3	95	0	0	0	1	0	3	0	1	73
Y.5	95	0	0	0	2	0	3	0	0	62
Y.7	99	0	0	0	1	0	0	0	0	87

Table 19—continued

(b) Subdivisions of the transactional category

Subject and year	Record	Report	Generalized narrative	Low-level analogic	Analogic	Speculative	Tautologic	Corative	Misc. informative	Miscellaneous
English:										
Y.1	3	9	0	3	0	0	0	0	0	0
Y.3	1	2	4	3	2	0	0	4	0	0
Y.5	1	7	4	5	4	4	0	1	3	0
Y.7	0	2	0	6	41	11	3	4	4	1
History:										
Y.1	0	32	14	26	4	0	0	0	0	0
Y.3	0	37	4	32	13	0	0	0	3	0
Y.5	0	3	0	14	74	0	0	0	4	0
Y.7	0	5	0	2	83	5	0	0	0	0
Geography:										
Y.1	3	6	31	42	1	0	0	0	2	1
Y.3	0	5	11	48	21	0	0	0	3	0
Y.5	0	0	0	78	20	2	0	3	0	0
Y.7	0	6	0	13	81	0	0	0	0	0
Relig. Educ.:										
Y.1	0	53	7	3	0	0	0	0	2	0
Y.3	0	45	2	4	4	0	0	0	0	0
Y.5	0	0	0	7	10	13	0	23	3	3
Science:										
Y.1	0	37	9	29	8	0	0	0	3	0
Y.3	0	25	11	18	31	0	0	0	10	0
Y.5	0	2	0	19	71	0	0	0	3	0
Y.7	0	1	3	2	72	7	10	0	2	0

(b) History is marked by its consistent use of informative writing, together with a movement away from the abstractive level of report, and into that of the higher analogic, in the fifth year.

(c) Religious education shares with history and science a movement away from the abstractive level of report after the third year, but is differentiated from them by its lesser use of informative writing and by its moderate use of expressive, persuasive and poetic writing—features which it shares to some extent with English.

(d) Geography is marked by its consistent use of informative writing and in particular by its use of the generalized narrative and lower analogic levels of the abstractive scale in the first three age levels. However, there is an increase in the lower level of the analogic in the fifth year, coupled with a decline in generalized narrative and indications of a rise in higher level analogic in the seventh year.

(e) Science is marked by its consistent use of informative writing, together with the movement away from the abstractive level of report, and into that of the higher analogic, most prominently in the fifth year. Note too the increase in writing in the upper levels of the abstractive scale (speculative/tautologic) in the seventh year.

The table throws further light on some of the divergences which we noted above. The pattern of writing for geography, for example, while it shares much with science and history, is also distinguished from them in a number of small ways: in particular by its less prominent use of the report level of informative writing in the first two age groups and by the amount of writing allocated to a generalized narrative level. We should add, too, its early and consistent use of the lower level of the analogic, together with indications of movement to a higher level only in the seventh year.

There are also a number of other points. The use of persuasive writing in religious education appears from the tables to be to some extent an isolated incidence in the fifth year, though there is still weight to be given to the fact that it appears in that subject and not in some others. The use of persuasive writing in English, though varied through age levels, is more consistent.

To be noted too are the indications of writing at mixed levels of the abstractive scale in science—a reflection perhaps of the tendency in that subject to complete reports of an experiment by an analogic classification of the data as illustrative of general findings—and also the movement towards more theoretical scientific writing in the seventh year. Such divergences open perspectives which, with more data, it might be interesting to explore.

However, there is also confirmation for the broader pattern we have noted. Thus the proportion occupied by informative writing in history, geography and science is never less than 76% of the year subtotals, while one notes within that proportion the expected convergence on the higher level of the analogic in the fifth and seventh years.

By contrast, the use made of informative writing in English and religious education before the seventh year is much less marked and the proportions of writing in functions other than the informative correspondingly higher. Thus, even with its increase in the fifth year, the proportion of informative writing in English is still only 27%, and in the first two age groups of the sample it is considerably lower. In religious education the proportion actually diminishes after the first year. As for the other functions—there is a significant proportion of expressive writing in both subjects, continuing in English through to the seventh year; while poetic writing, appearing somewhat variably in the totals for religious education, is strongly, even dominantly, marked in those for English. In the seventh year the pattern changes, the proportion of informative writing within English rising from 27% to 69% and that of the analogic subdivision from 4% to 41%; while there is a corresponding decline in poetic writing. One notes too that speculative writing, which gains a small entry in English in the fifth year, is also increased. As a result of such changes, the pattern of writing in English becomes much more like that of the other curriculum subjects in the seventh year, though even then the proportions of writing in the expressive and poetic categories are still relatively higher.

All in all the pattern to be derived from consideration of the subtotals for function by curriculum subject at the four age levels of the sample confirms the concentration of writing into the analogic category across the range of subjects, but gives indication also of divergences within particular subjects and especially of a contrasting pattern for English and religious education in the first three age groups.

By way of conclusion of this section, the outlines of our findings with regard to function may be presented in summarized form.

Summary

The overall tendencies of the sample suggest the dominance of transactional writing, and, within that category, of the analogic level of the informative subdivision. Analysis of the subtotals in the four age groups represented confirms this pattern, revealing a developing increase in analogic writing which is substantially accelerated in the fifth and seventh years. But while there is evidence of development in the ability to cope in writing with higher levels of abstraction, at the same time the incidence of writing at a speculative or tautologic level is comparatively low. In addition the evidence of writing in functions other than the transactional is relatively slight. Expressive writing is minimally represented throughout the sample and the amount of poetic writing, while significant in the first three age groups, declines markedly with the seventh year. Moreover the writing in both these functions is virtually monopolized by religious education and English. Finally, analysis of the various totals by curriculum subjects suggests that, while there are a number of divergences within each subject, the major contrast is to be found between the pattern of writing in geography, history and science, and that in religious education and English.

10 The interrelation of audience and function

The previous chapters have reported our findings in respect of audience and function—dimensions elaborated in the light of an overall reflection on the need for a multi-dimensional approach to the study of development in writing. We may now turn from consideration of these findings separately to their conjunction, using as data for this the cross-tabulation of audience by function. Such data, approached primarily as proportions of the total sample or of its subtotals at the four age levels, allow a more powerful presentation of patterns which we have already looked at, sensitive to the way in which audience and function are interrelated as two dimensions defining the configuration of writing in our sample. At the same time we may derive insight of a more particular nature into the actual association of various audience and function categories: specifically into the environment within which the principal function categories, on the evidence of our sample, appear to be developed in school. The latter step may be helped by considering some of the totals in the cells of the audience-by-function tables as proportions of each of the two category sets in turn (see Tables 25 and 26 below). Inspection of the figures in Table 20 suggests that the principal configurations of writing in our sample may be itemized as follows:

(*a*) Transactional writing (principally informative) for the teacher as examiner (42·9%) and, within that, classificatory writing for the teacher as examiner (analogic 17·9%; low-level analogic 11·3%).

(*b*) In roughly equivalent proportions—(i) Transactional writing for the teacher–learner dialogue (14·3%); (ii) poetic writing for the teacher–learner dialogue (13·2%).

(*c*) Report writing, mixed between examining audience (4·9%) and the teacher–learner dialogue (6·1%).

(*d*) Expressive writing for the teacher–learner dialogue (3·7%) and for the teacher as trusted adult (1·1%).

In part what is observable in the table is a reflection in combination of what we have hitherto observed separately: the overall domination of the teacher audiences, and in particular of the 'pupil to examiner' category, on the one hand; and, on the other, of transactional writing and the analogic level

Table 20   Audience by function (percentages of total scripts)

	Record	Report	Gen. narrat.	Low analog.	Analog.	Spec.	Taut.	Conat.	Misc. inform.	Misc. trans.
Self	—	0·1	—	0·1	0·2	—	—	—	—	—
Trusted adult	—	—	—	—	0·1	—	—	—	—	—
Trusted adult/ teacher–learner	—	—	—	0·1	—	—	—	—	—	—
Teacher–learner	0·4	**4·9**	1·4	2·5	2·4	0·9	0·1	0·9	0·7	0·2
Teacher–learner/ examiner	0·2	1·0	0·4	0·7	0·8	0·1	—	—	0·1	—
Examiner	0·3	**6·1**	3·7	**11·3**	**17·9**	0·9	1·1	0·1	1·4	0·1
Partic. relat.	—	—	—	0·1	0·5	0·1	0·2	—	—	—
Writer to readers	—	—	0·1	—	0·1	0·3	0·3	0·1	—	—
Teacher–learner/ writer to readers	—	—	—	—	—	—	—	0·1	—	—
Miscellaneous	—	0·1	0·1	0·1	0·5	0·2	0·1	0·2	0·2	—
TOTAL	0·8	12·2	5·7	14·7	22·3	2·4	1·7	1·3	2·3	0·3

Notes:
   (i) Each subtotal is shown as a true percentage (to one decimal place) and not as the sum of the percentages that comprise it.

of the informative scale. Such tendencies are confirmed within the table and it may come as no surprise to us that the proportionately larger cells reflect their conjunction.

What is added to what we have already seen is a more focused sense of the way these patterns are interrelated. Approaching (for the sake of clarity) from the perspective of function, we may note that within the overall domination of transactional writing it is transactional writing for an examining audience which occupies considerably the largest proportion of the sample. Forty-three per cent of the writing of the sample was allocated here—a figure three times as great as, for example, the amount of transactional writing for the teacher–learner dialogue. The expressive and poetic functions play, as we have seen, a subordinate role and the pattern of writing in them differs from transactional writing by being much more closely associated with the teacher–learner dialogue—and expressive writing with the 'child to trusted adult' category as well. Expressive and poetic writing, taken together, occupy a proportion of approximately one quarter of the writing in the sample, of which four-fifths is for the teacher–learner dialogue. Marked though the association is, within the broad lines of the sample overall these proportions are subordinate to the place of transactional writing.

In fact, the number of scripts allocated to the analogic level of the informative scale, for 'pupil to examiner' alone, exceeds the grand totals of either the expressive or the poetic categories—a point which might, again, have

Total Trans.	Trans./express.	Express.	Express./poetic	Poetic	Immature	Pseudo-inform.	Cummy run	Misc.	Trans-lations	Total
0·3	—	—	—	0·1	—	—	—	—	—	0·4
0·1	0·1	**1·1**	0·1	0·3	0·1	0·1	—	0·1	0·1	1·7
0·1	0·1	0·3	0·1	0·2	0·1	—	—	—	—	0·7
14·3	0·9	**3·7**	1·8	**13·2**	2·4	0·4	1·2	0·2	—	38·0
3·2	0·1	0·1	—	0·2	0·1	0·2	0·1	—	—	3·9
42·9	0·1	0·2	0·1	0·9	0·1	2·9	1·1	0·4	0·9	49·4
0·7	—	—	0·1	0·2	—	0·1	—	—	—	1·1
0·7	—	0·1	—	1·1	—	—	—	—	—	1·8
0·1	—	—	—	1·1	—	—	—	—	—	1·1
1·4	—	0·1	—	0·4	0·1	—	—	0·1	0·1	2·0
63·6	1·1	5·4	2·1	17·5	2·7	3·6	2·4	0·7	1·0	

(ii) Figures in bold type denote major groupings for the row or column concerned.

been deduced from our separate consideration of function and from the over-all domination in the sample of informative writing for the teacher as examiner. Closer inspection of other subdivisions of the informative scale reveals the partially discrepant pattern of the report category, which is fairly strongly associated with the teacher–learner dialogue—in part this is a reflection, as we shall see, of the tendency for the writing of report to be most strongly marked in the lower age-ranges of the sample. We may note too that persuasive and speculative writing fall into something of the same pattern, though the figures are small.

The same data may also be approached from the perspective of audience. What is suggested from this perspective is the difference in the overall pat-terns for the 'pupil to examiner' and teacher–learner dialogue audiences—the former being much more closely associated with the informative writing in the sample and the latter, while associated in some measure with informative writing, more dispersed across the persuasive, expressive and poetic categories. However, even the totality of writing for the teacher–learner dialogue occupies a considerably smaller proportion of the total sample than that taken by trans-actional writing for an examining audience.

The pattern year by year

Turning now to the patterns of audience by function at the different age levels, the detail offered by Tables 21–4 may be incorporated. Inspection of

Table 21   Audience by function by year: first year (percentages of year totals)

	Record	Report	Gen. narrat.	Low analog.	Analog.	Spec.	Taut.	Conat.	Misc. inform.	Misc. trans.
Trusted adult	—	—	—	—	—	—	—	—	—	—
Trusted adult/ teacher–learner	—	—	—	0·2	—	—	—	—	—	—
Teacher–learner	1·0	8·5	3·0	3·5	0·5	—	—	0·2	0·3	0·2
Teacher–learner/ examiner	—	1·9	0·9	1·2	0·2	—	—	—	—	—
Examiner	0·5	11·0	5·6	11·8	1·4	—	—	—	1·0	0·2
Partic. relat.	—	—	—	—	—	—	—	—	—	—
Writer to readers	—	—	—	—	—	—	—	—	—	—
Teacher–learner writer to readers	—	—	—	—	—	—	—	—	—	—
Miscellaneous	—	0·3	0·2	—	—	—	—	—	—	—
TOTAL	1·6	21·7	9·6	16·7	2·1	—	—	0·2	1·4	0·3

Table 22   Audience by function by year: third year (percentages of year totals)

	Record	Report	Gen. narrat.	Low analog.	Analog.	Spec.	Taut.	Conat.	Misc. inform.	Misc. trans.
Trusted adult	—	—	—	—	0·2	—	—	—	—	—
Trusted adult/ teacher–learner	—	—	—	—	—	—	—	—	—	—
Teacher–learner	0·2	6·7	1·3	2·3	1·3	—	0·2	1·0	0·2	—
Teacher–learner/ examiner	0·6	1·5	0·4	0·8	0·4	—	—	—	0·2	—
Examiner	—	8·4	5·7	13·6	9·0	—	1·1	—	1·9	—
Partic. relat.	—	—	—	—	—	—	—	—	—	—
Writer to readers	—	—	—	—	—	—	—	—	—	—
Teacher–learner/ writer to readers	—	—	—	—	—	—	—	—	—	—
Miscellaneous	—	—	—	—	—	—	—	0·2	—	—
TOTAL	0·8	16·7	7·5	16·7	10·9	—	1·3	1·1	2·3	—

Total trans.	Trans./express.	Express.	Express./poetic	Poetic	Immature	Pseudo-inform.	Dummy run	Misc.	Trans-lation	Total
—	—	1·2	—	—	0·2	0·2	—	0·2	—	1·7
0·2	—	—	—	0·2	0·2	—	—	—	—	0·5
17·2	0·9	4·9	2·8	14·8	7·1	1·0	2·3	—	—	51·0
4·2	0·2	0·2	—	0·3	0·2	0·5	0·2	—	—	5·7
31·5	—	0·2	—	0·3	0·2	6·6	0·3	0·3	—	39·5
—	—	—	—	0·2	—	—	—	—	—	0·2
—	—	—	—	0·2	—	—	—	—	—	0·2
—	—	—	—	0·3	—	—	—	—	—	0·3
0·5	—	—	—	0·2	0·2	—	—	—	—	0·9
53·6	1·0	6·4	2·8	16·5	8·0	8·3	2·8	0·5	—	

Total trans.	Trans./express.	Express.	Express./poetic	Poetic	Immature	Pseudo-inform.	Dummy run	Misc.	Trans-lation	Total
0·2	—	1·3	0·2	0·2	—	—	—	—	0·2	2·1
—	—	0·4	0·2	0·4	—	—	—	—	—	1·0
13·2	1·5	4·6	1·9	19·5	1·1	0·4	1·9	0·4	—	44·6
3·8	0·2	—	—	0·4	—	0·2	—	—	—	4·6
39·8	—	0·2	0·2	0·8	0·2	3·3	0·8	0·4	0·2	45·8
—	—	—	0·2	0·2	—	—	—	—	—	0·4
—	—	—	—	0·4	—	—	—	—	—	0·4
—	—	—	—	1·0	—	—	—	—	—	1·0
0·2	—	—	—	—	—	—	—	—	—	0·2
57·3	1·7	6·5	2·7	22·8	1·3	3·8	2·7	0·8	0·4	

Table 23   Audience by function by year: fifth year (percentages of year totals)

	Record	Report	Gen. narrat.	Low analog.	Analog.	Spec.	Taut.	Conat.	Misc. inform.	Misc. trans.
Trusted adult	—	—	—	—	—	—	—	—	—	—
Trusted adult/ teacher–learner	—	—	—	—	—	—	—	—	—	—
Teacher–learner	—	2·3	0·7	2·6	2·3	1·9	—	1·4	1·4	0·2
Teacher–learner/ examiner	—	—	0·2	0·2	0·5	—	—	—	—	—
Examiner	0·2	1·6	1·9	14·9	25·4	0·7	—	0·2	0·7	—
Partic. relat.	—	—	—	0·2	0·2	—	—	—	—	—
Writer to readers	—	—	0·2	—	—	0·2	—	—	—	—
Teacher–learner/ writer to readers	—	—	—	—	—	—	—	0·2	—	—
Miscellaneous	—	—	0·2	0·5	—	0·2	—	0·2	0·5	—
TOTAL	0·2	4·0	3·3	18·4	28·4	3·0	—	2·1	2·6	0·2

Table 24   Audience by function by year: seventh year (percentages of year totals)

	Record	Report	Gen. narrat.	Low analog.	Analog.	Spec.	Taut.	Conat.	Misc. inform.	Misc. trans.
Self	—	0·4	—	0·2	0·7	—	—	—	—	—
Trusted adult	—	—	—	—	—	—	—	—	—	—
Trusted adult/ teacher–learner	—	—	—	—	—	—	—	—	—	—
Teacher–learner	—	0·7	—	1·6	6·0	2·2	0·2	1·1	0·9	0·4
Teacher–learner/ examiner	—	—	—	0·2	2·4	0·4	—	—	0·2	—
Examiner	0·2	1·6	0·9	4·5	42·3	3·3	3·6	0·2	1·8	—
Partic. relat.	—	—	—	—	1·8	0·2	0·7	—	—	—
Writer to readers	—	—	—	—	0·2	0·9	1·1	0·4	—	—
Teacher–learner/ writer to readers	—	—	—	—	—	—	—	—	—	—
Miscellaneous	—	—	—	—	2·0	0·7	0·4	0·2	0·2	—
TOTAL	0·2	2·7	0·9	6·5	55·5	7·8	6·0	2·0	3·1	0·4

Total trans.	Trans./express.	Express.	Express./poetic	Poetic	Immature	Pseudo-inform.	Dummy run	Misc.	Translation	Total
—	0·2	1·4	—	0·2	—	—	—	—	—	1·9
—	—	0·5	—	0·2	—	—	—	—	—	0·7
12·8	0·2	3·0	1·2	15·4	—	—	0·2	0·2	—	33·1
0·9	—	—	—	—	—	—	0·2	—	—	1·2
45·7	0·2	—	—	2·1	—	0·5	2·8	0·5	2·6	54·3
0·5	—	—	—	0·2	—	0·2	—	—	—	0·9
0·5	—	—	—	2·8	—	—	—	—	—	3·3
0·2	—	—	—	1·9	—	—	—	—	—	2·1
1·6	—	—	—	0·9	—	—	—	—	—	2·6
62·2	0·7	4·9	1·2	23·8	—	0·7	3·3	0·7	2·6	

Total trans.	Trans./express.	Express.	Express./poetic	Poetic	Immature	Pseudo-inform.	Dummy run	Misc.	Translation	Total
1·3	—	—	—	0·4	—	—	—	—	—	1·8
—	—	0·2	—	0·7	—	—	—	—	—	0·9
—	0·2	0·2	—	—	—	—	—	—	—	0·4
13·1	0·7	2·0	0·9	1·6	—	—	—	0·2	—	18·5
3·3	—	—	—	—	—	—	—	—	—	3·3
58·4	—	0·2	—	0·4	—	—	0·7	0·2	1·3	61·5
2·7	—	—	0·2	0·2	—	—	—	—	—	3·1
2·7	—	0·2	—	1·3	—	—	—	—	—	4·2
—	—	—	—	1·3	—	—	—	—	—	1·3
3·6	—	0·4	—	0·4	—	—	—	0·2	0·2	4·9
85·1	0·9	3·3	1·3	6·5	—	—	0·7	0·7	1·6	

these figures suggests that:

(a) The proportion of transactional writing associated with the teacher–learner dialogue remains roughly consistent after the first year.
(b) The proportion of transactional writing associated with an examining audience increases substantially in each age level of the sample.
(c) The proportion of expressive writing for the teacher–learner dialogue remains steady but low through the first two age levels of the sample, declining somewhat in the fifth and seventh years.
(d) The pattern of poetic writing is relatively complex—predominantly for the teacher–learner dialogue, and increasing that proportion in the third year; branching out towards writing for an unknown public audience in the fifth, and dropping sharply in the seventh.
(e) There is a striking convergence of the writing in the sample into the analogic category for an examining audience in the seventh year.

From the perspective of the principal functions we may note again the increasing domination of the transactional function in its association with the teacher as examiner. The most striking feature of this—indeed perhaps of these tables as a whole—is the pattern which has been reached by the seventh year. In that year, as will be seen from the table, about 85% of the writing was judged as transactional, over 58% as transactional for an examining audience; and no less than about 42% of the writing was allocated to one cell alone—analogic writing for the teacher as examiner. As for the other functions —expressive writing, having maintained a steady though low proportion of the sample, in conjunction with the teacher–learner dialogue, in the first two age levels, declines somewhat in the fifth and seventh years. Poetic writing, though, is subject to rather greater change: we may note in particular the tendency to move towards writing for an unknown public audience in the fifth year, prior to the demise of the poetic category in the seventh.

A number of further points are suggested in relation to the subdivisions of the informative scale. We may confirm that the pattern of report, for example, which occupies a substantial proportion of the writing in the first two age levels of the sample, is marked by its more or less equal association both with writing for the teacher as examiner and with the teacher–learner dialogue. Also, speculative writing shares something of this pattern, being associated fairly strongly in its rise in the fifth year with the teacher–learner dialogue and preserving something of this association, though to a less marked extent, in the seventh year.

Approaching the same data from the perspective of audience, a number of interesting points emerge. The overall pattern, as we have already seen, is marked by the substantial increase of writing for the teacher as examiner, together with some move towards writing for a more public audience in the fifth and seventh years. The converse of this is the decline, from the first year onwards, of writing for the teacher–learner dialogue. It may be noted though that the proportion of transactional writing for the teacher–learner dialogue, while declining slightly after the first year, remains constant through-out the remaining age levels of the sample. The implications of this have their bearing on the interpretation of the overall decline in writing for the teacher–learner dialogue, which, as we have noted, is simply the product of the transfer of transactional scripts to the 'pupil to examiner' category between the first and third years. As for the later years of the sample—the decline in the fifth year is substantially the product of the movement of poetic scripts towards writing for an unknown public audience; while the striking decline in the seventh is very largely bound up with the sharp drop in poetic writing. Similarly the rise in writing for the teacher as examiner is more the product of a switch of other non-transactional kinds of writing into the transactional and 'pupil to examiner' categories than of a transfer of scripts within transactional writing itself. Such a consideration reminds us that the growing concentration of the sample is a concentration both of audience and function.

At its most general, an approach from the perspective of audience to the figures of audience by function suggests that we may see two broad patterns at work in the sample. There is an area of relative stability marked by the association of informative writing with an examining audience: such writing already occupies 31·5% of the writing in the first year. Alongside this there is an area of relative openness marked by the association of the teacher–learner dialogue, which in the first year occupies 51% of the total sample, with the whole range of functions. After the first year, the weight of the writing for the teacher as examiner shifts towards the analogic level of the informative scale and the range of writing in other functions (initially in association with the teacher–learner dialogue) converges into the 'pupil to examiner' pattern.

The reciprocity of audience and function

Further insight may be gained into the specific association of certain function and audience categories by treating the totals in the cells of the audience-by-function tables not merely as proportions of the total sample and its subtotals, but as reciprocal proportions of the two cross-tabulated variables. Such an interpretation allows us to formulate with more precision the degree of association between any particular category or range of categories of audience and any particular category or range of categories of function—offering in parti-cular some idea of the environments within which the principal function categories, on the evidence of the sample, appear to be developed in school. While it may be assumed that any association between categories reflects some sort of interaction between them, we may envisage the possibility that some relationships are dependent ones such as to offer guidance into the probable environments of certain categories of function.

The pattern of relations to be derived from the sample overall is given in Tables 25 and 26. Table 25 presents the scripts in each cell as column percentages—that is to say as proportions of categories of audience in relation to categories of function. Table 26 presents the same totals as row percentages—that is to say as proportions of categories of function. The notes on the tables given below follow a similar pattern.

Inspection of these figures suggests the following:

Audience (see Table 25)
   (*a*) A strong association of the 'child to trusted adult' audience with expressive writing and to a lesser extent with poetic writing—whereas no such association with transactional writing is evident.
   (*b*) Some association of the teacher–learner dialogue with all categories of function (with the sole exception of the tautological level of the informative function). In addition the following points may be noted:
     (i) The teacher–learner dialogue is associated more or less equally with transactional categories (taken together) and with poetic writing.
     (ii) As we shall note later, it is much less closely related to transactional writing than is the audience category 'pupil to examiner'.
     (iii) Though it shows some degree of association with expressive writing this is much less marked than the association of expressive writing with 'child to trusted adult'.
   (*c*) The overriding association of 'pupil to examiner' with transactional writing, lack of evident association with expressive writing and minimally evident association with poetic writing.
   (*d*) The strong association of the audience category 'pupil to teacher, particular relationship' with transactional writing and in particular with the analogic and tautologic levels of the informative; and some association with poetic writing.
   (*e*) The overriding association of the audience category 'writer to his readers' with poetic writing.

Function (see Table 26)
   (*a*) The strong association of all informative categories (taken together) with the 'pupil to examiner' audience, and to a lesser extent with the teacher–learner dialogue; but not with the audience categories 'child to trusted adult' or 'writer to his readers'.
   (*b*) The increasing association of informative writing with the 'pupil to examiner' audience as the level of abstraction increases, subject to two qualifications:
     (i) There is a minority of theoretical scripts in the 'writer to his readers' category;

Table 25 Audience by function: column percentages (audience)*

	Trusted adult & trusted adult/ teacher–learner (n=46)	Teacher–learner (n=751)	Teacher–learner/ examiner (n=77)	Examiner (n=975)	Partic. rel. (n=21)	Teacher–learner/ writer to readers & writer to readers (n=58)
Record	—	1	4	1	—	—
Report	—	13	25	12	—	—
Generalized narrative	—	4	10	8	—	—
Low-level analogic	—	7	17	23	—	—
Analogic	—	6	21	36	43	—
Speculative	—	2	—	2	—	9
Tautologic	—	—	—	2	14	9
Persuasive	—	3	—	—	—	5
Miscellaneous informative	—	2	—	3	—	—
TOTAL TRANSACTIONAL	—	38	77	87	57	23
Expressive	57	10	5	—	—	—
Poetic	20	35	—	2	19	72
Immature	—	6	—	—	—	—
Pseudo-informative	—	1	5	6	—	—
Dummy run	—	3	—	2	—	—
Transactional/expressive	—	2	—	—	—	—
Expressive/poetic	—	5	—	—	—	—

* Where column total is twenty scripts or more and cell entry is three or more scripts. Percentages to nearest whole number.

Table 26 Audience by function: row percentages (function)*

	Trusted adult & trusted adult/ teacher–learner	Teacher– learner	Teacher– learner/ examiner	Examiner	Partic. rel.	Teacher–learner/ writer to readers & writer to readers	n
Record	—	47	20	33	—	—	15
Report	—	40	8	50	—	—	241
Generalized narrative	—	24	7	66	—	—	112
Low-level analogic	—	17	5	77	—	—	291
Analogic	—	11	4	81	2	—	440
Speculative	—	38	—	38	—	10	48
Tautologic	—	—	—	65	9	15	34
Persuasive	—	70	—	10	—	10	30
Miscellaneous informative	—	29	—	60	—	—	45
TOTAL TRANSACTIONAL	—	23	5	67	1	1	1256
Expressive	24	69	—	3	—	—	107
Poetic	3	75	1	5	1	12	345
Immature	—	89	—	—	—	—	53
Pseudo-informative	—	11	6	80	—	—	71
Dummy run	—	51	—	45	—	—	47
Total 'additional categories'†	2	46	4	47	—	—	171
Transactional/expressive	—	77	—	—	—	—	22
Expressive/poetic	—	85	—	—	—	—	41

* Where row total is fifteen scripts or more and cell entry is three or more. Percentages to nearest whole number.
† Comprising immature, pseudo-informative and dummy run.

(ii) speculative writing is exceptional in being equally strongly associated both with the teacher–learner dialogue and with the 'pupil to examiner' category.

(c) Conversely to (b): the increasing association of informative writing with the teacher–learner dialogue as the level of abstraction *decreases*.

(d) Association of persuasive writing with the teacher–learner dialogue; and to a lesser extent with 'pupil to examiner' and 'writer to his readers'.

(e) The association of expressive writing with the teacher–learner dialogue and to a lesser extent with 'child to trusted adult'.

(f) The strong association of poetic writing with the teacher–learner dialogue and to a lesser extent with writing for an unknown public audience.

By way of simplifying the scattered observations above, we may group the various associations in terms of the principal function categories. From this perspective we are concerned with three main sets of associations:

[handwritten note: Associations devised from data]

(a) Transactional writing with the following audiences: 'pupil to examiner', the teacher–learner dialogue, 'pupil to teacher, particular relationship', 'writer to his readers';

(b) Expressive writing with the following audiences: the teacher–learner dialogue and 'child to trusted adult';

(c) Poetic writing with the following audiences: the teacher–learner dialogue, 'writer to his readers', 'pupil to teacher, particular relationship', 'child to trusted adult'.

We may notice, further, about these sets that they are differentiated both by the particular categories which are involved (or not involved) and by the differing degrees of involvement, where categories overlap. Transactional writing, for example, is associated both with an examining audience and with the teacher–learner dialogue, but much less closely with the latter than either expressive or poetic writing. We shall need to pay some attention too to the reciprocity of the relations between any two categories of audience and function. It is significant for example that the trusted adult audience is associated most closely with expressive writing; but at the same time expressive writing itself is more closely associated with the teacher–learner dialogue than with any other audience.

In commenting on such associations it may also be helpful to put them within the wider picture of the sample as a whole. As we have seen in Chapter 9 transactional writing forms the largest proportion of writing in the sample, steadily increasing its share of the total from 54% to 84% between the first and fourth age level of the sample, and forming the bulk of writing in history, geography and science (though a lesser proportion of the work in religious education and English before the seventh year). As will be seen from Table 26, the majority of such writing is for an examining audience, and in this is unlike the corresponding pattern for expressive or poetic writing. Thus 67% of transactional writing was judged to be for an examining audience—a proportion, as we have seen, of nearly 42% of the total sample. By contrast there was hardly any evidence of association between expressive writing and an examining audience; and only 5% of poetic writing was judged to be of this kind.

Association, then, with an examining audience may be described as a distinguishing feature of the transactional writing in our sample, though it seems unlikely that such a relationship could be described as a dependent one. Support is lent to this last assumption by the proportions of transactional scripts associated with the teacher–learner dialogue, with 'pupil to teacher, particular relationship', and with writing for a public audience. Scripts of this kind—associated with audiences other than the teacher as examiner—form only a quarter of the transactional writing in the sample, but a substantial proportion nevertheless of the writing in the related audience categories. In addition, as we have seen, there is some evidence of closer association of transactional writing with the teacher–learner dialogue in the early years of the sample and at the lower levels of abstraction. Neither of these points is compatible with positing any kind of dependent relationship between transactional writing and examining audience; and indeed it seems no more than common sense to see that this is unlikely to be the case. In fact, if we give weight to the increase of association as the age levels of the sample rise and, further, to the part played by the different patterns of use in curriculum subjects, it seems likely that emphasis is more properly placed on the demands made on the pupil's writing by the curriculum and differing educational practice—these determining both an examining audience and transactional writing alike.

It seems likely that some of the broader questions and implications of our findings may turn on the central contrast marked in our sample between transactional writing on the one hand and, on the other, expressive and poetic writing. Neither expressive nor poetic writing command anything like the proportion of the sample of transactional writing, though the number of poetic scripts is substantial before the seventh year; also, the writing in these categories is in both cases virtually monopolized by English and religious education—though not, it should be emphasized, to the exclusion of transactional writing in these subjects. The point to underline though is the discernibly different pattern of audience underlying the writing in these functions. For where association with an examining audience might be described as being a distinguishing feature of the transactional writing in the sample, the same role is broadly occupied for expressive and poetic writing by the teacher–learner dialogue. And here it seems more likely that we may legitimately hypothesize, in a weak sense at any rate, some sort of dependent relationship. To put the matter merely negatively, it seems theoretically unlikely that either expressive or poetic writing would develop in association with an examining audience; and the absence of such an association may be counted perhaps as some confirmation for the presuppositions of the function model in this respect. It seems possible too that the fact that there is little evidence of, in particular, expressive writing in the sample may be connected with the relatively low incidence of the teacher–learner dialogue as an audience —a point which, taking into consideration the interrelation of function and audience, is further supported by the cumulative convergence of the sample into the analogic category in the seventh year. None of this, however, amounts to saying more than that there is some support in the findings for the presupposition that certain sorts of writing demand certain sorts of environment in which to flourish.

We should add that the patterns of expressive and poetic writing, while sharing the association with the teacher–learner dialogue, differ as regards association with the categories of 'child to trusted adult' and 'writer to his readers' (public audience). While only a relatively small proportion of expressive writing is linked with the 'child to trusted adult' audience, the total is nevertheless a substantial proportion of the scripts in that audience category, and some account too may be taken of the fact that no other category of function is associated as closely. A separate link is marked in the sample between poetic writing and 'writer to his readers'—principally, as we have seen, a development of the fifth year and constituting 72% of the writing allocated to the 'writer to his readers' category. For the same sort of reasons as given earlier it seems unlikely that the link between poetic writing and 'writer to his readers' is a dependent one; but it is one which might have been expected. The onus perhaps is more to explain why, with a considerably higher proportion of scripts, such an association should, on the evidence of the sample, be so much less marked in transactional writing. If we give weight, though, to the divergence between expressive and poetic writing (as well as to what the two functions share)—to the unique association, that is, between expressive writing and the 'child to trusted adult' audience on the one hand, and on the other to the signs of movement in poetic writing out towards an unknown public audience—it seems likely that we may perceive some further confirmation for the presuppositions of the function model in this respect. Our overall hypothesis of development as a process of differentiation is perhaps neither established nor falsified by the particular dominant pattern of convergence marked in the sample; on the other hand, the different pattern of expressive and poetic writing is suggestive of something of that movement, from writing close to the self to more finely differentiated purposes and wider audiences, which underlies the hypotheses of our research.

Summary

Inspection of the distributions of audience by function at its most general suggests in the sample an area of relative stability marked by the association of transactional writing (principally informative) with writing for the teacher as examiner and an area of relative openness marked by the association of the teacher–learner dialogue with a range of functions—a pattern established from the first year. From the perspective of change and development in the sample, inspection of the subtotals at the four age levels suggests a movement of writing for an examining audience into the analogic level of the informative scale predominantly, and a wider convergence of other non-transactional kinds of writing into this pattern. From the perspective of the association of certain audience and function categories, a central contrast is also to be made between transactional writing on the one hand and, on the other, expressive and poetic writing. On the evidence of the sample, informative writing is largely developed in school in the environment of the teacher as examiner, while expressive and poetic writing are most closely associated with the teacher–learner dialogue. The latter association, it may be suggested, is to some extent a dependent one and—together with the divergence (also marked) in expressive and poetic writing towards the categories of 'child to trusted adult' and 'writer to his readers' respectively—may afford some confirmation of our research hypothesis that development in writing ability is a process of dissociation, or progressive differentiation.

11 Some implications

Standing back from it all, how much are we the wiser? We have spent time looking at a broader range of the writings produced in secondary schools than we have ever been able to do before, and we have studied them with one eye constantly on the processes likely to have been operating to produce them. Though we have to remind ourselves repeatedly that the sample of writing was too small and too unrepresentative to allow us to generalize confidently about 'what goes on in schools', nevertheless we are in a distinctly better position to speculate on that question than we were before we began. Even within the range of the work of five hundred pupils, we have found, for example, differences by types of school which must be in some measure characteristic of organizational variations in the system as a whole.

Moreover, if we are not in the position to predict from our findings the kinds of writing activity likely to be found in a given school, or a given school situation, what we have done is to devise a method of studying what goes on which might with advantage be directly applied to such a school to find out. It is, of course, this that we set out to do. Nevertheless, to demonstrate that the method is worth using again, we need to show that in using it on our sample we have found out the sort of thing we wanted to know. This is for us no matter of idle speculation since, while the report was being produced, we were taking our inquiry two stages further: first in the four-year follow-up study, and secondly in the development project which is still in operation.

First, then, are the things we can say about writing activity in the schools *questions* of our sample of any educational significance? Secondly, where our evidence proves inconclusive, can we anticipate that the follow-up study or the development project will supply any of the answers? And finally (always assuming that we escape the verdict, 'back to square one!') where do we go from here?

Writing for a public audience

Having in the early stages of the research considered a range of possible relationships between a writer and his reader, and gradually worked down to those that seemed most likely to operate in school (rejecting for example the

Belief —

role of 'teacher as enemy' only half-frivolously suggested), and then having arrived at operational definitions of ten categories for sense of audience, it was of course something of an anticlimax to find that two of those ten accommodated 92% of the scripts. We emerge, none the less, holding on to the belief that work in school ought to equip a writer to choose his own target audience and, eventually, to be able, when the occasion arises, to write as someone with something to say to the world in general. And we believe many more children would develop the ability if they had more opportunities and a stronger incentive. The trickle of scripts in category 4 (writing for a public audience) in our sample begins in the first year, increases rapidly in the fifth year and is sustained in the seventh. We might add that our everyday experience of reading the printed word would suggest that what is at issue here is more a matter of how the writer regards himself than it is one of ability (beyond a certain minimum level).

We can derive some evidence from the sample to suggest that writing for a public audience develops out of writing in a teaching rather than a testing situation. Of the split category verdicts involving audience category 4, twenty were paired with the teacher–learner dialogue and only seven with 'pupil to examiner'; pursuing the matter of context further, if we take judgements rather than verdicts, we have category 4 associated twice with 'child to trusted adult', seven times with 'pupil to teacher, particular relationship' and sixty-six times with the teacher–learner dialogue—a total of seventy-five, as against seventeen times with 'pupil to examiner'.

It is interesting to note the following characteristics of the sixty-seven scripts allocated either to the public audience category or to a split category including it:

(a) Fifty-two were produced for work in English.
(b) Forty-eight were in function category 3 (poetic)—one by a fifth-year boy for work in religious education, the rest in English.
(c) Of the remaining nineteen (two in the fifth year and the rest in the seventh), six were in function category 1.1.7 (tautologic), five in function category 1.1.6 (speculative), and three in function category 1.2.2 (persuasive).

Two problems emerge: why is it that up to the fifth year writing for a public audience is virtually restricted to the poetic (twenty-two out of thirty-five scripts)? And why in the seventh year, when transactional writing, mainly in the speculative and tautological categories, shows a move into the public audience category (sixteen scripts), does poetic writing for a public audience show a marked decline (from twenty-two scripts to twelve)?

To take the second question first: the context of school work brings about, as we have shown, a considerable decline in poetic writing as a whole in the seventh year. It seems likely that poetic writing, which in the earlier years flourished in a relationship we have described as a teacher–learner dialogue, is maintained in the fifth year because it is recognized as of value as an examinable product; but that, the way our examinations are at present set up, it is no longer examinable at A level. We shall be looking more generally in a later section at the possible effects of examinations on the writing that goes on at school.

The first problem is a more interesting one. Why should poetic writing move into a public audience so substantially before transactional writing even begins to do so? Putting the question rather differently, why is it that language in the role of participant (where A tells B) is less likely to supersede particular intercommunication than is writing in the role of spectator (where A *shares experience*—real or imagined—with B)? To state the problem that way is perhaps to begin to solve it. There can be no reason for sharing an experience in words beyond the satisfaction derived by both writer and reader in the utterance. This means that the writer secures an audience by *interesting* him. (The role of the teacher in the teacher–learner dialogue so far as spectator-role writing is concerned is first and foremost to be interested in the writer and what he writes: without that relationship such writing is inevitably a 'dummy run' and a particularly pointless one.)

The reader of a piece of writing in the participant role, however, does not have to be interested in what he reads—as every schoolboy knows. The tie between writer and reader is one of utility: we genuinely inform when we tell somebody something we want him to know, or have reason to believe he wants to know. Now there are very few occasions indeed when information is required of a school child by a multiple unknown readership. If he is to break through to a public audience, therefore, the kind of wares he must offer cannot be those specific to particular and limited transactions: he must, in other words, be able to *interest* an audience of strangers—and this means that he must offer his own interpretations of facts or events, his speculations, his ideas. This indeed is what we find to be the case in the sample—eleven out of the nineteen transactional pieces for a public audience were work in the speculative and tautologic function categories by seventh-year students.

Development in spectator-role writing—the move from expressive to poetic—constitutes in fact an increasing refinement of the verbal object, a heightening of the order imposed upon words and what they portray. Such an ordering makes it at one and the same time more satisfying to the writer and of greater potential appeal to an unknown reader. In effect, development in spectator-role writing is from the earliest stages a move in the direction of a public audience.

The increase of ability to meet the demands of participant language tasks—the move from expressive to transactional in our model—has not the same direct association with the move to a public audience. True, its first steps are to become less context-bound, more explicit—better able to communicate effectively with a reader who does not share the writer's context. But, at the other end of the scale, highly developed transactional writing may be addressed to a particular and restricted readership: the reader is a party to some transaction, and if the transaction is effectively completed nothing more is necessarily demanded in the way of capturing his interest as a reader or appealing to other readers. For transactional writing to be addressed to a public audience requires, then, a particular kind of transaction—one that can hope to woo an unintending audience into becoming a party to it.

That school children should share their experiences ever more widely by gradual stages to the point where they write in the poetic for a public audience is something we should expect to happen before they are ready to offer their speculations, interpretations or opinions to strangers. What we do not know is how far the one process can pave the way for the other.

Teaching and testing

But what of the many? Nine-tenths of the scripts were put in the audience categories of the teacher–learner dialogue and 'pupil to examiner', and, as we have seen, the interplay of these two categories forms the main plot in our story so far as sense of audience is concerned. 'Pupil to examiner' claimed nearly 49% of the scripts, teacher–learner dialogue, nearly 39%.

It is important to remind ourselves that the sense of audience categories were defined in terms of _relationships_. Where the identity of the reader remains the same, as may be the case with the teacher categories (2.1 to 2.4), it is the relationship alone that varies. The writer has, as it were, to re-define himself in a way complementary to the role he assigns to the teacher as reader on any given occasion. He does this in accordance with expectations drawn from experience, and to that experience both the writer's behaviour and the teacher's have contributed. We have suggested that in this way two sets of expectations are set up side by side in the pupil's school work, and sometimes, no doubt, side by side within the same subject with the same teacher. The two sets of expectations represent two situations, one 'closed', the other 'open'.

Where one or the other of these is consistently operated in a subject, they are likely, we suggest, to reflect two different conceptions of the learning process; and no doubt differences in the nature of subjects will influence the construction a teacher places on the learning process. Polarizing the distinction, we should say that the closed view sees teaching as instruction, while the open view sees learning as exploration and discovery. Methodologies appropriate to the two views would clearly have divergent implications for the teacher's role and hence for teacher–pupil relationships.

But the plot in our story is more complicated than that. We have suggested, from the evidence of our findings, that teachers who have set up the open situation in the early years of the secondary school may switch to a closed situation in the fifth year and maintain it through to the seventh. We are reminded that, when a team of educational experts from the USA visited the English departments of selected schools in this country in 1967, one of the major conclusions they reported[1] was to the effect that widespread autonomy on the part of teachers led to an interesting diversity of practice in the earlier years of the secondary school, but that this yielded quite sharply some time during or after the fourth year to the demands of the public examinations.

The evidence from our sample, broadly viewed, might be summarized as follows. Taking a baseline in the first year we find that at this point the two patterns, the open and the closed, are present in roughly equal proportions. There is a relatively open pattern, concentrated on the teacher–learner dialogue, across the range of the function categories, and involving work in English, religious education and some history. By the fifth year some (not all) of the transactional writing has disappeared from this open pattern and, within it, the poetic writing shows some tendency to move into a public audience. In the seventh year, the open pattern declines sharply. Alongside this there is, from the first year upwards, a relatively closed pattern, concentrated on the 'pupil to examiner' audience, confined to transactional writing, and involving work in science, geography and some history. It is this pattern that in the seventh year assimilates the work in other subjects and so presents a decisive change in the total picture.

From years one to five the chief movements seem to be (*a*) from report to analogic within the transactional, and (*b*) the concentration of most transactional writing into the 'pupil to examiner' audience. Then in the seventh year, while there is some extension into the higher transactional categories (speculative and tautologic), the landslide is into the analogic, and principally at the expense of writing in the poetic. This pattern, it seems to us, is most consistent with an interpretation that sees the mounting effect of examination demands as dominant.

For the research team, having in mind the expectations we brought to the task, it is ironic that we have been able to sketch in these main movements without any reference at all to expressive writing. But this is a point that we shall consider directly in a following section.

We do not for a moment suppose that the relationships we have ascribed to the writings in respect of audience categories represent the relationships existing in fact between the writers and their teachers. We can well imagine that many of the scripts we have classified 'pupil to examiner' have in reality been written for a shadowy figure of an 'external examiner' whom teachers and pupils have conspired together to conjure up. We can well imagine that the practical activities associated with work in science and geography, for example, may provide ample opportunity for a teacher–learner dialogue at the spoken level, and that such talk forms the basis upon which relationships are maintained. It seems to us, nevertheless, that the relationships embodied in the written tasks should not in such cases run counter to those holding more generally, and that when they do a vital educational function for the writing is neglected.

What study we have made over these years of the processes involved in writing—a study represented above in Chapter 2—has convinced us that there is more to it, and more to be gained from it, than can be expected to take place at the drop of an invigilator's hat.

We have suggested in Chapter 8 that some of the patterns of writing we have seen may bear a very indirect relation to teachers' intentions: that the role a writer takes up may reflect a 'drift' that has multiple causes in the school situation. Let us make a similar point in more general terms here: we do not suppose that these patterns of function and audience in the writing in our sample were *planned*. What we do believe, however, is that a greater general awareness of the potential roles of language in school, with a clearer notion of what actually goes on, might have led to the better management of resources of time and effort.

Learning and the learner

We spent many hours reading scripts, and those hours were not without their moments. It was at the first of our Saturday briefing meetings that the following came to light—written by one of the first-year girls in the sample:

It is quite easy to make oxygen if you have the right equipment necessary. You will need a test tube (a large one), a stand with some acid in it. You will need also a Bunston burner, of course you must not forget a glass tank too. A thin test tube should fix neatly in its place. When you have done that fill the glass tank and put the curved end upwards. Put the glass tank on the table and fill with water. Very soon you will find that you have made oxygen and glad of it.

We wondered whether the girl's science teacher was glad she was glad of it. We wondered also whether this was the sort of thing that science teachers were afraid of, the reason why they fought shy of the kind of writing in which a learner directly documents experience as he feels its first impact; not at this stage working upon it to sort out what belongs to the world experienced and what to the individual who experiences. Surely, the moment would come when the writer of this piece could learn without difficulty that it is one thing to describe an experiment (for the purpose of repeating it if she wanted to, or for the sake of someone else who wanted to try), and another thing to describe how she felt about it when first she performed it. Meanwhile, her being glad about it, and prepared to say so, augurs well, one might suppose, for the expenditure of such effort as she might need to make her description more accurate, more informative, and so more useful.

It will by now be perfectly clear that we were disappointed to find so little writing in function category 2, the expressive, in our sample. From 6% in the first year its share dwindled steadily to 4% in the seventh year; what there was of it was virtually shared between two subjects, English and religious education. Our disappointment arises from our belief that expressive writing, whether in participant or spectator role, may be at any stage the kind of writing best adapted to exploration and discovery. It is language that externalizes our first stages in tackling a problem or coming to grips with an experience. Moreover, it represents, we believe, the move into writing most likely to preserve a vital link with the spoken mode in which up to this point all a child's linguistic resources have been gathered and stored.

As we said in Chapter 3 above, our initial proposal included the hypothesis that the writing development we were setting out to explore would prove to be a process of *dissociation*, a process of progressive differentiation, of learning by dividing. When we developed our function categories and incorporated expressive writing as the central term, it was because we had come to see expressive writing as the relatively undifferentiated starting point from which the dissociation would take place (bearing in mind, however, that mature expressive writing was one of the forms into which it would evolve). Clearly, we have been unable to prove or disprove this hypothesis in the course of Stage I of the research. If, as we had predicted, the development of writing abilities showed itself as a growing range of kinds of writing shaped by thinking processes, we should have expected to find in the sample a great deal of expressive writing in the early years, in all subjects, and an increase in later years of analogic, speculative and theoretical writing, as well as persuasive and poetic—all these compensating for a reduction in the expressive; and at the same time, a proportion of expressive writing maintained and developing into its maturer forms and purposes.

It would appear, however, that the pressures to write at an analogic level of the informative—and in the main for an audience of the teacher as examiner —were great enough both to inhibit early expressive writing and to prevent any but minimal development into the more abstract levels of the informative; strong enough at the same time to cut down drastically in the seventh year the output of the poetic. As we have already indicated, we believe an explanation for this unexpected narrowing of the range must be sought in the whole curriculum and its objectives. The small amount of speculative writing certainly suggests that, for whatever reason, curricular aims did not include the fostering of writing that reflects independent thinking; rather, attention was directed towards classificatory writing which reflects information in the form in which both teacher and textbook traditionally present it.

There would seem to be no intrinsic reason why writing for an examiner audience should preclude independent thought. On the other hand, where the demands of an unknown audience of external examiners are too rigidly interpreted, a situation may arise in which both teachers and pupils are on the defensive; and they may then feel that the only safe guide is the syllabus in the form in which teachers have structured it and textbooks reinforce it. In such circumstances many pupils may be taking on the forms of classificatory writing without engaging in the thinking processes required to give full meaning to what is learnt.

Since we took our sample, there have been many changes in schools. Mixed-ability groups have taken the place of many streamed classes and this has reduced the amount of class teaching; integrated studies and team-teaching have brought in more group discussion and more individual inquiry; many national projects have appeared and many more have been developed locally. All this might suggest that a sample taken in 1974 would show very different results. Our impression is that there is still a great deal of writing done in school, and much of it is now done on work-sheets. Though as yet there has been no serious study of written answers on work-sheets, our experience would indicate that, with the pressure of external examinations still maintained, an even greater reduction of choices may have taken place. It begins to look as though organizational changes in the circumstances in which learning takes place may make little difference in the face of the effect of the examination upon school writing.

Returning to take a general look at our sample, and with our dissociation hypothesis in mind, we should have liked to see much more openness as regards what children can achieve in writing, fewer of the limitations which we have attributed to a restricted view of the curriculum and the restrictive effect of examinations. We should like to see deliberate attempts made in the future to discover why the expectations generated in school act so powerfully to inhibit expressive writing, and what can be done to counter this effect. What the sample as we find it suggests is the surprising degree to which learning situations in different subjects, with different syllabuses, and with the whole background of potentially different roads from experience into words and back to experience—the degree to which such learning situations (to judge by the writing) grow more and more like each other, more and more concentrated on one use of the written word.

We see our categories and their theoretical backing as possible means towards an understanding of what goes on in writing and what might go on. We certainly do not see it as any solution to turn them into a sequential programme and *teach* them.

Research prospects and problems

Our four-year follow up study has provided data, still in process of analysis, which should shed light on our major developmental hypothesis. Knowing a good deal about the school context in which the writings have been produced, seeing work over a continuous span of time and across subjects in the curri-

culum, we should be able to perceive what (in open and favourable circumstances) goes with what, and what leads to what, in terms of our categories.
Moreover, for the first time in the research we shall pay some attention to
the quality of performance: not in a global sense, of course, but in terms of
writing tasks and the effectiveness with which their specific demands are met.
Some of our speculations about the nature of the writing process will be
checked against what the writers have to say and write about their own writings.
And we shall have information on individual reading levels and interests to
see what light these may shed on the writing. Above all, our association with
seven schools over the four years has given us optimum circumstances in which
to try out specific effects—to angle for the expressive, to tempt into the speculative, to offer a guaranteed peer-group audience, and so on. One of the points
on which we shall look for evidence will be the relationship between writing
for a public audience in the poetic and doing so in the transactional.

THE DEVELOPMENT PROJECT

At the time of writing this report, the Schools Council 'Writing Across the
Curriculum' project had been in operation for more than three years, concentrating first upon the eleven- to thirteen-year-olds and latterly upon the
fourteen- to sixteen-year-olds. Its intention was to work with teachers in their
schools on the language problems they raised; seeing whether the ideas that
have gone into the research reported here could assist in framing practical
hypotheses to be tried out *in situ*. Clearly this constituted an entirely new
phase of the inquiry, a stage of experimental innovation.[2]

The effects of some kinds of teacher intervention have already been observed. Thus, experimental approaches to writing for those who find it most
difficult have suggested that deliberate attempts to encourage expressive
writing are not effective unless they are accompanied by as deliberate an
effort to counter the inhibiting assumptions about writing that pupils bring
to the task. The key problem has been seen as one of helping such pupils to
draw upon their experience as talkers. The writing situation has to be close
enough to a familiar talk situation for the acquired skill to be used in a modified
form; and yet the writing must produce for the writer some satisfaction he
could not equally well have achieved by the less laborious process of talking.
Another experiment was one which set out to eliminate every trace of the
'examiner relationship' from a teacher's written responses to what his pupils
wrote: the effect was described as dramatic.

Interventions such as these have come from individual teachers or small
groups working together with the assistance of members of the project team.
Two other kinds of activity are being pursued: first, the development of
language policies by groups of different subject teachers within a school
working towards a policy adopted by the whole staff; second, for local education authorities and professional associations to expand and develop these

small group experiments by means of conferences and courses which cut across the curriculum boundaries, to look at theoretical ideas about the relation of writing and talking to thinking and learning—and to organize their own interventions and innovations on a wider scale than is possible without such organizational support.

PROBLEMS

The field of inquiry is vast and includes both urgent practical matters and others of fundamental importance to our theoretical paradigms.

Two particular pieces of work are required to complete the job we have begun. As we have confessed, we had intended from the start to take scripts allocated to the various categories of writing we have proposed and submit them to the kind of linguistic analysis which would reveal what particular features in the total resources of a language were being employed in any one script: hence to discover whether clusters of features would emerge which would characterize a kind of writing. Since our categories have proved meaningful by a number of criteria in our work so far, this analysis seems more than ever worth doing.

We venture to hope that one outcome of these procedures might be to establish differences between the two spectra—expressive to transactional and expressive to poetic. It is a crucial feature of our approach that the first cut we make in the model for function is between participant-role and spectator-role uses. It is this feature that has been most criticized, particularly by linguists. Our response is to feel that eventually some way will be found of making this essential first cut that will satisfy our critics.

The second task is not unrelated to the first and is also one we have referred to earlier. Can we find a means of identifying and describing the language resources a writer is drawing upon in a particular piece of writing, and so go on to plot, over a period of time and a corpus of writings, his growth in resources? It seems likely that a writer draws upon his linguistic experience both as a speaker and as a writer/reader in order to write. In what relation do the two processes stand, and does the relationship vary with individuals? We would certainly suppose that the internalizing process—say of the forms of the written language met in reading—will have selective laws of its own: and that perhaps 'writing to a model' (either as a teaching technique or out of deficit on the part of a writer) may fail to respect those laws. Recent studies of reading have stressed 'linguistic awareness' as something essential to reading and extra to competence in speech: there is clearly an area of common interest here that we need to pursue.

Of all the other matters we might place on the agenda, we select a very familiar problem that our investigation has raised afresh. We need, it seems to us, two avenues of investigation into examining procedures with regard to their use in schools. First we need to discover ways of arriving at reliable evaluations of language behaviour that is not measurable in any simple direct fashion. We cannot go on allowing the threshold of school achievement—across the curriculum—to be kept down to the level of directly measurable language performances, such as the use of analogic informative writing.

Secondly, we need further experiments in the *forms* of examining with the object of devising examination procedures which *articulate more easily* with the whole range of work (examinable, not yet examinable, and predictably *un*examinable) which teachers are committed to producing in their classrooms.

What does it matter?

We conclude by asking, 'How important is writing, anyway?' It is often enough claimed that in this telecommunications age the importance of writing is declining rapidly; indeed, that many young people leaving school today will seldom need to use it, and then only in its simplest forms (say, in our categories of report and generalized narrative and, for simple instructions, regulative). The rest, it is said, will be done by word of mouth. Even if this prophecy proved largely true, we should still want to claim a *developmental* role for writing in school—that is to say, that the talk by which children will govern their lives will require mental abilities that will best be developed by the practice of writing.

Research workers in Jerusalem, concerned with the differing educational needs of children of European immigrants and those of Middle Eastern origin, have developed the hypothesis that even before a child can read or write, and, at a later stage, regardless of whether he is in the habit of reading and writing, the speech forms he uses bear the stamp of his family history in respect of their relationship to a written language. They speak therefore of 'the reading person', recognizable by the nature of his mental processes as his speech reveals them; and their educational programme sets out to foster the emergence of 'reading persons' irrespective of their origins.[3]

It must be said that, seen from the standpoint of anthropology, the whole case against the importance of writing seems flimsy indeed. Goody and Watt[4] mark the chapters of their story in millennia, and the effect of a written language upon all aspects of society has, over more than one millennium, been profound indeed by their account. A written record arrests time, so to speak: once a record of past behaviour and past beliefs becomes widely available, a sense of difference between present and past is able to develop; from this to scepticism is an inevitable step, and the next is to arrive at hypothesis and experiment. The nature of thinking is altered. 'For writing, by objectifying words, and by making their meanings available for much more prolonged and intensive scrutiny than is possible orally, encourages private thought.'[5] The telecommunications age may effect changes, but they will be modulations of that theme, and no reversal.

In a recent paper Bruner[6] has proposed the term 'analytic competence' to designate a stage beyond innate linguistic competence or socially induced communicative competence. He describes it as involving 'the prolonged operation of thought processes exclusively on linguistic representations, on propositional structures, accompanied by strategies of thought and problem solving appropriate not to direct experience with objects and events but with ensembles of propositions'. He notes the resemblance between his analytic competence and Piaget's 'formal operations'.

We would certainly associate the kind of mental ability Bruner has described with some of the characteristics Goody and Watt see promoted in a society by the use of the written word: and it would be our hunch that the practice of the written word in school will be a principal means by which an individual acquires it.

It is perhaps our particular contribution to add that the higher mental processes Bruner has referred to are associated with the mode of organization by which language in the role of participant reaches the peak of its achievement. What we have been discussing in this section so far might be seen as part of the study of the rules of use of transactional language. To complete the picture we need to envisage other principles leading to a different kind of order, that which Susanne Langer[7] has begun to describe in relation to a work of art. These rules of use for language in the spectator role may as yet be no more than shadows, but there is substance in what children daily achieve in school through their use of writing in the spectrum from expressive to poetic.

Finally, and in all common sense: while class sizes remain stubbornly at their present level, writing has to stand in for a great deal of interpersonal speech. There will be many children whose relations with their teacher have to be established and maintained principally by what each writes for the other.

We can confidently conclude, therefore, by saying that we shall carry on from where Roger Ascham[8] set us in 1570—though, since it was translating Latin he had in mind, we shall need to twist the tail of his injunction: 'After this the child must take a paper book, and sitting in some place where no man shall prompt him, by himself, let him'—write!

Notes and references

1   J. R. Squire and R. Applebee, *Teaching English in the United Kingdom: A Comparative Study*.

2   The project ran from 1971 to 1976. Its main publication was a book for teachers, *Writing and Learning Across the Curriculum 11–16* by Nancy Martin et al. (Ward Lock Educational, 1976).

3   A. Stahl, 'The Structure of the Written Language of Children from Middle Eastern and European Cultures' (unpublished synopsis, 1971); Y. Sternberg, 'A Typology of Verbal Communicative Situations as a Basis for Analysing Cultural Deprivation'.

4   J. Goody and I. Watt, 'The Consequences of Literacy', in P. P. Giglioli (ed.), *Language and Social Context*.

5   Ibid., p. 346.

6   J. S. Bruner, 'Language as an Instrument of Thought', in A. Davies (ed.), *Problems in Language and Learning*.

7   Susanne Langer, *Mind: An Essay on Human Feeling*.

8   Roger Ascham, *The Scholemaster*.

Appendix I
Instructions for allocation of scripts to function categories

(These instructions were supplied to assessors as part of the function categories briefing document—see p. 88)

I CATEGORY ASSESSMENT SHEETS
   With each set of scripts you should find two different types of assessment sheets.
   (*a*) One sheet numbered 1–100 on which there is room to record your assessment only. *Please return this sheet with the scripts.*
   (*b*) Four sheets for more detailed recording, with columns for *script number, category* (as in '*a*' above), *short title* (i.e. the title on the script, or, if that is lengthy, the gist of it), and *notes if any*. (Please make notes on any script you allocate to category 4.1. Make other notes only when you think it's necessary. Use the back of the sheet for longer notes.)
   As a safeguard against loss in the post will you please post the more detailed sheets to us in a separate envelope. Postage will be refunded.

2 CHECKING
   Each set of scripts is numbered 1–100. The letter before the number identifies each set of a hundred. Ignore the number on the right.
   Before entering assessments check that the number on the script tallies with the number on the sheet.

3 TEACHERS' INSTRUCTIONS
   Most, not all, of the scripts are accompanied by teachers' instructions and/or notes. You should read these instructions in conjunction with the scripts.

4 NOTES ON PROCEDURE
   (*a*) Decide on one of the three major categories before considering sub-divisions.
   (*b*) In difficult cases a *return* to the major categories has often been found helpful.

(*c*) Scripts in category 4.2 (school context) usually exhibit some of the features of the mature categories. When you have allocated a script to any subdivision of category 4.2, add in brackets the mature category you think this script most resembles.

5   DOMINANCE

(*a*) Where possible you should allocate a script to a definite category, only making use of points (*b*) and (*c*) below where you feel there is a strong case for so doing. It is true that many scripts have features of more than one category, but you should allocate by an impression of dominance rather than place a script in two categories.

(*b*) Sometimes you will feel that you have accurately located two categories which apply to a script, but feel that you have no means of deciding which is dominant. Or you may feel that a script lies between two categories. In such cases, if you feel that to place the script in one category rather than another would be to give false information about it, then insert a stroke between the two relevant categories, e.g. 2/3.

(*c*) You might find a script which shifts its category. For example it might start off as a 1.1.2 type script, but change dramatically half way through to a 1.1.5 type script. If you feel that such a script could not be properly allocated to a single category by dominance, then assess the script by inserting a 'to' between the relevant categories e.g. 1.1.2 to 1.1.5.

6   COPIED WORK

Decide on the function, disregarding that it is copied.

7   TRANSLATION

Ignore these scripts. Just enter *translation* instead of a category. (This applies also to scripts where translations from Latin are followed by a brief stylistic comment.)

8   SCRIPTS IN TWO DISTINCT PARTS

Assess only the first part. You should find that the second part has been crossed out.

Appendix II
Coding reliability

We arrived at an estimate of the reliability of our classification of the scripts into audience and function categories by first modifying a calculation used by Loban, Squire and others when employing nominal categories.[1]

Squire used a second coder on a proportion of the scripts. We used three assessors throughout. Agreement between the three judgements on any one script was objectively scored (for the purpose of calculating agreement) by turning each judgement and the resulting verdict into a 'split category' and scoring one mark for each half-category agreement. This gave a score of six when all three judgements were the same, and four when two agreed but not the third; and in more complicated cases worked as illustrated (1.1.3 is our generalized narrative category, 1.1.4 is the low-level analogic):

(a) 1.1.3, 1.1.3/1.1.4 and 1.1.4 gave the verdict 1.1.3/1.1.4. The judgements were converted to: 1.1.3/1.1.3; 1.1.3/1.1.4; 1.1.4/1.1.4
and the verdict to: **1.1.3/1.1.4**; **1.1.3/1.1.4**; 1.1.3/**1.1.4**
It is clear that four half-categories coincide (see bold type), and the score is four.

(b) 1.1.3, 1.1.3/1.1.4 and 1.1.3 gave a verdict of 1.1.3, but scored five on the same principle.
Judgements: 1.1.3/1.1.3; 1.1.3/1.1.4; 1.1.3/1.1.3
Verdict: **1.1.3/1.1.3**; **1.1.3**/1.1.3; **1.1.3/1.1.3**

(c) 1.1.3/1.1.4, 1.1.3 and 1.1.2 (report)/1.1.3 gave a verdict of 1.1.3, although no two judgements coincided, since it yielded a score of four.
Judgements: 1.1.3/1.1.4; 1.1.3/1.1.3; 1.1.2/1.1.3
Verdict: **1.1.3**/1.1.3; **1.1.3/1.1.3**; 1.1.3/**1.1.3**

(d) Where agreement fell below a score of four, a 'no verdict' was recorded, and this of course scored zero—for example, 1.1.1(record)/1.1.4, 1.1.2/1.1.4 and 1.1.3/1.1.4; or 1.1.3, 1.1.3/1.1.4 and 1.1.2.

Coding reliability was then calculated as follows—first by applying the formula:

$$\frac{6A+5B+4C}{6(A+B+C+D)}$$

where A is the number of cases of full agreement, scoring six, B the number scoring five, C the number scoring four, and D the number of 'no verdicts'.

Next, account was taken of the proportion of agreement expected by chance, using Scott's pi:[2]

$$pi = \frac{\text{observed agreement} - \text{expected agreement}}{1 - \text{expected agreement}}$$

Observed agreement is the coding reliability index; expected agreement is the sum of the squares of the proportions of scripts in each category.[3]

Applying this to the audience categories gave us:

Verdicts scoring 6	1046
Verdicts scoring 5	201
Verdicts scoring 4	749
Total verdicts	1996
'No verdicts'	126
Total assessed	2122

$$\frac{6(1046)+5(201)+4(749)}{6(2122)} = 0.807$$

Expected agreement for the distribution of audience categories was calculated as 0.393. Applying the correction therefore:

$$\frac{0.807-0.393}{1-0.393} = 0.682$$

This is our first, and more stringent, estimate of coding reliability. However, it ignores the fact that further assessors from the research team reworked the 126 'no verdicts' and reduced their number to 18. Calculating their coding reliability on these scripts gave an index of 0.676, amended by Scott's pi to 0.466. Their lower level of agreement is accounted for, of course, by the fact that the previous 'screening' had singled out the difficult decisions.

If we now combine the two assessments—the original and the team's reworking—we have:

$$\frac{6(1046+25)+5(201+29)+4(752+54)}{6(2122)} = 0.847$$

and after applying pi this becomes 0.748. This constitutes our second, and no doubt rather lenient, estimate of coding reliability for the audience categories.

The function categories gave a lower set of figures, but when allowance is made for the much lower expected agreement (i.e. for the more difficult task), the coefficients for the two sets are not very different.

Verdicts scoring 6	694 (original)	40 (team)	734 (combined)
Verdicts scoring 5	141 ,,	34 ,,	175 ,,
Verdicts scoring 4	903 ,,	180 ,,	1083 ,,
Total verdicts	1738 ,,	254 ,,	1992 ,,
'No verdicts'	384 ,,	130 ,,	130 ,,
Total assessed	2122 ,,	384 ,,	2122 ,,

First estimate of coding reliability (based on original assessment only): 0·671, amended by *pi* to 0·635.

Team reworking only: 0·481, amended to 0·425

Combined to yield second estimate of coding reliability for function categories: 0·755, amended by *pi* to 0·729.

Notes and references

1   W. Loban, *The Language of Elementary School Children*; J. R. Squire, *The Responses of Adolescents While Reading Four Short Stories*.

2   See O. R. Holsti, *Content Analysis for the Social Sciences and Humanities*, pp. 135–42.

3   We are grateful to Dr Arthur Applebee for his advice on the method of carrying out this calculation.

Appendix III
Details of distribution of scripts

A Distribution of scripts into audience categories by sex

Category	Boys	Girls	Totals
Child to self	6	4	10
Child to trusted adult	11	22	33
Teacher–learner dialogue	389	428	817
Pupil to teacher, particular relationship	12	9	21
Pupil to examiner	553	471	1024
Expert to known laymen	1	0	1
Child to peer group	0	2	2
Group member to working group	2	2	4
Writer to his readers	15	22	37
Child to trusted adult/teacher–learner dialogue	4	9	13
Teacher–learner dialogue/pupil to examiner	47	38	85
Teacher–learner dialogue/writer to his readers	13	9	22
Miscellaneous	18	17	35
TOTALS	1071	1033	2104

Contingency coefficient: 0·09 ($P < 0.1$).
Column groupings: 'expert to known laymen', 'child to peer group', 'group member to working group' and 'miscellaneous'.

B   Distribution of scripts into function categories by sex

Category	Boys	Girls	Totals
Record	12	3	15
Report	125	116	241
Generalized narrative	56	57	113
Low-level analogic	164	128	292
Analogic	244	198	442
Speculative	21	27	48
Tautologic	19	15	34
Persuasive	14	14	28
Expressive	42	67	109
Poetic	164	187	351
Immature categories	18	35	53
Pseudo-informative	43	28	71
Dummy run	24	23	47
Mixed 'lower' informative*	17	19	36
Speculative/tautologic	6	3	9
Informative/persuasive	0	5	5
Informative/expressive	11	12	23
Expressive/poetic	14	28	42
Other mixed categories	10	3	13
Translations	12	8	20
TOTALS	1016	976	1992

Contingency coefficient: 0·16 ($P < 0·001$).
Column groupings: nil.
* Comprises report, generalized narrative, low-level analogic and analogic.

C Distribution of scripts into audience categories by types of school

Category	Sec.	Com-prehens.	Gram-mar	Dir. Grant	Ind.	F.E.	Totals
Child to self	0	0	3	1	6	0	10
Child to trusted adult	11	9	7	4	2	0	33
Teacher–learner dialogue	256	144	234	72	101	10	817
Pupil to teacher, particular relationship	1	4	9	5	2	0	21
Pupil to examiner	201	150	388	138	115	32	1024
Expert to known laymen	0	0	1	0	0	0	1
Child to peer group	1	0	1	0	0	0	2
Group member to working group	0	1	3	0	0	0	4
Writer to his readers	1	0	14	13	9	0	37
Child to trusted adult/ teacher–learner dialogue	4	4	3	1	1	0	13
Teacher–learner dialogue/pupil to examiner	28	16	26	8	5	2	85
Teacher–learner dialogue/writer to his readers	2	1	13	3	3	0	22
Miscellaneous	7	0	13	7	8	0	35
TOTALS	512	329	715	252	252	44	2104

Contingency coefficient: 0.24 ($P < 0.001$).

Column groupings: 'child to trusted adult' and 'child to trusted adult'/teacher–learner dialogue'; 'writer to his readers' and 'teacher–learner dialogue/writer to his readers'; 'child to self', 'pupil to teacher, particular relationship', 'expert to known laymen', 'child to peer group', 'group member to working group' and miscellaneous.

D Distribution of scripts into function categories by types of school

Category	Sec.	Com-prehens.	Gram-mar	Dir. Grant	Ind.	F.E.	Totals
Record	0	4	10	1	0	0	15
Report	73	39	70	21	37	1	241
Generalized narrative	47	26	29	1	10	0	113
Low-level analogic	93	51	88	23	23	14	292
Analogic	61	35	183	74	61	28	442
Speculative	1	1	20	16	10	0	48
Tautologic	0	1	13	14	6	0	34
Persuasive	0	0	26	2	0	0	28
Expressive	30	27	27	14	11	0	109
Poetic	80	53	126	46	46	0	351
Immature categories	34	15	2	0	2	0	53
Pseudo-informative	21	18	25	4	3	0	71
Dummy run	10	14	19	1	3	0	47
Mixed 'lower' informative*	9	10	14	2	1	0	36
Speculative/tautologic	1	0	4	1	3	0	9
Informative/persuasive	1	0	4	0	0	0	5
Informative/expressive	3	5	9	3	3	0	23
Expressive/poetic	11	11	9	5	6	0	42
Other mixed categories	1	2	6	1	3	0	13
Translations	1	1	2	5	11	0	20
TOTALS	477	313	686	234	239	43	1992

Contingency coefficient: 0·41 ($P < 0·001$).

Column groupings: speculative and tautologic; mixed 'lower' informative,* speculative/tautologic and informative/persuasive; record, 'other mixed categories' and translations.

* Comprises report, generalized narrative, low-level analogic and analogic.

E Distribution of scripts into audience categories by year

Category	Year 1	Year 3	Year 5	Year 7	Totals
Child to self	0	0	0	10	10
Child to trusted adult	10	11	8	4	33
Teacher–learner dialogue	315	246	166	90	817
Pupil to teacher, particular relationship	1	2	4	14	21
Pupil to examiner	246	251	239	288	1024
Expert to known laymen	0	0	1	0	1
Child to peer group	0	0	2	0	2
Group member to working group	1	1	1	1	4
Writer to his readers	1	2	14	20	37
Child to trusted adult/teacher–learner dialogue	3	5	3	2	13
Teacher–learner dialogue/pupil to examiner	35	29	6	15	85
Teacher–learner dialogue/writer to his readers	2	5	9	6	22
Miscellaneous	5	0	9	21	35
TOTALS	619	552	462	471	2104

Contingency coefficient: 0.32 ($P < 0.001$).
Column groupings: 'child to trusted adult' and 'child to trusted adult/teacher–learner dialogue'; 'child to self', 'expert to known laymen', 'child to peer group', 'group member to working group' and miscellaneous.

F   Distribution of scripts into function categories by year

Category	Year 1	Year 3	Year 5	Year 7	Totals
Record	9	4	1	1	15
Report	125	87	17	12	241
Generalized narrative	55	40	14	4	113
Low-level analogic	96	87	79	30	292
Analogic	12	57	122	251	442
Speculative	0	0	13	35	48
Tautologic	0	7	0	27	34
Persuasive	1	9	9	9	28
Expressive	37	34	21	17	109
Poetic	95	119	106	31	351
Immature categories	46	7	0	0	53
Pseudo-informative	48	20	3	0	71
Dummy run	16	14	14	3	47
Mixed 'lower' informative*	8	12	8	8	36
Speculative/tautologic	0	0	3	6	9
Informative/persuasive	2	0	1	2	5
Informative/expressive	6	9	4	4	23
Expressive/poetic	16	15	5	6	42
Other mixed categories	3	4	3	3	13
Translations	0	2	11	7	20
TOTALS	575	527	434	456	1992

Contingency coefficient: 0.57 ($P < 0.001$).

Column groupings: persuasive and informative/persuasive; 'other mixed categories' and translations.

* Comprises report, generalized narrative, low-level analogic and analogic.

Distribution of scripts into audience categories by subjects

Category	Eng.	Hist.	Geog.	Relig. Ed.	Biol.	Chem.	Phys.	Soc. St.	Classics	Mod. Lang.	Misc. I*	Misc. II†	Misc. III‡	Totals
Child to self	1	7	0	0	0	0	0	0	0	2	0	0	0	10
Child to trusted adult	29	0	0	4	0	0	0	0	0	0	0	0	0	33
Teacher–learner dialogue	566	49	30	100	15	4	5	14	5	18	4	2	5	817
Pupil to teacher, part. rel.	11	5	0	1	3	0	0	0	0	0	0	1	0	21
Pupil to examiner	153	198	187	34	159	80	57	5	20	29	56	38	8	1024
Expert to known laymen	1	0	0	0	0	0	0	0	0	0	0	0	0	1
Child to peer group	1	0	0	0	1	0	0	0	0	0	0	0	0	2
Group member to working group	2	1	0	1	0	0	0	0	0	0	0	0	0	4
Writer to his readers	32	0	0	0	2	0	0	0	0	0	0	3	0	37
Child to trusted adult/teacher–learner dialogue														
Teacher–learner dialogue	10	1	0	2	0	0	0	0	0	0	0	0	0	13
Teacher–learner dialogue/pupil to examiner	25	24	11	8	4	2	2	0	0	3	1	1	4	85
Teacher–learner dialogue/writer to his readers	20	0	0	2	0	0	0	0	0	0	0	0	0	22
Miscellaneous	17	2	2	4	6	0	0	0	0	3	0	1	0	35
TOTAL	868	287	230	156	190	86	64	19	25	55	61	45	17	2104

Contingency coefficient: 0·54 ($P < 0.001$).

Column groupings: 'child to trusted adult' and 'child to trusted adult/teacher–learner dialogue'; 'writer to his readers' and 'teacher–learner dialogue/writer to his readers'; 'child to self', 'expert to known laymen', 'child to peer group', 'group member to working group' and miscellaneous.

Row groupings: biology, chemistry and physics; social studies, classics, modern languages; miscellaneous I, II and III.

* Miscellaneous I = practical subjects.
† Miscellaneous II = sixth-form minority studies.
‡ Miscellaneous III = art, music.

H Distribution of scripts into function categories by subjects

Category	Eng.	Hist.	Geog.	Relig. Ed.	Biol.	Chem.	Phys.	Soc. St.	Classics	Mod. Lang.	Misc. I*	Misc. II†	Misc. III‡	Totals
Record	11	0	2	0	0	0	0	0	0	0	0	0	2	15
Report	42	55	10	54	28	23	8	2	3	5	8	0	3	241
Generalized narrative	16	13	34	5	10	6	4	2	3	0	18	0	2	113
Low-level analogic	35	55	106	6	38	9	10	1	2	3	20	2	5	292
Analogic	96	104	39	7	78	33	27	0	0	28	7	22	1	442
Speculative	30	2	1	4	6	0	0	0	0	2	0	3	0	48
Tautologic	7	0	0	1	5	4	0	0	0	0	0	17	0	34
Persuasive	21	0	0	7	0	0	0	0	0	0	0	0	0	28
Expressive	92	1	0	15	0	0	0	0	0	1	0	0	0	109
Poetic	322	5	2	17	2	1	0	0	1	0	1	0	0	351
Immature cats.	27	6	0	4	2	0	0	10	0	4	0	0	0	53
Pseudo-informative	3	16	17	10	6	2	8	1	0	2	6	0	0	71
Dummy run	41	2	0	3	0	0	0	0	0	0	0	1	0	47
Mixed 'lower' informative¶	9	5	4	1	5	5	3	0	0	3	0	0	1	36
Speculative/tautologic	6	0	0	1	1	0	0	0	0	0	0	1	0	9
Informative/persuasive	2	0	1	1	1	0	0	0	0	0	0	0	0	5
Informative/expressive	18	0	0	3	0	0	0	0	0	0	0	0	2	23
Expressive/poetic	38	0	1	2	0	0	0	0	0	1	0	0	0	42
Other mixed cats.	5	2	1	2	0	1	1	0	0	0	1	0	0	13
Translation	1	0	0	0	0	0	0	0	15	4	0	0	0	20
TOTALS	822	266	218	143	182	84	61	16	24	53	61	46	16	1992

Contingency coefficient: 0·65 (P<0·001).
Column groupings: persuasive and informative/persuasive; mixed 'lower' informative¶ and speculative/tautological; record, 'other mixed categories' and translations.
Row groupings: biology, chemistry and physics; social studies, classics, modern languages, miscellaneous I, II and III.
* Miscellaneous I = practical subjects.　† Miscellaneous II = sixth-form minority studies.
‡ Miscellaneous III = art, music.　¶ Comprises report. generalized narrative. low-level analogic and analogic.

Glossary of linguistic terms

Addressee—the listener to speech, or reader of a piece of writing.

Addressor—the speaker or writer.

Audience—see *sense of audience*.

Analogic—writing which makes generalizations and relates them in an explicitly logical or hierarchical way. (Also see *low-level analogic*.)

Analogic-tautologic—see *speculative*.

Classificatory—a general term to describe writing in which the principle of organization is one of relating classes of phenomena. Thus it is more abstract than those forms which are organized on a time sequence or a spatial order, but less abstract than any form of theorizing. In our model the term covers *low-level analogic* and *analogic*.

Communicative—a use of language in which the prime intention is to pass on information, opinions, instructions etc. to the reader. Compare Sapir's term 'referential' and our term 'transactional': the three have a broad overlap but are not identical.

Conative—language used to instruct or persuade.

Context of culture—understood in its broadest sense, the context of any utterance includes the past experiences of the participants: this broad sense is sometimes termed the 'context of culture'.

Context of situation—the situation (events, physical and social circumstances) in which an utterance is made, seen in relation to the utterance.

Dummy run—exercise and demonstration of the ability to perform a writing task which fails to take up the demands of the task that would be appropriate to it if it were a genuine verbal operation.

Expressive—a use of language which relies upon a reader's interest in the *writer* as well as in what he has to say.

Function—the conventional or typical purpose which a piece of writing is designed to serve.

Generalized narrative—writing tied to particular events and places but detecting a pattern of repetition in them, which is expressed in generalized form.

Generalized other—Mead's term for what is 'internalized' in the socializing process of representing to oneself, in general terms, the characteristic behaviour, needs and likely responses of other people.

Immature categories—in our scheme, undisassociated categories, practice play etc.

Impelled writing—where the topic has completely absorbed the writer so that he seems not to be in control of his writing but to be controlled by it.

Informative writing—the first main subdivision of transactional writing: subdivided into *record, report, generalized narrative, low-level analogic, analogic, speculative* and *tautologic*.

Internalized other—a term taken from George Mead to refer to what is internalized when we represent to ourselves the characteristic behaviour, needs and likely responses of another person.

Involved writing—where the writer has made the task his own and begins to write to satisfy himself as well as his teacher.

Low-level analogic—writing consisting of genuine generalizations but loosely related; i.e. the logical or hierarchical relationships between them are not perceived and/or not made explicit.

Pseudo-conative—writing which fails to embody the role of persuader or instructor demanded by the task set and is instead directed to the teacher for the purpose of being marked or graded.

Pseudo-informative—writing which fails to embody the role of informant demanded by the task set etc. (see previous entry).

Perfunctory writing—where the writer satisfies only the minimum demands of the task.

Persuasive—writing which attempts to influence action, behaviour or attitude in cases where compliance cannot be assumed.

Poetic—writing as a verbal construct, a patterned verbalization of the writer's feelings and ideas.

Record—eye-witness account or running commentary.

Regulative—language which lays down a course of action to be followed, makes demands and issues instructions where compliance is assumed.

Report—writing which gives an account of a particular series of events or the appearance of a particular place.

Sense of audience—a writer's interpretation of his reader's expectations as they affect his writing.

Special categories—categories in our scheme created by the special contexts of education, that is, *pseudo-informative, pseudo-conative* and *dummy run*.

Speculative—writing which speculates about generalizations; the open-ended consideration of analogic possibilities.

Tautologic—writing consisting of hypotheses and deductions from them; theory backed by logical argumentation.

Theoretical—in our terminology, writing in the *speculative* and *tautologic* categories.

Transactional—language to 'get things done' or participate in the world's affairs: i.e., in our model, to inform, persuade or instruct.

References

Applebee, A. N. 'The Spectator Role: Theoretical and Developmental Studies of Ideas about and Responses to Literature, with Special Reference to Four Age Levels.' Unpublished Ph.D. thesis, University of London, 1973.

Ascham, Roger. *The Scholemaster*. London, 1570.

Auden, W. H. *Collected Shorter Poems 1927-57*. Faber, 1966.

Bain, A. *English Composition and Rhetoric: A Manual*. Longmans Green, 1866.

Barnes, D., Britton, J., and Rosen, H. *Language, the Learner, and the School*. (Revised Edition.) Penguin Books, 1971.

Ballou, F. W. 'Scales for the Measurement of English Composition', *Harvard-Newton Bulletin*, No. 2. Cambridge, Mass.: Harvard University, 1915.

Becker, H. S. 'Social Class Variations in the Teacher-Pupil Relationship', *Journal of Educational Sociology*, **25**, 4, 1952. Reprinted in *School and Society* (ed. Open University School and Society Course Team), Routledge & Kegan Paul and Open University Press, 1971.

Berger, P. L. and Luckmann, T. *The Social Construction of Reality*. Penguin Books, 1966.

Bilbrough, H. 'The Effect of the Title Upon Performance in English Composition.' Unpublished M.Ed. thesis, University of Manchester, 1955.

Britton, J. N., Martin, N. C., and Rosen, H. *Multiple Marking of English Compositions: an account of an experiment* (Schools Council Examinations Bulletin No. 12). HMSO, 1966.

Britton, J., Martin, N. C. and Rosen H. 'Abilities to Write', *New Education*, **2**, 10, 1966.

Britton, J., and Newsome, B. 'What is learned in English Lessons ?', *Journal of Curriculum Studies*, I, 1, November 1968.

Brooks C. and Warren, R. P. *Fundamentals of Good Writing*. Dobson, 1952.

Bruner, J. S., *et al. Studies in Cognitive Growth*. New York: John Wiley, 1966.

Bruner, J. S. 'Language as an Instrument of Thought', in A. Davies (ed.) *Problems in Language and Learning*. Heinemann, 1975.

Campbell, G. *The Philosophy of Rhetoric* (2 vols). London, 1776 (second edition 1801).

Cassirer, E. *An Essay on Man*. New Haven: Yale University Press, 1944.

Cazden, C. B. *Child Language and Education*. New York: Holt, Rinehart & Winston, 1972.

Chomsky, C. 'Reading, Writing and Phonology', *Harvard Educational Review*, **40**, 2, 1970.

Chomsky, N. and Halle, M. *The Sound Pattern of English*. New York: Harper & Row, 1968.

Dick, K. (ed.). *Writers at Work: The Paris Review Interviews*. Penguin Books, 1972.

Emig, J. *The Composing Process of Twelfth Graders* (NCTE Research Report No. 13). Champaign, Illinois, 1971.

Firth, J. R. 'The techniques of semantics', *Papers in Linguistics, 1934–51*. Oxford University Press, 1965.

Ford, C. T. 'Development in Written Composition During the Primary School Period', *British Journal of Educational Psychology*, **24**, 1, 1954.

Goldman-Eisler, F. 'Speech Analysis and Mental Processes', *Language and Speech*, **1**, 1958. See also *Language and Speech*, **4**, 1961.

Goodacre, E. J. *Teachers and Their Pupils' Home Background*. Slough: National Foundation for Educational Research, 1968.

Goody, James and Watt, I. 'The Consequences of Literacy' in Giglioli, P. P. (ed.), *Language and Social Context*. Penguin Books, 1963; reprinted 1972.

Gosling, G. W. H. *Marking English Composition*. Victoria: Australian Council for Educational Research, 1966.

Grierson, H. J. C. *Rhetoric and English Composition*. (Second edition.) Edinburgh: Oliver and Boyd, 1945.

Gumperz, J. J. 'Types of linguistic community', *Anthropological Linguistics*, **4**, 1, 1962.

Gusdorf, G. *Speaking* (trans. P. Brockelman). Chicago: Northwestern University Press, 1965.

Habermas, J. 'Towards a Theory of Communicative Competence', *Inquiry*, 4, 1971.

Halliday, M. A. K. 'Language in a social perspective', in 'The Context of Language'. *Education Review*, **23**, 3, 1971.

Harding, D. W. 'The Role of the Onlooker', *Scrutiny*, **VI**, 3, 1937.

——. 'Psychological Processes in the Reading of Fiction', *British Journal of Aesthetics*, **II**, 2, 1962.

——. *Experience into Words*. London: Chatto and Windus, 1963.

——. *Social Psychology and Individual Values*. (Revised edition.) Hutchinson, 1966.

——. 'Considered Experience', *English in Education*, **I**, 2, 1967.

——. 'Raids on the Inarticulate', *Use of English*, **19**, 2, 1967.

——. 'Practice at Liking: A study in Experimental Aesthetics', *Bulletin of the British Psychological Society*, **21**, 70, 1968.

Harris, R. J. 'An Experimental Inquiry into the Function and Value of Formal Grammar in the Teaching of English.' Unpublished Ph.D. thesis, University of London, 1962.

Hartley, L. P. *Mrs Carteret Receives and Other Stories*. Hamish Hamilton, 1971.

Hirst, P. H. and Peters, R. S. *The Logic of Education*. Routledge and Kegan Paul, 1970.

Hoggart, R. 'The Reith Lectures', *The Listener*, 25 November 1971. *The Reith Lectures*. BBC, 1971.

Holloway, J. *Language and Intelligence*. Macmillan, 1951.

Holsti, O. R. *Content Analysis for the Social Sciences and Humanities*. New York: Addison–Wesley, 1969.

Hughes, Ted. *The Iron Man: A Story in Five Nights*. Faber, 1968.

Hunt, Kellogg W. *Grammatical Structures Written at Three Grade Levels* (NCTE Research Report No. 3). Champaign, Illinois, 1965.

Hymes, D. 'The Ethnography of Speaking' in J. A. Fishman (ed.), *Readings in the Sociology of Language*. The Hague: Mouton, 1968.

——. 'Competence and Performance in Linguistic Theory' in Huxley, R. and Ingram, Z. (eds.), *Language Acquisition: Models and Methods*. London and New York: Academic Press, 1971.

Jakobson, R. 'Linguistics and Poetics' in Sebeok, T. A., *Style in Language*. New York: Wiley, 1960.

Joos, M. *The Five Clocks*. New York: Harcourt Brace Jovanovich, 1961.

Keats, John, ed. S. Colvin. *Letters of John Keats*. Macmillan, 1928.

Kelly, G. *The Psychology of Personal Constructs*. New York: Norton, 1955.

Kohl, H. *Thirty-six Children*. Penguin Books, 1972.

Kuhn, T. S. *The Structure of Scientific Revolutions*. (Second edition.) Chicago: University of Chicago Press, 1970.

Langer, S. K. *Philosophy in a New Key*. (Fourth edition.) Cambridge, Mass.: Harvard University Press, 1960.

——. *Mind: An Essay on Human Feeling*. (Vol. I.) Baltimore: Johns Hopkins Press, 1967.

Loban, W. *The Language of Elementary School Children* (NCTE Research Report No. 1). Champaign, Illinois, 1963.

Lowry, M. *Under the Volcano*. Jonathan Cape, 1967.

Luria, A. R. and Vinogradova, O. S. 'The dynamics of semantic systems', *British Journal of Psychology*, 50, 1959.

Lyons, J. *Structural Semantics: Analysis of Vocabulary of Plato*. Oxford: Blackwell, 1964.

Malinowski, B. 'The problem of meaning in primitive languages', Supplement 1 to Ogden, D. K. and Richards, I. A., *The Meaning of Meaning*. Routledge and Kegan Paul, 1923.

McLeod, A. 'This is what came out', *English in Education*, 3, 3, 1969.

Mead, G. H. *Mind, Self and Society*, Chicago: University of Chicago Press, 1934.

Mellon, J. C. *Transformational Sentence Combining: A Method for Enhancing the Development of Syntactic Fluency in English Composition* (NCTE Research Report No. 10). Champaign, Illinois, 1967.

Moffett, J. *Teaching the Universe of Discourse*. Boston: Houghton Mifflin, 1968.

Morris, C. *Signs, Language and Behaviour*. New York: Prentice Hall, 1946.

Paris Review—see Dick, K.

Orwell, George, *Nineteen Eighty-four*. Secker & Warburg, 1949. Reprinted Penguin Books, 1970.

Piaget, J. and Inhelder, B. *The Psychology of the Child* (trans. H. Weaver). Routledge & Kegan Paul, 1969.

Polanyi, M. *Personal Knowledge*. Routledge & Kegan Paul, 1958.

Poole, R. *Towards Deep Subjectivity*. Penguin Books, 1972.

Purves, A. C. and Rippere, V. *Elements of Writing about a Literary Work: A Study of Response to Literature* (NCTE Research Report No. 9). Champaign, Illinois, 1968.

Richards, I. A. *The Philosophy of Rhetoric*. Routledge & Kegan Paul, 1936.

Rosen, H. 'An investigation of the effects of differentiated writing assignments on the performance in English composition of a selected group of 15/16 year old pupils.' Unpublished Ph.D. thesis, University of London, 1969.

Sapir, E. *Culture, Language and Personality*. Berkeley and Los Angeles: University of California Press, 1961.

Sartre, Jean-Paul. *The Psychology of Imagination*. (Translation by the Philosophical Library, Inc., New York.) Methuen, 1940.

Schonell, F. J. *Backwardness in the Basic Subjects*. Edinburgh: Oliver & Boyd, 1942.

Searle, J. *Chomsky's Revolution in Linguistics*. New York Review Special Supplement, 1972.

Seegers, J. C. 'Forms of Discourse and Sentence Structure', *Elementary English Review* 10. NCTE: Champaign, Illinois, 1933.

Siegel, S. *Nonparametric Statistics for the Behavioral Sciences*. New York: McGraw-Hill, 1956.

Sidney, Sir Philip. *Astrophel and Stella*, London 1584. (Reprinted in *Silver Poets of the Sixteenth Century*, ed. G. Bullett. Everyman's Library. J. M. Dent, 1957.)

Smith, F. *Understanding Reading*. New York: Holt, Rinehart & Winston, 1971.

——. (ed.) *Psycholinguistics and Reading*. New York: Holt, Rinehart & Winston, 1973.

Squire, J. R. *The Responses of Adolescents While Reading Four Short Stories* (NCTE Research Report No. 2). Champaign, Illinois, 1964.

Squire, J. R. and Applebee, R. *Teaching English in the United Kingdom: A Comparative Study*. NCTE: Champaign, Illinois, 1969.

Steinmann, M. (ed.). *New Rhetorics*. New York: Charles Scribner, 1967.

Sternberg, Y. 'A Typology of Verbal Communicative Situations as a Basis for Analysing Cultural Deprivation, *Educational Review*, **22**, 2, 1970.

Tajfel, H. and Wilkes, A. L. 'Effects of a Classification on Judgments of Length', *Proceedings of Annual Conference of the British Psychological Society*, 1960.

Van Bruggen, J. A. 'Factors affecting regularity of the flow of words during written composition.' *Journal of Experimental Education* **15**, 12, 1946.

Vygotsky, L. S. *Thought and Language* (trans. Hanfmann, E. and Vakar, G.). Cambridge, Mass.: MIT. Press, 1962.

Wallas, G. *The Art of Thought*. C. A. Watts, 1926.

Whateley, R. *Elements of Rhetoric*. Oxford, 1828.

White, P. *Tree of Man*. Penguin Books, 1970.

Winterowd, W. R. *Rhetoric: A Synthesis*. New York: Holt, Rinehart & Winston, 1968.

Wiswall, Z. E. 'A study of sentence structure in eighth grade composition', *Elementary School Journal*, 26, NCTE: Champaign, Illinois, 1926.

Yevtushenko, Y. *Poems*, ed. H. Marshall. Pergamon, 1967.

Zola, Emile, *Germinal*, trans. L. W. Tancock. Penguin Books, 1969.

Index